SanFrancisco™
Component Framework

SanFrancisco™
Component Framework

An Introduction

Paul Monday
Mary Dangler
James Carey

ADDISON–WESLEY

An Imprint of Addison Wesley Longman, Inc.

Reading, Massachusetts • Harlow, England • Menlo Park, California
Berkeley, California • Don Mills, Ontario • Sydney
Bonn • Amsterdam • Tokyo • Mexico City

AWL Direct Sales
Addison Wesley Longman, Inc.
One Jacob Way
Reading, Massachusetts 01867
(781) 944-3700

Visit AW on the Web: www.awl.com/cseng/

*Library of Congress Cataloging-in-Publication Dat*a

Monday, Paul.
    SanFrancisco component framework : an introduction / Paul Monday, Mary Dangler,
    James Carey.
        p.   cm.
    Includes bibliographical references (p.).
    ISBN 0-201-61587-8
        1. Application software—Development.   2. SanFrancisco (Computer file).   3.
    Business—Data processing.   I. Title.   II. Dangler, Mary.   III. Carey, James. 1962-

    QA76.76.D47 M66 1999
    005.2'76 21—dc21   99–043462

ISBN 0-201-61587-8

Text printed on recycled and acid-free paper

1 2 3 4 5 6 7 8 9 10—CRS—0302010099

First printing, November 1999

Contents

Part III   The Common Business Objects   95

Chapter 6 *An Introduction to the Common Business Objects* 97

Chapter 7 *Common Business Object Categories* 111

Chapter 8 *Using the Common Business Objects*   155

Part IV   The Core Business Processes   173

Part V   The Client   251

Chapter 12   *Preparing to Build a Client Application*   253

Chapter 13   *Using Commands in an Application*   271

List of Figures

Preface

IBM's SanFrancisco component framework helps software developers—IBM's business partners—to build business applications for their own use or for distribution to their customers. The SanFrancisco component framework is not designed to be used directly for performing business tasks such as keeping track of inventory. Instead, it provides a flexible infrastructure of preprogrammed, tested, and debugged components that solve difficult problems in object-oriented computing and business domains. IBM's business partners then customize the SanFrancisco component framework to create applications that contain business logic and interfaces tailored to their specific needs.

Procedural Versus Object-oriented Techniques

Today's large, heterogeneous systems perform a broad array of tasks including managing inventory levels in warehouses, handling business ledgers, dealing with accounts receivable and accounts payable, and many more. Many of these large systems were built using *procedural* programming, a technique designed for creating smaller systems with a more limited range of tasks. Many large systems are even built on top of, or as extensions to, smaller systems. In such an environment, systems become unstable and unmanageable. Procedural techniques are no longer efficient or effective when a large, heterogeneous system is produced.

Object-oriented techniques, on the other hand, provide methods of analysis, design, and implementation that fit more closely the heavy demands of complex applications. Furthermore, object-oriented techniques, such as polymorphism, subclassing, and aggregation, help developers adjust to changing requirements by modifying and enhancing a system with minimal disruption to existing applications. Existing applications may not even need to be recompiled to take advantage of new policies and updated capabilities. Finally, object-oriented techniques allow system creators to reap the benefits of reusing designs and implementations produced by others, thus allowing them to focus on extending and customizing a system for their needs. Development is more efficient and effective when it maintains a tight focus on the unique business logic of a particular module rather than trying to focus on the system as a whole. The SanFrancisco component framework helps developers take maximum advantage of object-oriented techniques.

Goals and Objectives of the SanFrancisco Component Framework

Unlike many other projects, the SanFrancisco project has been driven from its inception by the real-world requirements of its users rather than by technology built in a lab. This requirements-driven, top-down model is a familiar one to software developers—it reflects the working environment in which they produce applications for their customers. This approach differs from a typical technology-driven approach, or bottom-up approach, which many development efforts use. This insight is the result of a 1995 meeting in San Francisco between IBM and its business partners. In this meeting, the developers presented a range of difficult problems they faced in their day-to-day tasks of creating applications.

Chief among the requirements was flexibility. To remain competitive, applications had to meet current requirements while at the same time providing the adaptability developers needed to meet future requirements from the customer base.

One result was that SanFrancisco was built with the object-oriented Java programming language. Through its rich array of built-in class libraries, Java provides portability among various hardware platforms as well as robust support for network-based applications. At the same time, its extensibility allows the SanFrancisco component framework to add numerous layers to the Java base. A key enhancement, for example, is SanFrancisco's Foundation layer, which takes care of generic, low-level details so that developers can concentrate on building the parts of an application that meet specific business requirements.

The problems presented by the business partners in 1995 were specific and wide-ranging. The original goals and objectives of the SanFrancisco project included solutions to the following problems:

- Large parts of applications needed to be rewritten for a variety of reasons, such as solving year 2000 problems, updating networking capabilities of an application, and dealing with the Euro currency.

- People needed to be retrained or hired to obtain the skills necessary for updating the portions of applications. The combination of a shortage of skilled computer professionals and long training times for creating new skills made the transition to new technologies expensive or even impossible. It was especially difficult to train procedural application developers—who might be using a waterfall development model with an implementation language such as COBOL—to use the object-oriented development and programming environment.

- Often, existing business systems could not be adapted fast enough to take advantage of the dynamic business environment. Furthermore, because systems were often being adapted to serve purposes for which they were not intended (such as Internet accessibility and processing of additional data), applications became increasingly fragile over time and with each new capability added to the system.

- Systems had to be deployed on or ported from new platforms—often because of mergers or acquisitions—creating large-scale porting efforts and ensuing problems with maintenance and infrastructure modifications.

It was from this base of customer requirements that the SanFrancisco project was launched. This precedent of top-down, rather than bottom-up, development continues today as hundreds of international business partners provide input into the content and structure of SanFrancisco.

The SanFrancisco Solution

The infrastructure of the SanFrancisco framework (the "plumbing" for object communication and most system services) is the Foundation layer. The Foundation layer, in addition to providing the system services, defines a strict programming model for use throughout the SanFrancisco component framework. On top of this layer is a set of common business classes, patterns, and techniques called the Common Business Objects layer. On top of this framework are sets of interrelated classes, patterns, and techniques, such as general ledgers, warehousing, accounts receivable, and accounts payable, that are tailored to the needs of particular business domains. The expertise to determine the structure and contents of the layers is provided by application developers and domain specialists for the particular framework being built.[1]

Within each of the business domains for which SanFrancisco provides a framework, analysts locate common processes as well as places where systems may require custom logic. For example, the credit checking policy at a small hardware store may vary substantially from the credit checking policy at an on-line bookseller. The small hardware store may have a credit policy that extends credit to many customers based on good faith rather than on actual credit records, which an on-line bookstore is likely to use. For such cases, San-Francisco provides default behavior (such as a default credit checking policy) but documents it as a customization point, allowing a system developer to replace it through an extension mechanism. Customization through extension points isolates the custom logic so that the application's logic remains unchanged. SanFrancisco mechanisms automatically take advantage of a replaced policy.

A key benefit of the SanFrancisco component framework is that a development team can take advantage of the framework's wide-ranging potential for *reuse* of its components. The development cycle does not differ substantially from that of any other object-oriented approach. Analysts, designers, and programmers take additional time to map requirements, patterns, and functions to those provided in SanFrancisco.

Typically, the SanFrancisco component framework fulfills about 40 percent of an application's needs within its supported business domains (such as General Ledger, Warehouse Management, Order Management, and so on), and it may provide significantly more. The amount of reuse depends on how closely an application maps to the provided requirements, design patterns, and common business objects (and their implementations). Implementation reuse is valuable in cutting the number of lines of code that developers must write to implement business logic. Analysis and design reuse can go a long way toward reducing the complexity and sheer number of decisions that must be made in building large business systems.

No matter how much reuse occurs, developers benefit from the thousands of hours spent by the SanFrancisco development team working with solution developers to create a robust architecture and design for the SanFrancisco classes. When developers use the framework, they gain—in addition to a

---

[1]SanFrancisco is a single framework that encompasses many frameworks that apply to different business domains. Each of the frameworks encompassed by SanFrancisco is built with the same programming model. Often, the term *SanFrancisco application business components* is used. It is interchangeable with the SanFrancisco framework, and both are used in this book. Using broad definitions of components and frameworks, the SanFrancisco framework as a whole adheres to both definitions. (Keep in mind that the term *components* is not synonymous with JavaBeans, even though JavaBeans are components.)

design that encourages extension and reuse—object-oriented design patterns and a robust programming model for consistency and coding guidance.

Reading This Book

This book addresses the SanFrancisco framework using a layered approach that parallels the framework itself. The only exception is the first part of the book, which serves as an introduction to frameworks in general and to the San-Francisco framework in particular.

As you proceed through the book, the techniques we use to present examples and diagrams vary according to the conceptual level of the material. For example, SanFrancisco's Foundation layer contains the definition of the programming model along with basic functions and utilities. In Part II we present Unified Modeling Language (UML) depictions of many classes and Java code to show how some of the services in the Foundation layer are used. On the other hand, Part IV, The Core Business Processes, has little to do with Java code; instead, it describes particular business domains and explains how the SanFrancisco framework supports them. The samples show how to match an application's business requirements to similar requirements provided by SanFrancisco.

We use the various presentation techniques to reach the target audience of each specific area. After reading about the Foundation layer, a programmer will have an idea of how SanFrancisco is coded and will understand the structure, layout, and techniques used in SanFrancisco's programming model. Because the programming model is used in all layers of the SanFrancisco framework, discussion of how to program while using one of the business domains is not necessary. With respect to business domains and the SanFrancisco Core Business Processes layer, it is more important to understand the contents of the framework and the approach SanFrancisco uses to support the business domain. As a result, examples are presented in text and non-UML diagrams.

This book provides insight and knowledge about the contents of the SanFrancisco framework as well as how a development shop codes an application that uses it. We delve into various business domains, but first provide a business-oriented background before presenting how the SanFrancisco framework addresses a domain.

The structure of the book is as follows:

- Part I gives an overview of how the SanFrancisco framework fits with an object-oriented development process and describes the overall architecture of SanFrancisco. The framework contains several layers. Each layer has a specific purpose and provides capabilities that allow developers to implement business requirements. After reading Part I, you should understand how the SanFrancisco framework fits into the development process. You should also understand the rationale for the layered approach and should be familiar with the contents of the layers. Part I should be read in its entirety by all readers.

- Part II provides deeper insight into the Foundation layer of SanFrancisco, which contains many of the object-oriented services (such as object persistence, transactions, and distribution). It also establishes the programming model that you use when programming with the SanFrancisco framework. Although many services are provided in this layer, there are no classes that correlate directly to a business application's needs (such as a currency class). On the other hand, there are primitive classes, collections, and helper classes that are used when the business content is built in the upper layers.

- Part III discusses the Common Business Objects (CBO) layer of SanFrancisco, the first layer to provide requirements-level reuse and implementations of those requirements. This layer provides a set of design patterns and principles that can be reused in their own right within an application. Requirements in this layer address the handling of business partners, currency, euro transition, and so on. These requirements are implemented using the design patterns and implementation classes defined within this layer, which are built using classes from the Foundation layer.

- Part IV is a discussion of the Core Business Processes (CBP) layer, where the most reuse for particular business environments can be garnered. Here, the perspective changes from traditional object-oriented development to analysis and design from the perspective of the business processes involved in a particular application. Whereas the earlier parts of the book largely involve reuse of patterns and implementation for developers, this part speaks more to customizations that are particular to a specific business system, explaining how to extend or enhance function within a framework to tailor it for a particular need. The chapters explain business domains using common examples before discussing how SanFrancisco supports the specific business domains.

- Part V talks about the creation of client applications, returning to programming and client implementation techniques. Whereas most of the book focuses on the framework and class extensions, at some point in development a final, deployable application must be built. In this part of the book, we discuss many SanFrancisco client development technologies, such as JavaBeans, as well as user interface building techniques.

The topics addressed in this book can be of value to many different people. No matter which of the following categories you fit into, make sure you read Part I. It explains the basis of SanFrancisco.

- *Analysts* will get the most from reading Parts III and IV, gaining familiarity with the contents of the Common Business Objects layer and Core Business Processes layer and learning how to exploit these layers for reuse when completing analysis of their own application requirements. An analyst should at least survey Parts I and II to understand the SanFrancisco structure and programming model. Surveying Part V will give analysts an idea of how the developers will complete the application for which the analysts design the business logic.

- *Designers* will have much the same task as analysts but should focus more closely on the patterns and implementations discussed in Parts III and IV. Designers should also have some knowledge of the technologies that will be crucial for implementors. As a result, a greater focus on Parts I, II, and III is necessary, and an understanding of Parts IV and V is useful.

- *Implementors* should focus on Parts I, II, and V. It is useful for an implementor to have at least a cursory understanding of how analysts and designers come to a particular conclusion, so an understanding of Parts III and IV can be helpful. With SanFrancisco, software implementors themselves are split into two groups: the framework implementors and the client implementors. Implementors who are putting the designs into use will have much less need for Part V and a heavier reliance on Parts III and IV of this book than those who are actually building clients.

Although we encourage reading the book from cover to cover, we understand that it caters to many different audiences. If your project is committed to using SanFrancisco, it is useful for everyone on the project to have a good understanding of the roles and responsibilities of each of the members of the team. At a minimum, the book explains the motivation for the framework and outlines its benefits. It also looks at the various layers of SanFrancisco and helps you understand each of them in the perspective for which it is most appropriate. Finally, the samples and code will give readers a good starting point for a project involving SanFrancisco.

Where to Find Out More about SanFrancisco

On the accompanying CD is the SanFrancisco Evaluation edition. After you install it, you will find a wealth of on-line documentation, including

- SanFrancisco Programmer's Guide. This reference explains the SanFrancisco programming model in detail. The programming model is introduced in Part IV of the book.

- SanFrancisco Business Requirements Guides. Complete listings of business requirements and processes that are implemented for the various domains currently addressed by SanFrancisco.

- JavaDoc. Complete JavaDoc for all publicly accessible classes.

On-line documentation. There are thousands of pages of documentation that attempt to fulfill the needs of everyone from a manager to an implementor. In addition to the on-line documentation, the SanFrancisco Web site contains white papers, business case studies, redbook information, and several user's guides for individual business domains. The site is located at http://www.software.ibm.com/ad/sanfrancisco.

Providing complete Rose diagrams for the contents of the SanFrancisco framework is not possible in an introductory book. If you would like to use the Rose diagrams and go further with the SanFrancisco framework, contact IBM for access to the diagrams and other related materials.

Additional books dealing with SanFrancisco that cater to different domains and contents in the framework will become available from Addison Wesley Longman. Many of the books will be written by authors who helped develop the technologies in SanFrancisco.

Acknowledgments

The authors would like to take a moment to pretend they are rock stars and thank the variety of people who made this book possible, helped ensure its technical accuracy, and, of course, helped it look nice and read cleanly.

First, we thank Robert Schmidt, the IBM manager who helped make all of this happen. Next, we would like to thank Mike Hendrickson, Julie Debaggis, Paul Becker, John Fuller, and Ross Venables for their patience and acceptance of the book and authors. A book about such a large, cutting-edge project is risky. We understand that and would like to thank Mike and the AWL team for their encouragement and help in getting this book published.

Our reviewers, Curt Brobst, Brent Carlson, Sholom Cohen, Howard Harkness, David Jordan, Haim Kilov, David Rine, Greg Rogers, and Will Tracz provided valuable and timely feedback. We thank them for their time and efforts. We looked forward to the reviews for days, and, after receiving them, we often regretted asking for their opinions. Without their reviews, however, the quality of this book would not have been nearly as high as it is now.

Finally, our grammar and spelling would not be as good as they are without the help of the copy editor, Betsy Hardinger.

In addition, Jim would like to thank his family—Anne, Marinda, and Joseph—for their support and patience. Thank you for giving me a reason to come home at night.

Mary would like to thank her husband, John, for his patience while she spent so much of her "free time" writing this book. She would also like to thank Bob Patton, formerly of Homestead High School, for getting her started toward her career in computer science. We've come a long way from those programmable calculators!

And last but not least, Paul would like to thank his parents, brother, and friends for all their support. He would also like to thank his new family, Andrea and Shaun. This isn't exactly a Rugrats book, and it probably won't be a movie, but thank you for tearing me away from the red ink and making life worth living.

Enjoy the book.

Part I

Introduction

To understand how the SanFrancisco component framework fits into a development process, you must understand the context in which the framework was created: its motivation, its building blocks, and its layers. To create an understanding of the SanFrancisco component framework, we present two introductory chapters that cater to all audiences.

Chapter 1, An Overview of SanFrancisco Development, provides insight into how frameworks fit into an object-oriented development process. Understanding how the framework is used leads to an understanding of the layers that make up the SanFrancisco component framework, as well as the layout of the book.

Chapter 2, Architecture Overview, looks at the contents and details of San-Francisco in more depth. It addresses the motivation for the layering approach used by SanFrancisco as well as the contents of the various layers. The chapter also discusses how to use the documentation provided by SanFrancisco.

An Overview of SanFrancisco Development

1

The SanFrancisco component framework is not, in itself, a development process. Examining how the SanFrancisco component framework fits *into* a development process will give you insight into how the component framework was developed and how you can derive the most benefit from it.

A key concept is the duality of the SanFrancisco component framework. On the one hand, there are many places where classes and implementations in SanFrancisco fulfill an application's needs exactly; this is why these elements are often referred to as *components*. On the other hand, throughout the components, extension points and modification points are provided that follow *patterns* and are better thought of as *frameworks*. Each term—*components* and *frameworks*—is applicable to different locations within the overall SanFrancisco component framework.

This chapter does not discuss actual implementations of components and framework mechanisms. Rather, it explains techniques you can use to adapt component and framework usage in an existing object-oriented development process.

Typically, you should adopt a well-known object-oriented development process throughout development with the SanFrancisco component framework. In this book we focus on the key phases of most object-oriented processes:

- Requirements gathering
- Object-oriented analysis (OOA)

- Object-oriented design (OOD)
- Object-oriented programming (OOP)
- Testing

The tools, documentation, and representations of classes and models used in the process can vary. Frequently, the large size of the systems to be built with the SanFrancisco framework may preclude your using index cards and whiteboards to diagram classes and relationships. Furthermore, the full SanFrancisco framework release provides analysis and design-level class models in unified modeling language (UML). Throughout this book, we use UML to depict relationships between classes, but developers can use any tool set or object-oriented design methodology and tools.

Keeping these things in mind, let's look at an overview of the object-oriented development process. Then we'll discuss how the existing development process can be enhanced to make the best use of frameworks.

The Object-oriented Development Process

The discussion of the object-oriented development process in this chapter does not embrace any single implementation of object-oriented development processes. Rather, we discuss the typical steps that are embodied in most object-oriented development processes. If you want a fuller treatment, many books are available on techniques and development process implementations.

A typical object-oriented development process is iterative. Iteration spans the entire process—often referred to as the *macro* development process—as well as the constituent steps. Object-oriented development starts with a requirements stage and proceeds through several steps, including analysis, design, and implementation. Each phase gets input from the previous stages and provides an output to the next stages of development. The project proceeds in a planned way from the system requirements, produced by the domain analysis team, to a system implementation, which is written in an object-oriented language.

Often, new requirements and capabilities are discovered at a later stage, affecting earlier stages. *Planned iteration* allows you to refine the output of each stage of the process based on late discoveries. For example, system designers often discover a system behavior that the application requirements did not take into account or did not adequately identify. This new requirement is fed back to the requirements documentation, which then proceeds through analysis and back into the design stage. On a smaller scale, an individual task, such as analysis, may go through successive iterations within itself. Furthermore, the requirements cycle and analysis cycle may occasionally go through iterations before reaching a design cycle.

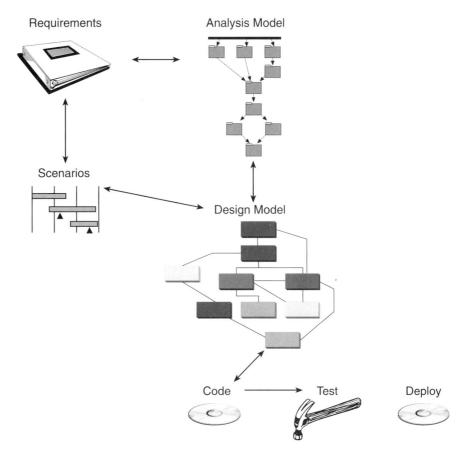

Requirements

Analysis Model

Scenarios

Design Model

Code   Test   Deploy

Figure 1-1. Object-oriented Development Process

Typically, there are six phases to the object-oriented process: requirements gathering, scenario design, analysis, design, programming, and testing (see Figure 1.1). Some processes blend scenario creation with requirements gathering or the object-oriented analysis stage, or testing may be combined with the coding phase.

Requirements Gathering

The requirements gathering phase, also known as a domain analysis phase, establishes the core requirements of a system. The system may be completely new, or it may be an addition to or modification of an existing system. Either way, the purpose is to gather the requirements for the system.

Typically, a small team of domain specialists, system architects, and developers sets out to determine the project's size and scope and write a high-level description of the requirements that the project must fulfill. The team may also produce a prototype or proof of concept implementation in this phase. A prototype aids in determining risk factors associated with the project.

It is crucial to exit this stage of development with a realistic view of the project's scope, risk, and project management style. Keep in mind that although it is tempting to close off the documentation of the requirements stage upon exiting, this stage remains alive. Remember, object-oriented processes are all about iteration. As analysis progresses, an aspect of the system may be uncovered that produces an additional requirement. Maintaining the requirements team is crucial so that it can evaluate whether a new requirement fits with the system and affects other results of the requirements gathering stage.

The output of a requirements phase typically includes the following:

- Documentation about the domain being addressed
- Information about what the system must do to fulfill the needs of its users and perhaps some specific information about how requirements are fulfilled
- Optional system prototypes
- Risk assessments
- Statement of project management style

Scenario Creation

As previously mentioned, scenario creation often blends into object-oriented analysis or possibly the output of requirements gathering. The most important thing is that application scenarios be produced and documented. The style of documentation for this stage varies. Often, a series of UML use cases is produced. The use cases take into account how various pieces of a system, including a user, interact with the system. They reflect how business logic flows through the system as well as how a user may interact with it and the subsequent effects that the interaction may have on the system.

A *scenario* begins with an initial state and is initiated by communication with, or within, the system. The scenario ripples through a series of objects and terminates with a new system state. It may sound odd that we have objects defined so early in the development process, but this is when the analysis-level classes start taking shape. Often, analysis occurs before scenario creation, in which case you start with a set of classes to define the scenarios. The interactions that occur in the system are documented, thus making the states predictable and forming the basis for an application.

Output from this stage typically includes

- Domain-level scenarios or use cases
- Revised requirements

Object-oriented Analysis

The analysis phase focuses on the behavior of the system. However, the *how*—as in "How do I iterate over the Result collection"—and other detailed questions are left for later. During analysis, the system's major functions are explored, as are the behaviors a system can exhibit, ways the system can or cannot interact with other systems, and any oversights that may have occurred in requirements gathering or scenario development. Previous use cases or scenarios may be refined, and second-level use cases may be added.

Also during analysis, the system is initially partitioned into package-level diagrams and sometimes beyond: into rough class diagrams that delve lightly into the domain aspects of the system. These partitions have responsibilities within the context of the system assigned to them. Keep in mind that the analysis phase is weighted heavily toward the application from a domain and architect's perspective and not from a programmer's perspective.

Package-level diagrams are used for a variety of reasons, such as dividing a system into logical pieces. Packages can be nested in analysis models. Pieces and packages can be used to maintain lower complexity. Similarly, a package can be used to divide a system into its component subsystems.

Object-oriented analysis is one of the most critical phases of the development cycle. Unfortunately, if a development team is heavily weighted with programmers, OOA is sometimes overlooked or minimized, a sure path to project failure. On the other hand, projects have been known to get stuck in what is known as "analysis paralysis" when the domain specialists and system architects attempt to solve more problems than should be taken on during the analysis phase.

It's important to understand that analysis should uncover all the primary behaviors and many of the secondary behaviors of a system. Attempting to uncover every class, every artifact of each scenario, and every tertiary behavior within a system will drag a project down. This type of work should be left to the design and implementation stages. In fact, often the design phase starts to overlap the tail end of the analysis.

The output of the analysis phase typically includes

- Further revised requirements documentation
- Refined scenarios and second-level scenarios or use cases

- A domain-level class diagram
- A revised risk assessment for the project

Object-oriented Design

Object-oriented design bridges the domain-oriented analysis models to the design of the underlying implementation that is used to build the project. In a nutshell, a level of realistic detail is added to the analysis and requirements. Implementation questions—such as "How many elements can be in my collection?" and "What is the best type of collection to use?"—are answered.

In addition to designing the implementation, the design phase is concerned with management of the project as a whole. By this time, the analysis should have yielded enough details to let you create a release plan, testing criteria, and a realistic assessment of the risk associated with the project.

Architectural patterns are identified during this phase of development as the overall system architecture is built. There are many ways to approach system design and architecture. Whatever approach you use, it's important not to postpone difficult problems until late in the design; it can create problems when you try to produce a realistic project plan. Also, system designers should look for opportunities for reuse and ensure that what they are implementing in the design accurately reflects the vision passed down by the analysts.

Again, even though the overall system architecture is likely defined in this phase, it may be fatal to expect to have a complete system architecture before you turn to the next phase of development. As with all portions of an object-oriented development process, the design phase may have important information that gets fed back into the analysis phase.

Output of the design phase typically includes

- An overall system architecture
- Design patterns that will be used in implementation
- Project plans

Code

The coding phase of a project usually requires the work of substantially more developers than earlier stages. Moving from design into implementation can be difficult. If a rigorous architecture is followed throughout the earlier stages of development and if tools are used that generate particular file formats, however, code generators may be available to build much of the code for implementation. Typically, code generators can generate implementations for simple read/write properties as well as many more-complex patterns and templates. Code generators allow programmers to focus on custom business logic rather than on the typical repetitive patterns that occur in program models.

If you are using class libraries, it is in coding that the payoff will likely occur. For example, if the project needs a persistence model, programmers can use Java's JDBC classes—otherwise known as the Java Database Connectivity classes—in combination with the Java serialization interface to implement persistence. Some class libraries may enter the picture during the design phase, but it is more likely that they are leveraged at this level.

Programmers are normally required to participate in the unit test of their code. The goal is to provide a product that can be released into the larger test phase and subsequently to the customers.

Output of the coding phase typically includes

- Working—possibly unit tested—deliverables, which could be components or a complete application
- Complete end user documentation

Test

Testing occurs at many different levels. Scenario creation helps to test system requirements. Analysis and design further validate requirements and scenarios. Scenarios test other scenarios and help to find system problems early in development.

By the time coding occurs, many high-level tests are completed. As coding proceeds, unit testing proceeds. Unit testing is typically the first line of defense against implementation bugs. It ensures that the methods and components, or units, function as expected.

Then formal component and system tests are designed for a project. They test at a higher level of the system than what individual programmers can usually achieve. Whereas unit tests test all paths that the programmer is aware of through the code, component tests test the contracts and boundary conditions of the system components. Finally, the system test is used to test the various ways in which the components can be used in the larger context of the system. Typically, in system tests all the components of a system are finally fit together in a way that is similar to the way customers will use the components.

After all levels of testing are complete to a satisfactory level, a final product is shipped. At this point the entire object-oriented development process starts again from the top, with new requirements that are added, leftover requirements that may not have made it into the final release because of one project constraint or another, and perhaps even bug fixes.

Output of the testing phase typically includes

- A tested product that is ready to be installed by customers
- Complete, tested end user documentation

A Framework-enhanced Development Process

To be useful, frameworks should have well-defined locations in the development process where they can be reused. At these locations, documentation typically exists to aid the target audience at each stage in understanding the contents of the framework and getting reuse from it. For example, if a framework advocates reuse at the requirements phase, documentation that is targeted at domain analysts and system architects must exist.

In the SanFrancisco framework, reuse starts at the beginning of the development process—at the application requirements stage—and continues throughout the process. For the requirements stage, the documentation provided by SanFrancisco is tailored to domain analysts. It consists of application requirements that are fulfilled in the SanFrancisco Framework implementation and design patterns. For the design stage, SanFrancisco supports reuse in two ways. First, the requirements' reuse produces design-level models and documentation for the design phase. Second, SanFrancisco provides a set of design patterns and classes that can be used for fulfilling new requirements. For the implementation and testing stages, reuse occurs in many ways. First, the implementations of the requirements and design patterns supply much of the implementation code for the server-side components in an application. In addition, implementors can reuse client technologies that are packaged with SanFrancisco. The client technologies can simplify access to framework components, organize them for better performance, and even provide graphical user interfaces.

Enhancing the object-oriented development process to take into account a framework really consists of two elements:

- Mapping the framework
- Rigorous documentation

The mapping steps and documentation go through each of the steps of the object-oriented development process. Mapping steps give the development team time to pause and search for reuse in corresponding framework documentation. If reuse is found during a mapping step, it must be documented and passed to the next phase (because reuse at an early stage implies reuse at later stages). Furthermore, this reuse affects the project's risk assessment and schedule, and this information is fed back to previous development stages for reevaluation.

The mapping steps are added to requirements gathering, scenario development, analysis, and design. Latter stages of the development process gain from the early identification of a mapping. For example, identifying a requirement that is fulfilled in the SanFrancisco framework implies the availability of scenarios, class diagrams, and implementations of the scenarios. The testing phase also benefits substantially because the implementations are heavily tested.

To aid in understanding the many ways that the SanFrancisco Framework fits into OOD, the SanFrancisco Framework provides the SanFrancisco Application Development Roadmap. The Roadmap provides advice and guidelines for the activities to undertake during each phase of OOD. It also includes a set of checklists and templates that can be used for creating the work products that are a result of each phase. You need not use these templates and checklists in your own development cycle, but they may help you formulate the documentation that you will produce at each stage.

Requirements Mapping

Because reuse with the SanFrancisco Framework begins at the requirements phase, a mapping step should be added to the end of this phase. This added step gives the architects pause to discover whether there are application requirements that are fulfilled with the SanFrancisco Framework and that either matches, or nearly matches, those identified in the requirements phase.

An example is the *stock take* that occurs in warehouse applications. Stock take involves the maintenance of physical inventory in a warehouse. A requirements document exists in the *SanFrancisco Framework Business Reference* that addresses stock take directly:

```
WHS Stock Take

Abstract:

This process is used for counting physical stock.

Description:

Five major steps are included in a full stock take run / process:

1 Select stock to include in count

2 Perform physical count (purely manual step)

3 Enter result of count

4 Perform analysis of result (not included in the framework)

5 Update stock figures and create records of update
```

Domain analysts can use this documentation to map their requirements to the contents of the SanFrancisco framework. The documentation goes further, explaining how the requirement is implemented, how it is designed, and how the default processes can be overridden or extended. Also included in the requirements documentation are the tasks and scenarios in the SanFrancisco framework that implement the application requirements.

Discovery of this potential reuse in a warehouse application requires a mapping step, an opportunity for thinking, calculation, and matching. A mapping step doesn't always yield reuse, but experienced analysts often find mappings that are exact, almost exact, or close enough to garner some reuse in development. Often, you find new requirements in your own application. In that case you should seriously consider documenting it in the same manner as the framework documentation.

If there are matches or close matches, additional output from the requirements phase should include the following:

- Documentation of any high-level application requirements that are fulfilled, or nearly fulfilled, by the framework. It also identifies how the framework may have to be extended or changed to adapt the framework's implementation of the requirement to the application's version of the requirement.

- Modification of the risk assessments.

Scenario Mapping

As with the requirements phase, documentation in the SanFrancisco framework describes scenarios and tasks that the framework implements. This information is not in UML use cases; rather, it is in table format. The table is tied to the requirements documentation or can be accessed independently. This two-way access allows the following:

- You can reuse common scenarios that are usually identified from application requirements already implemented by the SanFrancisco framework. This reuse should quicken the pace of the scenario mapping phase compared with that of a typical object-oriented development process.

- Occasionally you discover scenarios that should have been identified in the requirements phase. Allowing direct access to scenarios allows discovery, whether or not an associated requirement was identified. After the scenario is identified, the team can identify the requirement that drove the SanFrancisco framework to identify the scenario, and that may help you identify missing requirements in the system as the requirements team defined it.

Any mapping discoveries made here should be adequately documented and passed to the analysis phase. This mapping phase may drive iteration back into the requirements phase for revisions.

Outputs of the scenario mapping stages include

- A list of application scenarios that are fulfilled by the framework
- Additional scenarios discovered by the framework that are not found in a specific application requirement

Object-oriented Analysis Mapping

Further mapping to existing SanFrancisco framework requirements and scenarios occurs during this phase. Also, with the additional input by the mapping exercises, the analysis step should give developers a jump on the creation of class diagrams; the SanFrancisco framework comes with analysis-level class diagrams that implement the requirements and scenarios.

Often, reuse of common business objects starts here. Whereas prior stages of development were highly focused on application domain information, now analysis can start moving away from the domain specifics. For example, suppose that an insurance application requirement states that all policy numbers are unique. It is likely that, in the requirements phase, the analysts were focused on locating a policy class or a similar match. At analysis time, a further level of detail is brought out in the insurance policy. An analyst now discovers that the Number Series requirements match the requirement of generating unique numbers for the policy classes. While this is not a complete match for the policy, it will prove useful through the course of application development.

Outputs of the analysis mapping stage include

- Detailed information on reuse discovered during analysis
- Modified analysis models that use and extend the framework analysis models

Object-oriented Design Mapping

Mapping steps, which can benefit from mapping exercises just as much as prior phases do, should continue during the design phase. Nonetheless, much of the reuse that occurs in design starts in prior phases.

If matching requirements and scenarios have been found earlier, designers can gather many of their design-level class diagrams from the SanFrancisco framework. The framework comes with these diagrams as well as design patterns. The latter are discussed in the SanFrancisco Programmer's Guide and the SanFrancisco Extension Guide. The design patterns are used to implement common business application constructs.

An example of a design pattern that may be discovered and reused during a design mapping stage is the Property Containment pattern. Property Containment (discussed later in the book) is useful for runtime modification of class attributes.

Outputs of the design mapping stage include

- Documentation of design reuse, including applicable design patterns discovered in the framework
- Modified design models that implement the design patterns

Implementation Mapping

By the time implementations of framework components and client applications are produced, the mapping steps should reveal most of the reuse that the implementations can exploit. On the other hand, there is no reason to stop the mapping steps at the final stages of a project.

Mapping during implementation can be useful because you can often find in a framework classes that can be used in a client application. For example, the SanFrancisco framework provides a Client Command framework that may be useful for alleviating a performance bottleneck. This discovery is likely to occur at implementation time.

Locating potential reuse in the implementation phase may be the result of an oversight on the designer's part or merely an unexpected detail that could not have been predicted. Either way, it is useful if the system implementors are aware of any client-side technologies the framework has to offer and are on the lookout for possible reuse of client technologies supplied by the framework. If reuse is discovered in the implementation phase, feedback to the design phase is crucial. An implementation that is not approved by system designers may have an unexpected impact on system flexibility or a characteristic that is not seen in the implementor's environment.

Documentation

As you develop applications using a framework, it's critical to remember the importance of documenting your design decisions so that they are comprehensible to people who will be working on future iterations of the software. Suppose, for example, that you implement your project in the Java language. By basing the documentation on the implementation code and developers' comments, the JavaDoc tool produces consistent and predictable programming-level documentation. Now suppose that you create your own documentation format for your classes and extensions. Unless you redocument all the Java portions of the application in this format, you will force future system maintainers and programmers to understand and work with both formats.

The Java example applies equally to framework development. If you expect your application to revolve around the architecture, design, and components of an existing framework, it is worthwhile to think about how future analysts and designers will use the documentation you produce. If you choose to use UML use cases and class diagrams, you need to ask yourself whether you have included enough information so that future system maintainers can understand where the system can be extended to add new functions, how the system was intended to be extended at that location, and what motivated particular design decisions. Keep in mind that if you choose a format and if the framework you use has chosen a different format, you need to consider how the two will mesh to create the overall picture of the system.

An Example

To illustrate where the mapping processes fit into a small scenario, let's look at a short case study that terminates after the requirements mapping phase of development. The case study is expanded later in the book. Here, a high-level view of the case study is sufficient to illustrate how the SanFrancisco framework fits into the object-oriented development process.

The requirements phase applies to both the pure object-oriented development process and the framework-enhanced version of the object-oriented process. For now, we forgo the details of how these requirements came to be, and we leave the requirements at a very high level. Let's just say that upon examining the needs of several customers, an application development group comes up with the following business application requirements during the requirements gathering phase. An application must be built that supports physical inventory by performing the following tasks:

- Set up and maintain business rules for taking inventory. An annual count of the entire inventory could be taken, but most businesses have instituted some form of cyclic count in which items are counted at various intervals depending on their relative importance.

- Determine the stock to count based on the defined business rules.

- Perform the physical inventory count.

- Record the result of the count.

- Analyze the result of the count.
- Update the inventory figures with the final count.

With these requirements in mind, the development process is now split into two separate tracks. On one track, development proceeds using the object-oriented, nonframework approach. On the other track, development proceeds using the object-oriented, framework-enhanced approach. (Keep in mind that here we are documenting these two tracks at a very high level. The primary difference is that the framework approach entails additional steps for mapping framework elements to the project requirements for possible reuse.)

After the requirements are defined, the framework user attempts to find matches or near matches in the framework. In our example the framework user finds the WHS Stock Take requirement in the SanFrancisco framework. Upon matching the framework contents, the framework supplies predefined scenarios to be used in the scenario creation phase. A set of domain-level class diagrams, design-level class diagrams, and the tested implementation is also available for the latter portions of the development process.

In the nonframework development track—or in the event that no mappings are found between the application requirements and the requirements that are fulfilled by the framework—development starts with the given requirements and continues directly to the scenario creation phase.

Note that the framework-enhanced process has a major advantage over the nonframework process. The SanFrancisco framework produces a matching requirement. As a result, much of the input and output of the scenario creation phase, the analysis phase, the design phase, the implementation phase, and the testing phase are already complete.

It goes without saying that even with the match found in the framework, the latter phases of development should be carried out. Analysis may revise the requirements and determine that some part of the system is not a perfect match with the SanFrancisco framework implementation of the WHS Stock Take. The same goes for the design and implementation phases.

Although this example appears contrived—it matches the warehouse stock take requirement presented earlier in the chapter—there are many cases in which the requirements in the SanFrancisco framework will match this closely. After all, domain analysts with application experience designed the requirements that the framework implements.

It's clear that in this warehouse stock take application, the framework users have leapfrogged the nonframework development shop in all aspects of the process. One thing left up to the framework users in this example is to build the application's user interface. This requires the team to create additional scenarios, resulting in impact on analysis, design, implementation, and testing. Of course, one should never minimize the impact of the user interface on the project as a whole.

Overall, the payoff for using the framework, the framework mapping exercises, and the reuse of framework elements (in the form of analysis, design, implementation, and testing) should allow the framework users to move up the release date for the project and beat the nonframework users to market.

Summary

The SanFrancisco framework, and frameworks in general, provide multiple elements that can be reused. These reusable elements include prefabricated analysis-level and design-level class models as well as use cases, scenarios, design patterns, and implementation code (and their documentation) that can be used to meet a variety of business requirements. Typically reuse is discovered in explicit mapping steps that are added to a traditional object-oriented development process.

Most projects fall somewhere in between the two extremes of potential framework reuse. Consider a project in which reuse is minimal. As development proceeds from the requirements phase to the testing phase, all the units and outputs of each phase must be produced within the process itself. If few or no mappings can be found between the project requirements and the framework components, much of the application must be designed, coded, and tested on site. As a result, the project derives little benefit from the experience of the framework designers.

On the other hand, if your project reuses SanFrancisco framework components, such as diagrams and documentation, at early phases in development, it reduces the amount of work that must be done in all phases. The earlier the reuse occurs, the more the benefits ripple to later phases, all the way through to testing. Framework implementations require little or no unit testing or component testing. The test cycle is responsible chiefly for testing newly implemented components and extensions and for conducting the system test.

Architecture Overview

Chapter 1 describes how to use SanFrancisco when you develop an application. This use, which involves a great deal of reuse, is driven by the same business motivation that drove IBM to develop SanFrancisco, which in turn provides the major driving force behind the architecture of SanFrancisco. This chapter describes the architecture as well as the vision behind it. Here you'll find the highest-level overview of what SanFrancisco provides and the background necessary to effectively read the remainder of this book.

SanFrancisco Architectural Vision

The architectural vision behind SanFrancisco is based on a number of interrelated goals:

- To enable solution developers to rapidly deploy business applications
- To free solution developers from having to worry about the underlying technology and thus to enable them to target any underlying technology
- To enable solution developers to concentrate on those aspects of their application that differentiate it from other applications having the same target customers

From these goals come the guiding architectural principles of SanFrancisco. The core principles fall into the following areas:

- To provide the maximum of reuse possible
- To provide isolation from the underlying technology
- To provide the core of the solution that would have to be supplied by any application in a particular domain
- To allow integration with existing systems

Let's look at each of these areas in detail.

Maximizing Reuse

There are many ways in which SanFrancisco can be used by solution providers, each use building from a different entry point. Each entry point must maximize reuse from its perspective without the clutter of the other reusable pieces. For this reason, each entry point to SanFrancisco is isolated within a *layer*. These layers can be thought of as independent, interrelated frameworks.

Frameworks in and of themselves maximize reuse by allowing customization of the components they provide. This customization enables framework developers to provide the core of the application, which the solution provider adapts to build an application. The ability to customize is the key to reusing any framework; thus the framework developer must provide for it in a consistent manner. This consistency promotes understanding, making it easier for the solution provider to use the framework. One of the best ways to ensure consistency is to identify patterns of customization and to capture them formally as design patterns. SanFrancisco's design patterns, as well as other customization techniques, are captured in detail in the SanFrancisco Extension Guide, which is included as part of the SanFrancisco product. In addition, SanFrancisco provides a code generator, which generates Java code from object models to simplify the use of many of these patterns.

Reuse of an item can be maximized only if its documentation is complete. It must cover all levels of reuse, from the requirements down to the implemented code, as discussed in Chapter 1. At first blush it may seem that the code itself should not be exposed. However, exposure allows much broader reuse because it not only clarifies what the class does but also lets us modify the class when necessary. You can discard small pieces of the exposed class. If it were opaque, you would have to discard the whole class.

The components provided on top of the framework are JavaBeans or other components that simplify the use of the framework. For simple uses, they provide reusable components. For more complex uses, they provide examples of how to create the components from the framework.

Isolation from Underlying Technology

Constantly having to rewrite your application to adapt to a new platform or to take advantage of the latest technology is time-consuming and expensive. Unfortunately, such changes are rarely isolated but instead ripple through the entire application. Ideally, you should be able to draw a clear "line in the sand," encapsulating the underlying technology as much as possible and freeing the majority of the application from the particular technology on which it is implemented. In SanFrancisco, the *SanFrancisco Programming Model* (SFPM) defines a set of base classes and application programming interfaces (APIs). It also specifies how they should be used to minimize dependency on the underlying technology.

The SanFrancisco code generator provides support for generating Java code that conforms to the SFPM. This tool simplifies using and conforming to the SFPM.

Focus on the Core

When you look at applications for a specific domain, there are parts that differ between the applications and parts that are common across the majority of the applications. The common parts supply the functions that must be supplied to have a viable application. The parts that aren't common are usually those that differentiate one application from another in the marketplace. SanFrancisco focuses on the common (or core) pieces so that you can focus on the pieces that differentiate your application. SanFrancisco designers worked with experts in each domain to identify which parts are which.

One aspect of focusing on the core is to ensure that the framework provides only those attributes and methods that the framework needs as well as those that all domain experts expect to find in the class. For example, an Address class that did not have an e-mail address attribute would be surprising to most experts, so SanFrancisco provides such an attribute even though it is not used directly by the framework. This approach keeps the classes focused and uncluttered. The other approach—adding everything anyone might ever want—would create huge classes having many attributes and methods.

Another aspect of focusing on the core is to ensure that the core parts can be customized for most applications—that is, focusing on the core uses. This focus is necessary because it isn't practical to support every possible customization. In other words, SanFrancisco did not make the framework more complex only to support a use that would be needed by a very small percentage of applications. This is not to say that these applications cannot be accommodated. It means only that customizing the framework for those cases will not be as easy.

Integration with Existing Systems

The ability to integrate with existing systems (sometimes called *legacy* systems) is another important aspect of SanFrancisco architectural vision. Integration involves the ability to gradually move to a SanFrancisco solution while sharing data with an existing system.

This integration capability requires isolation between the parts of SanFrancisco, allowing you to substitute existing application modules. For example, SanFrancisco ensures that all of the framework's interaction with the General Ledger (in the financial subsystem) goes through a well-defined interface. In this way, information being sent to the General Ledger can be redirected to a legacy General Ledger module. This redirection does not affect the subsystems that are sending information to the General Ledger.

Even if an existing application can be replaced with a SanFrancisco solution, sometimes the data in the database must remain in the same layout, either because of the difficulties of reformatting it or the existence of other applications that will continue to use the data. The Foundation layer provides support that allows the object structure to be mapped to the legacy layout. This mapping is not done by the object designer but rather is done in deployment when the relationship between the object and the database is defined. (This is not to say that object designers can be oblivious to mapping considerations. It means only that they do not have to be driven by them.)

SanFrancisco Architecture

The architectural vision just described is what drives the SanFrancisco architecture. This section provides an overview of the architecture: the pieces that make it up and how they relate to one another. It gives you the necessary background for understanding the more-detailed discussions later in this book.

The overall architecture of SanFrancisco is shown in Figure 2-1. Here you can see the layering of SanFrancisco, which allows different entry points into SanFrancisco and thus different levels of reuse. Moving from the top down, these layers proceed, with respect to a particular application domain, from most specific to most general.

The most specific layer is the *Core Business Processes* layer, which captures the main classes and processes for a particular application domain. Because it is the most specific layer, it is applicable only to the domains it covers. One such domain, Warehouse Management, contains the core classes and processes necessary to build a warehouse management application. These components are not provided as static components that must be used as is but instead are provided in a manner that allows easy customization. For example, Warehouse Management provides a stock replenishment process whereby you buy more

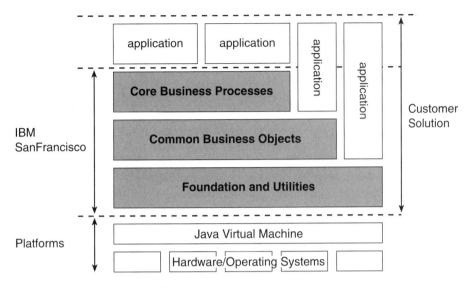

Figure 2-1. SanFrancisco Architecture

stock just before you run out. Every warehouse management application must support this process. It is provided so that you can easily customize the business rules driving the replenishment. The other domains covered are General Ledger, Accounts Receivable/Accounts Payable, and Order Management. Some core business processes are built directly on the underlying Common Business Object layer, whereas other core business processes are themselves built on top of other supporting core business processes.

The middle layer is the *Common Business Objects* layer. This layer consists of classes, processes, and mechanisms that are common across many application domains. This layer was populated in two ways. One was by domain experts identifying classes and processes needed by a broad array of business applications. The other way was by identifying commonalities between the domains supported in the Core Business Processes layer. The Common Business Objects layer will continue to grow over time as additional core business processes are developed.

The bottom layer is the *Foundation and Utilities* layer. This layer provides the basic services needed by a business application and isolates applications from the underlying technologies. The basic services include things such as storage and sharing of business objects and utilities to configure and control the basic services. It is in the Foundation layer that the SanFrancisco Programming Model is defined and supported. One example of the isolation provided here is that the developer, who must supply the business logic, can develop it independently of the particular database used to store the objects.

Each of these layers is built on all the layers below it. In other words, when you look at a particular layer, you see that it uses some of the classes and processes provided by the layers below it. It also means that when you are developing, you use classes and processes from not only the layer you are targeting but also the layers below it. For example, the Core Business Processes layer is on top of the Common Business Objects layer. A class that is provided by the Core Business Processes layer is built using a class or classes from the Common Business Objects layer or the Foundation layer. On the other hand, classes added during development can be built on classes from any of the layers.

When you are developing your application, you can use SanFrancisco at whatever level is appropriate for your needs. For example, as shown in Figure 2-2, if you are building a financial application, you could build it on the General Ledger and Accounts Receivable/Accounts Payable portions of the Core Business Processes layer. On the other hand, if your application were an insurance application, which SanFrancisco does not provide as part of the Core Business Processes layer, you would build it on the Common Business Objects layer. If you were creating a nonbusiness application, which might not benefit from the Common Business Objects layer, you would build it directly on the Foundation layer.

This does not mean that a financial application must be built on the Core Business Processes layer; you can decide to build the application on a lower level and not use the Core Business Processes layer at all. However, you would lose the advantage of having the Core Business Processes layer provide the

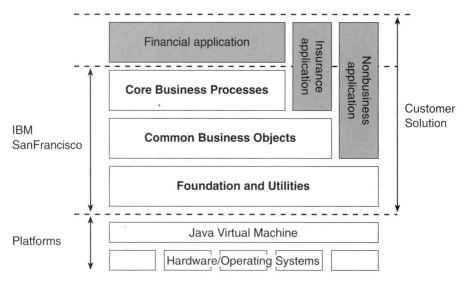

Figure 2-2. Building on SanFrancisco

processes that are common to all applications within, for example, the General Ledger and Accounts Receivable/Accounts Payable domains. Every General Ledger must somehow represent an account and must determine which accounts are valid. This support is provided by the General Ledger portion of the Core Business Processes layer.

The Core Business Processes

The core business processes (contained in the Core Business Processes layer) provide the most application-domain-specific portion of SanFrancisco (see Figure 2-3). Each core business process provides the common processes and classes for a particular business domain.

A common process is one that every business application in a particular domain would have. For example, warehouse management applications support stock take (also known as physical inventory), which involves physically counting the amount of various products stored in the warehouse on schedules determined by the business. The SanFrancisco Warehouse Management core business process provides this. Simply providing the process, however, is not enough. Even though all warehouse management applications (in particular, their inventory control portions) support stock take, the resulting action—

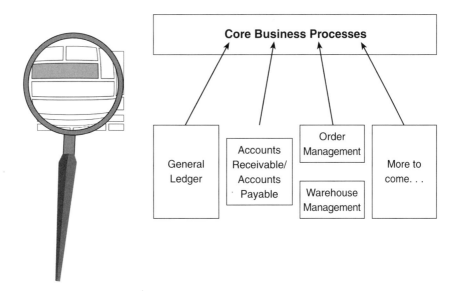

Figure 2-3. The Core Business Processes

taken as a result of finding differences between what you thought you had and what you actually have—can vary. For this reason, SanFrancisco provides the common processes in a manner that allows them to be easily customized through what is called *extension points*. To identify these common processes and specify how they enable customization, IBM enlisted the help of solution providers familiar with each domain.

To effectively use a core business process, you must understand it at many levels, especially at each level where reuse of the framework can occur (see Figure 2-4). The highest-level documentation for any of the core business processes is its User Guide, which provides a high-level domain entry point into the capabilities SanFrancisco provides. The User Guide discusses the support in terms that a domain person understands and then maps from this perspective to what is provided by SanFrancisco. This approach allows a domain expert to understand what is provided and an architect or developer to see how that relates to what SanFrancisco provides. In parallel with the User Guides are the

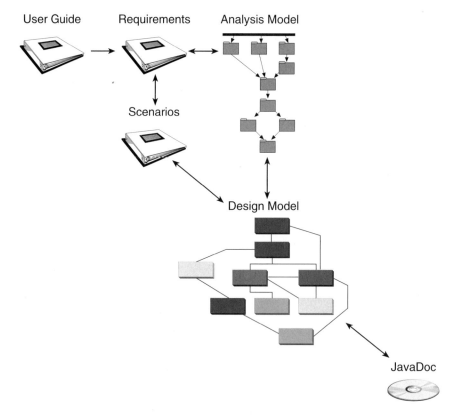

Figure 2-4. Core Business Process Documentation Structure

requirements. The requirements consist of domain-level *processes,* which are broken into individual *tasks.* The processes give you a domain-level view of the requirements broken down into activities that logically belong together. This is similar to what is provided by the User Guide and both the processes and the User Guide refer to the tasks that make up the processes. For each task, one or more *scenarios* supply a more detailed description of the task (or a portion of it).

For example, the Warehouse Management core business process requirements have a process for stock take, which contains a task for generating a stock take list (the list of which items to count). This task has a single scenario, which provides detail on what actually happens when the stock take list is generated.

Along with the requirements, object diagrams, called the *analysis model,* are supplied. These diagrams provide a domain-level view of the object model and relationships. The analysis model contains those classes that a domain expert will be most familiar with, such as a Warehouse class and a Product class in the Warehouse Management core business process.

From the scenarios and the analysis model, more details are provided by the *design model* and finally by the JavaDoc. The design model adds the design-level classes and relationships to the object model. The JavaDoc describes each method in detail, including in many cases the preconditions that must exist and any postconditions that will exist when the method is used. For the Core Business Processes layer (and the Common Business Objects layer), the source code is also provided. SanFrancisco provides all this documentation (User Guide to JavaDoc and source code) so that a solution provider can effectively map to the support provided by SanFrancisco. In this way, as discussed in Chapter 1, a solution provider can maximize reuse.

Often, the documentation will lead a solution provider to SanFrancisco support that is close to, but is not quite, what is needed. In this case the solution provider modifies the support to meet the particular need. The documentation and design of the core business processes aid in customizing the support by identifying extension points where the support is designed to be modified.

A catalog of extension techniques, called the Extension Guide, is provided with SanFrancisco. This catalog describes how to identify the extension points and the techniques (patterns) used to support them. For example, business logic can vary based on differing criteria. Sometimes the business logic is associated with a particular business object, such as a product, and at other times it is associated with a particular company. When defining the replenishment policy for a product, you may want a different policy for each product, or you may want one that is used for all products. The Extension Guide describes how to use the extension techniques and how to design them into your application.

The Extension Guide is valuable in two ways. First, it ensures that extension techniques are used consistently so that when the same customization approach is needed in two processes, the same technique is used. This makes it much easier to understand SanFrancisco. After you understand a particular use of an extension technique, you can apply that knowledge to all other uses of the technique. Second, the catalog provides an organized document for you to use as a reference when adding customization to your application.

Currently four core business processes are provided in SanFrancisco: Accounts Receivable/Accounts Payable, General Ledger, Order Management, and Warehouse Management. Accounts Receivable/Accounts Payable and General Ledger provide the core for a financial application. The General Ledger provides the function necessary for recording the financial history of the company. It supports receiving this information from other subsystems or applications through a generic interface. The General Ledger is the source of information you need to produce reports on earnings for the tax authorities and the owners of the company. Accounts Receivable/Accounts Payable (AR/AP) handles processing of customer and supplier invoices and payments, allowing you to manage what you owe and what you are owed. Warehouse Management introduces the basic concepts of warehouse, product, and inventory and extends them to provide robust warehouse and stock management. Order Management is built on top of Warehouse Management and provides a flexible and reconfigurable set of basic order types such as sales, purchase, quotation, back-to-back, and credit order. You can modify these order types and create new order types by using the features of the Order Management core business process.

The core business processes can be related to one another directly or indirectly. In direct dependence, one core business process is built on another. For example, Order Management is built on top of Warehouse Management. Indirect relationships are subtler; they show up as one core business process using a generic interface of another core business process. Part of this subtlety is that the generic interface is provided as part of a lower layer.

For example, as shown in Figure 2-5, Warehouse Management indirectly depends on General Ledger because Warehouse Management uses the generic interface to General Ledger, which is provided as part of the Common Business Objects layer. In the figure, when there is a change in stock in the warehouse, such as a damaged item being discovered, the assets of the business must be updated in the General Ledger. To do this, the interface to the General Ledger, provided as part of the Common Business Objects layer, is used. A similar situation exists between the AR/AP and the General Ledger core business processes. For example, when a payment that is processed by the accounts receivable application is made, the status of the customer account and the cash account in the general ledger must be updated to reflect the payment.

A *generic interface* provides a means of getting information into a core business process without the need to know all the details of that core business process; that is, a generic interface isolates the supplier from the consumer of the information. This isolation allows suppliers to use the interface without having

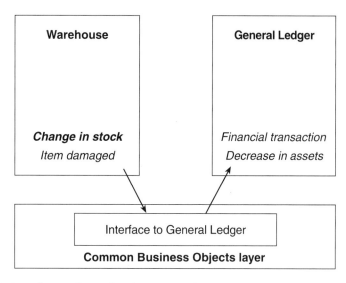

Figure 2-5. Interface to General Ledger Example

to know whether a consumer exists, and it allows the consumer to be replaced without affecting the supplier. For example, when the Warehouse Management core business process supplies information to the general ledger, it does not care whether an application based on the General Ledger core business process receives it, a legacy general ledger receives it, or the information is discarded (in the unlikely case that there isn't a general ledger). This type of interface is currently provided for the General Ledger and AR/AP core business processes. These interfaces are an important aspect of the core business process. However, because they are used by one or more other core business processes and to emphasize the fact that they do not depend on the target core business process, they are provided as part of the Common Business Objects layer.

You can use a core business process when you are developing an application that includes its particular domain. However, it is up to you to decide which (and how many) of the core business processes to use. For example, if you are developing a financial application, it could be written on top of both the General Ledger and AR/AP core business processes. You must also decide how much of the core business process to use. In some cases you may omit whole pieces of the core business process. The normal practice, however, involves customizing the classes and processes provided (using the extension points) and adding processes and classes unique to your application.

The Common Business Objects

Even though business applications cover a wide variety of domains, there is still an underlying set of common processes and classes that are shared by most or all of them. Leveraging solution provider experience and its own experience developing the core business processes, IBM identified many of these common processes and classes. They are provided in the Common Business Objects layer and are usually called common business objects. They are split into three main groups: general business objects, financial business objects, and generalized mechanisms (see Figure 2-6).

The *general business objects*, the most recognizable to all domains, are the business objects needed by most business applications. Examples are Company, Currency, and Customer (Business Partner). Because they are part of the Common Business Objects layer, they can be reused and shared among applications.

The *financial business objects* are the common business objects related to the financial aspects of business. SanFrancisco provides two types: general business objects that are financially oriented, such as Bank, Bank Accounts, Invoicing, and Financial Calendar; and business objects related to transferring financial status into the financial subsystems. The latter category consists of the direct support of the generic interfaces, discussed in the preceding section, and indirect support from financial integration, which supports mapping from one

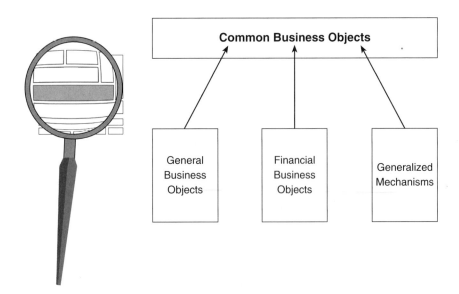

Figure 2-6. Common Business Objects Layer

domain's items to the accounts in the General Ledger—for example, allowing the warehouse management application to update the general ledger using products, warehouses, and stock types, instead of knowing the details of the general ledger's accounting structure.

The final group of processes and classes provided in the Common Business Objects layer is the *generalized mechanisms*, which provide defined solutions to recurring business application problems. Generalized mechanisms are also known as patterns. They are described in more detail later in this chapter.

Breaking the Common Business Objects layer into these three groups is somewhat arbitrary. The groups are intended only to help understanding and not as a statement of how each item in a particular group must be used. For example, the processes and classes associated with currency are considered a common business object but could just as easily have been considered a financial business object.

The documentation provided for the general business objects and the financial business objects is the same as that of the core business processes. Figure 2-4 shows the structure of the documentation. On the other hand, the generalized mechanisms are documented in the SanFrancisco Extension Guide. All the SanFrancisco patterns are documented in the Extension Guide because they are involved with the various extension techniques. The Extension Guide provides information on what a pattern is, when to use it, which customization it supports, and how to use it.

The Common Business Objects layer, unlike the Core Business Processes layer, provides independent pieces from which you can pick and choose. This arrangement is similar to that of a class library except that the individual pieces consist of a set of related processes and classes. For example, you can decide whether you want to use the currency class in SanFrancisco, but if you need to use the Exchange Rates classes with it, you will do so via the processes and relationships defined in SanFrancisco.

The Foundation

The Foundation layer provides the technical underpinnings needed for business applications (see Figure 2-7). It is a middleware solution that solves the common problems you face when developing an object-oriented business application. It provides the underlying mechanisms needed by all applications, such as the services to support distributed objects, concurrent access to objects, and the ability to store object data to a database. There are three main pieces in the Foundation layer: the Foundation Object Model, services, and the utilities. Rules for using the Foundation are defined by the SanFrancisco Programming Model (SFPM).

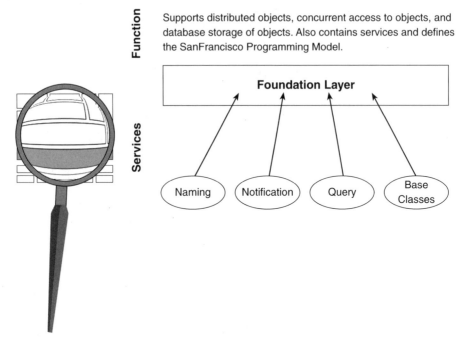

Figure 2-7. The Foundation Layer

The Foundation Object Model encapsulates the Foundation services by defining classes that encapsulate the services. The object model defines classes that should be extended by application developers when they build new business objects. For example, when a business object must be shareable and persistent, it should be created by subclassing the Entity class. (If the object does not need to be shareable, a Dependent class, which is persisted as part of an Entity, should be used.) The object model also provides classes that act as interfaces to the services. For example, the BaseFactory class provides life-cycle services such as creating and deleting object instances. Other classes help with implementing business objects; for example, collections are used for implementing one-to-many relationships. The SanFrancisco Programming Model defines how to use the Foundation Object Model, shielding developers from the technology being used within the Foundation layer. As a result, additional platform support can be added and newer technology can be used with minimal impact to an application that conforms to the SFPM.

The services, which you are shielded from, are the underlying mechanisms. They include things such as the Object Request Broker (ORB), which allows a client to work with remote objects, security authentication and authorization, including persisting business object data, locking business objects, querying a group of objects, accessing legacy data, and implementing externalization.

The final piece of the Foundation layer is the utilities, which aid in administration, configuration, and deployment of an application built on SanFrancisco. The utilities include user administration, server and datastore configuration, and other system management functions.

Although applications can be written directly on the Foundation layer, most business applications are built on the Common Business Objects layer because of the additional support it provides for business applications.

Patterns

Three forms of design patterns are used within SanFrancisco: those that are completely implemented, those that are partially implemented, and those that define how the task should be done and are then customized in each use.

The patterns that are completely implemented are used directly as is. Both of them are provided as part of the Foundation layer. The completely implemented patterns are as follows:

- Factory Class Replacement. This variation on the abstract factory pattern ensures that all instances of the class are instances of the new subclass of the class.

- Property Containment. The ability to associate an arbitrary object with an Entity by key.

The generalized mechanisms capture those patterns that are partially implemented and can be reused directly. For example, when the result of adding up a large amount of information is needed often or quickly, it makes sense to store and maintain the totals of common interest. Code to accomplish this function, called *cached balances*, is one of the generalized mechanisms. These partially implemented patterns are used just like miniature frameworks. Currently, the generalized mechanisms include support for the following patterns:

- Commands. A base class is provided for representing business tasks, calculations, and other actions that control or modify business objects.

- Keys and Keyables. Provide a means of separating a set of criteria from an algorithm that uses it.

- Cached Balances. Provide a means of caching totals and retrieving them based on a set of criteria.

- Extensible Item. Provides support for instance-by-instance dynamic inheritance.

- LifeCycle. Provides support for controlling the dynamic inheritance of an Extensible Item.
- Hierarchy Level Information. Provides support for controlling a hierarchy of LifeCycles.

The third form of patterns used in SanFrancisco is the traditional design patterns. In addition to the design patterns described in the book *Design Patterns*, by Erich Gamma et al. (Addison-Wesley, 1995), SanFrancisco also identifies some new design patterns. These design patterns define a solution that must be applied specifically each time it is used. Following are the new patterns identified by SanFrancisco:

- Policy. This pattern is a variation of the Design Patterns strategy pattern, which adds scope to the policy.
- Chain of Responsibility Driven Policy. This is a compound pattern in which a chain of responsibility is used to find the correct policy to use.
- Token Driven Policy. This pattern adds the ability to determine which policy will be used based on a token that typically represents a business process.
- Controller. This is a special collection that is associated with a context. It supports sharing of items in the collection across the context or isolation between the contexts.
- Keyed Attribute Retrieval. This pattern is a collection whose items can be retrieved using special criteria (keys).
- -Ables/-Ings. This pattern decomposes function to allow it to be added dynamically more flexibly and easily as part of the Extensible Item support.
- Generic Interface. This pattern defines a means of getting information into a subsystem so that the user of the interface is independent of the target subsystem.
- List Generation. This pattern defines how to generate lists, such as the list of items to pick to fill an order.

A number of these patterns are supported by the code generator; for example, the Controller pattern is almost completely generated.

SanFrancisco uses patterns when adding extension points. This leverages the advantage that patterns have in creating consistency and makes it easier to understand how things are done. In the case of extension points, once you understand the pattern used to support an extension point you can quickly understand other extension points that are supported by the same pattern.

Client Programming

The various layers of SanFrancisco address server-side components. Client programming with SanFrancisco is the responsibility of the application programmers who use SanFrancisco for their server-side logic. A client programmer should have some knowledge of the SanFrancisco Programming Model, established by the Foundation layer, and must understand the classes that are provided by the server-side component developers.

There are some technologies provided by SanFrancisco that can be used in the final client application. Because the client interface is often perceived as a distinguishing feature of an application, SanFrancisco does not limit itself to any single client technology.

Typically, an application provider determines the type of client and interface he or she wants to use for access to the server-side logic. For example, a client may decide that the user application must be a Web-based, thin client with no installation required. Access to server-side components in this environment is likely best done with Java servlet or Java server page technology, possibly combined with use of JavaBeans. As a result, the client application programmer can ignore the SanFrancisco Graphical User Interface framework but should pay particular attention to the use of SanFrancisco Command classes and SanFrancisco beans.

On the other hand, a client application programmer may determine that his or her environment cannot depend on a Web server or servlet-based processing. This client does not mind having a SanFrancisco framework installation physically residing on each of the client machines. With this environment, the client application programmer will want to look into the SanFrancisco Graphical User Interface framework or the component-based SanFrancisco GUI beans as well as other types of user interface technologies that can provide a suitable front end.

Basically, the approach that the SanFrancisco component framework takes to client-side application programming is to expect a wide variety of user interface types to access the server-side components. Guidance for the various access paths is provided via the SanFrancisco Programming Model and through miniature frameworks (such as the SanFrancisco Graphical User Interface framework and the Client Command framework).

Summary

This chapter provides an overview of the SanFrancisco architecture, and it introduces the major concepts and terms used by SanFrancisco. It talks about the three layers of SanFrancisco.

- Core Business Processes contains the core business objects and processes for a particular domain, such as General Ledger.

- Common Business Objects contains the business objects, processes, and mechanisms that are needed by many different business applications, such as the business objects and processes for working with currencies or the cached balances generalized mechanism.

- Foundation provides isolation from the underlying technology and defines the SanFrancisco Programming Model.

This chapter provides the background necessary to read the remainder of this book. It talks about SanFrancisco from the Core Business Processes layer down to the Foundation layer. This order is the most effective for introducing the overall concepts. The remaining parts of the book, on the other hand, are organized working from the Foundation layer up to the Core Business Processes layer. This order is more effective when you're learning the details of each of these layers because the layers build on one another. You may not need to know the details of each of the parts, or you may want to read them in an order more appropriate to your needs. Having read this chapter, you have the background necessary to read them in whatever order is appropriate for you.

Part II

The Foundation

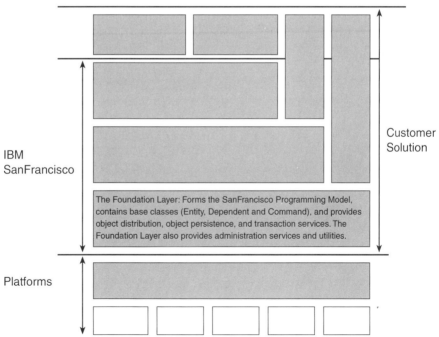

IBM
SanFrancisco

Customer
Solution

The Foundation Layer: Forms the SanFrancisco Programming Model, contains base classes (Entity, Dependent and Command), and provides object distribution, object persistence, and transaction services. The Foundation Layer also provides administration services and utilities.

Platforms

The Foundation Layer

As discussed in Chapter 2, Architecture Overview, the Foundation layer of the SanFrancisco Application Business Components is a middleware solution that solves the common problems you face when developing object-oriented solutions. The Foundation layer provides the basic plumbing needed by all applications, such as the services to support distributed objects, concurrent access to objects, and storage of object data to a database.

Chapter 3, An Introduction to the Foundation, provides a high-level overview of the functionality contained in this layer.

The Foundation layer goes beyond simply providing distributed application services; it also encapsulates them in objects. This design shields the solution developer from the underlying technologies being used. Chapter 4, The Foundation Object Model, describes this encapsulation.

The SanFrancisco Programming Model is a set of rules that are used for developing new SanFrancisco business objects or for using existing business objects. Chapter 5, Using the Foundation, describes this programming model in the context of a simple sample application. This chapter also covers configuration and administration of SanFrancisco applications.

3 An Introduction to the Foundation

There are many issues involved in developing distributed, object-oriented business applications. Many software developers are making the move from procedural languages to object-oriented techniques and languages such as Java because they promise reusability and "write once, run anywhere" platform neutrality. Although there are definite benefits to be realized, there are also new technical issues to address. Issues that were solved in a procedural world using well-defined techniques now need new solutions and techniques in the world of objects—issues such as figuring out how to persist the data you have encapsulated in those objects, how to share the objects between processes and on a network, how to maintain data integrity, and how to make changes to objects atomically across multiple servers. Ideally, these issues should be solved in a user-friendly way to minimize the impact on application programmers. Because the traditional procedural solutions to these issues do not map to an object-oriented language and design, what we need is an object-oriented infrastructure, more commonly termed *middleware*, that supplies these distributed object *services*. The Foundation layer of the SanFrancisco Application Business Components is just that: a middleware solution that solves the common problems you face when developing object-oriented solutions.

The Foundation layer consists of three pieces, as shown in Figure 3-1. First there is a set of Foundation services—things such as the Object Request Broker (ORB), which allows a client to work with remote objects by proxy. The Foundation services also include security, consisting of authentication and authorization; persistence of business object data; naming, for things such as user

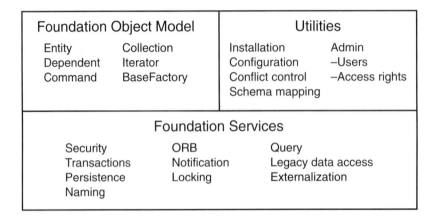

Foundation Object Model		Utilities	
Entity	Collection	Installation	Admin
Dependent	Iterator	Configuration	−Users
Command	BaseFactory	Conflict control	−Access rights
		Schema mapping	

Foundation Services		
Security	ORB	Query
Transactions	Notification	Legacy data access
Persistence	Locking	Externalization
Naming		

Figure 3-1. Logical Pieces of the Foundation Layer

aliases; notification, to allow objects to register an interest in events created by other objects; locking of business objects; and transaction support, query of a group of objects, legacy data access, and externalization (to allow streaming of data).

Built on top of these base Foundation services is the Foundation Object Model, which encapsulates the Foundation services and is meant to be extended by application developers. The object model provides a set of base classes that can be subclassed to build new business objects. You can create a business object that must be shareable and persistent, for example, by subclassing the base Entity class. The Entity class provides the functionality to allow an object to be shareable and persistent without any extra effort by the implementor. The object model also provides concrete classes that act as an interface to a service. For example, the BaseFactory class provides life-cycle services, such as creating and deleting object instances, and transaction services, such as begin and commit. There are also concrete classes to help with implementing business object class relationships such as collections, which allow grouping of objects. SanFrancisco's implementation of the object model as the interface into the Foundation services shields developers from the Foundation's underlying technology. With the rapid and ongoing development of Java, SanFrancisco will be able to take advantage of new technologies within the Foundation as they become available without affecting applications already implemented on the Foundation Object Model.

The Foundation also provides a set of utilities to aid in administration, configuration, and deployment of an application built on SanFrancisco. These utilities aid in administering users of the system as well as authorization to system resources, configuration of servers and datastores, and other system management functions.

Foundation Services

The Foundation services are the object-oriented middleware referred to earlier (see Figure 3-2). The services provide the functionality to allow persisting object data, sharing objects between processes and on a network, maintaining data integrity, and making changes to objects atomically across multiple servers.

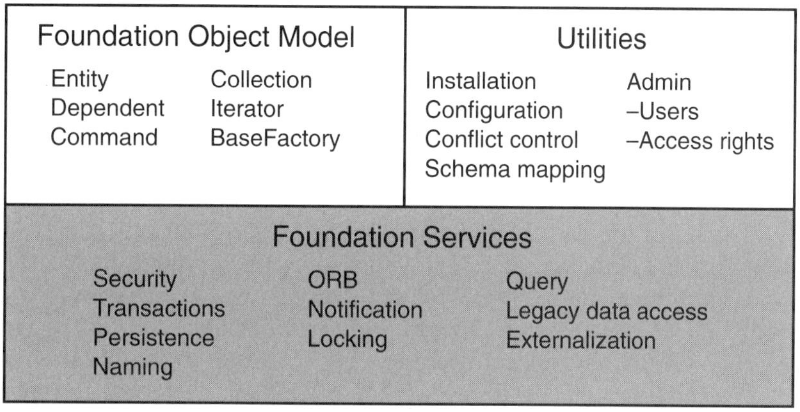

Foundation Object Model		Utilities	
Entity	Collection	Installation	Admin
Dependent	Iterator	Configuration	−Users
Command	BaseFactory	Conflict control	−Access rights
		Schema mapping	
Foundation Services			
Security	ORB	Query	
Transactions	Notification	Legacy data access	
Persistence	Locking	Externalization	
Naming			

Figure 3-2. The Foundation Services

The Object Request Broker is what allows you to work with remote objects by proxy—that is, as if they were local. The SanFrancisco ORB is built on top of Java's remote method invocation (RMI) support. Extensions have been made to allow for maintaining transaction scope and security information across remote method calls. SanFrancisco allows the programmer a choice of accessing objects by proxy or by copy. When objects are accessed by proxy, every method invocation is a remote method call. Working with objects by copy allows a copy of the object's data to be made locally so that method invocations are also done locally. There are advantages to both approaches, and the decision can be based on the nature of the objects and the application. In fact, an object instance can be accessed remotely in one case and locally in another. When developing high-performance distributed applications, you quickly learn that you need to keep network traffic to a minimum.

The transaction support in SanFrancisco involves the typical transaction protocol of begin, commit, and roll back. This functionality lets you encapsulate object operations within atomic transactions. Because objects can exist on multiple servers, both single-phase and two-phase commit protocols are available.

Typical Java objects exist only within the scope of a running application. The persistence mechanisms within the Foundation allow your business objects to be *persisted*, or saved, to some type of system storage, thereby extending the life of the object. Persistent objects exist until they are explicitly deleted. This mechanism is encapsulated within the implementation of the Foundation Object Model, and no extra programming is necessary. Persistence to POSIX files or a relational database is supported.

Support of existing relational database data is provided through the schema mapping services. *Schema mapping* allows the object schema (classes, instances, and attributes) to be mapped to a database schema (tables, rows, and columns). Schema mapping can be used to reflect the mapping of your existing tables so that your object data can be stored to them. When you create new tables, you can also use schema mapping to determine their structure.

SanFrancisco supports object locking services, which let you ensure data integrity while allowing multiple clients to access object instances. Traditional pessimistic locking (read/write) as well as optimistic locking is supported.

In typical database-oriented applications, you may query encapsulated application data using Structured Query Language (SQL). In SanFrancisco, you use the object query, a service found in the Foundation layer, to execute queries involving the attributes of your object. You express these queries in Object-Oriented Structured Query Language (OOSQL).

Typical notification support is also part of the Foundation services. *Notification* allows objects to register an interest in an event that may be generated by other objects. When an object generates the event, any object that has registered an interest is notified.

Foundation Object Model

As depicted in Figure 3-3, the Foundation Object Model encapsulates the Foundation services and is meant to be extended by application developers. The object model provides a set of *abstract* classes (those meant to be subclassed) and a set of *concrete* classes (objects that can be used as is). The abstract classes are subclassed by a solution developer to build new business objects. The set of concrete classes acts as an interface to a service or helps with implementing business object class relationships. Because this layer shields the application developer from its underlying technology, SanFrancisco can evolve and take advantage of new technologies in the future without affecting existing applications built on the object model.

Figure 3-4 depicts the core classes in the SanFrancisco Foundation Object Model. The Base class provides capabilities needed by most SanFrancisco business objects. These capabilities allow an object to be an argument on a remote method call, to be compared, to be put in a collection, and to be made persistent. The BusinessObject class adds additional behavior to work with contained objects.

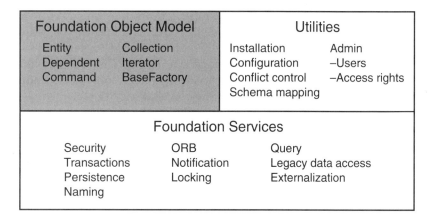

Figure 3-3. The Foundation Object Model

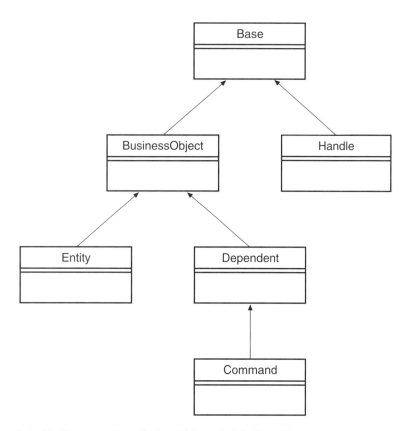

Figure 3-4. SanFrancisco Foundation Object Model: Core Classes

Entity, Dependent, and Command are the three classes from which new business objects are derived. Entities are used to encapsulate business data and operations on the data. Entities are designed to support shared, persistent objects that must be accessed independently. They can be named, locked, and secured, and they can participate in transactions. Each Entity has a unique identification within the network so that it can be located. This unique ID is encapsulated within the Handle object. Handle objects can be stored as part of an application or stored in another object for later use in accessing the business object they reference. Dependent classes are used for lightweight objects that may encapsulate a small amount of data. To be meaningful to the application, a typical Dependent object needs context provided by a containing Entity object. Dependents are not shared and are persistent only if they are contained within a persistent Entity. Command classes represent business tasks, calculations, and other actions that control or modify business objects. Some Commands support undoing and redoing of actions.

Examples of concrete classes that allow access to the Foundation services are the Global class and the BaseFactory class. The Global class lets you initialize a SanFrancisco application and allows access to security services. The Base-Factory class contains operations to manage the life cycle of objects (such as creating and deleting Entities) and is also the interface to transaction services such as begin and commit.

The Foundation Object Model also contains concrete classes to help with implementing business object class relationships, specifically *collections*. A set of persistent collection classes is supplied to implement a one-to-many relationship between classes.

Chapter 4 discusses the Foundation Object Model in further detail.

SanFrancisco Programming Model

The SanFrancisco Programming Model is a set of rules to follow when you either implement new business objects or use existing business objects (see Figure 3-5). The programming model consists of two parts. The Business Object Developer Programming Model is a set of rules to be used for extending the SanFrancisco Foundation Object Model. These rules contain information on how to implement a subclass of an Entity, Dependent, or Command class, how to implement one-to-many relationships between classes, and so on. The Client Programming Model is a set of rules on how to use existing SanFrancisco business objects. It contains information on how to create instances of Entities, Dependents, and Commands, how to access existing instances, how to copy objects, and so on. The programming models exist to ensure that an application developer creates well-behaved SanFrancisco objects and applications. Several

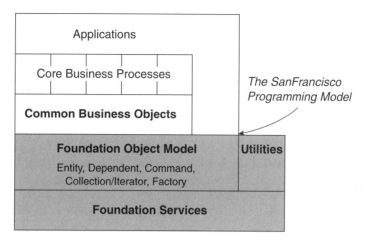

Figure 3-5. The SanFrancisco Programming Model

tools, such as code generators, help ensure adherence to the rules while easing the work of the programmer.

Chapter 5, Using the Foundation, provides details on the programming models within the context of a sample application.

Foundation Utilities

Utilities are provided in the Foundation (see Figure 3-6) to aid in maintaining user IDs and passwords for users of the system and authorizing those users to access system resources. The utilities are also used for configuration of servers and datastores and other system management functions.

Foundation Object Model		Utilities	
Entity	Collection	Installation	Admin
Dependent	Iterator	Configuration	–Users
Command	BaseFactory	Conflict control	–Access rights
		Schema mapping	
Foundation Services			
Security	ORB	Query	
Transactions	Notification	Legacy data access	
Persistence	Locking	Externalization	
Naming			

Figure 3-6. The Foundation Utilities

The Configuration utility is used to configure which server object instances should be created on and which storage type (for example, a DB2 or Oracle database) should be used for persisting object instances. Object location and datastores are strictly a matter of configuration; no programming is necessary to indicate where objects should be located and how they are persisted, so you can change this information with no impact on application code. The Server Management utility is used to configure the servers within your SanFrancisco network and specify their responsibilities.

In a business application or group of integrated applications, there may be actions that must not run concurrently because it could lead to wrong or inconsistent results. In this context, an action is seen as any piece of code that can be regarded as a unit. The Conflict Control utility helps you define potential conflicts and make sure that conflicting actions are not run at the same time.

Security and User administration is done using the Users and Access Rights utilities. These utilities allow you to create users and groups of users within the system via traditional user IDs and passwords and then to specify which users have access to resources and actions within the system.

The Schema Mapping tool assists with creating the schema mappings that specify how your business objects should be persisted to a relational database—that is, how your classes, instances, and attributes map to appropriate database tables, rows, and columns. If you are persisting to POSIX files, no mapping is necessary.

Chapter 5, Using the Foundation, discusses using the utilities to administer and configure a sample SanFrancisco application.

Summary

The Foundation layer consists of a set of middleware services—the plumbing needed by any distributed, object-oriented application. Built on top of these services is a Foundation Object Model that is meant to be extended by the solution developer and shields the developers from the underlying technology. A set of utilities allows installation, configuration, and administration necessary for application deployment.

4 *The Foundation Object Model*

The Foundation Object Model of the SanFrancisco component framework encapsulates the Foundation services and is meant to be extended by application developers (see Figure 4-1). The object model provides a set of base classes that can be subclassed to build new business objects as well as a set of collection classes used to implement object relationships.

Foundation Object Model		Utilities	
Entity	Collection	Installation	Admin
Dependent	Iterator	Configuration	−Users
Command	BaseFactory	Conflict control	−Access rights
		Schema mapping	
Foundation Services			
Security	ORB	Query	
Transactions	Notification	Legacy data access	
Persistence	Locking	Externalization	
Naming			

Figure 4-1. Foundation Object Model

The Big Three

All business object subclasses extend either Entity, Dependent, or Command. All the common business objects and core business process objects are derived from these three base classes. New business objects necessary for an application will also extend these classes either directly or indirectly (the latter by subclassing existing classes).

Object Containment and Ownership

It is important to understand relationships between business objects. SanFrancisco supports the concept of object *ownership* as well as that of object *containment*. These terms are similar to the object-oriented terms *containment by value* and *containment by reference*. When a business object instance is owned, its lifetime is tied to its owning object; when its containing object is deleted, the owned object is also deleted. The SanFrancisco Programming Model suggests that naming conventions be used to convey this object ownership in method names. For example, a Customer object that owns an Address instance would have a setOwnedAddress() method. In this example, when a Customer instance is deleted, the Address is also deleted. When a business object instance is merely contained by another object, its lifetime is not tied to the containing object.

Transient Versus Persistent Objects

Business object instances in SanFrancisco can be either transient or persistent. *Transient* instances are similar to Java objects in that they do not live beyond the scope of the process they were created in. *Persistent* object instances are created via configuration information so that the object data persists in a datastore beyond the life of the creating process. Persistent instances are activated into a home server process when they are accessed by any client. Persistent instances must be explicitly deleted. Entity instances can be transient or persistent. Dependents and Strings are transient if they are not contained within another persistent object.

Entity

The Entity class is an abstract class (see Figure 4-2) that can be subclassed to create a concrete business object class. Entity subclasses are common and typically encapsulate the main business data within a SanFrancisco application. A programmer extends the Entity class whenever there is a need for a business object that is inherently persistent, that can be shared among multiple processes, and that can participate in a transaction. No additional programming

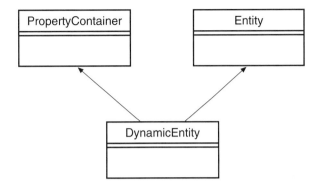

Figure 4-2. Entity

effort is required to make an Entity subclass instance persistent, and programmers can be totally unaware of the physical datastore that eventually contains
the instances. When an instance of a persistent Entity subclass is instantiated
(either created from scratch or retrieved from the datastore), it behaves in the
same way as any regular Java object. Client programs can call methods on
those instances even if they live in separate address spaces, possibly on a
remote system. Every Entity instance has a networkwide unique identity and
therefore can be located by services throughout the network. The Handle class
encapsulates this unique identification of the object instance. Handle objects
can be stored as part of an application or in another object for later use in
accessing the Entity they reference.

DynamicEntity is a specialization of Entity. A DynamicEntity subclass
instance has the additional capability that data can be added to it at runtime.
This added data is referred to as a *property* and is accessed via a String key.
DynamicEntity implements the PropertyContainer interface to add this capability to the base Entity class. Properties can be Strings or instances of a Dependent or Entity subclass. PropertyContainers also support a chaining behavior
that allows the retrieval of a particular property from an object instance to be
delegated to a parent object if the property is not found on the child. There are
several uses for the PropertyContainer functionality, such as when a solution
developer has created a SanFrancisco application and wants to specialize or
customize it for a particular customer. If one customer needs an additional
piece of data on a business object, adding the data as a property could be one
solution. In some cases, the additional information is not needed in all
instances but only in some instances in certain situations. In that case, properties can be added only to the instances that need the additional data, an easier
approach that has some benefits over creating a subclass for all object
instances. Properties are also one way to extend the SanFrancisco common
business objects and core business processes and still allow coexistence with

other applications that extend the same classes. Each application can add the data it needs to the existing objects without affecting other users of the objects.

Dependent

The Dependent class is an abstract class that can be subclassed to create a concrete business object class. Dependents are typically used for lightweight business objects that do not exist on their own. To be meaningful to an application, a typical Dependent object needs context provided by a containing Entity object. Dependents are named with a *D* prefix to distinguish them from Entities (DTime, for example). When a business object references a Dependent subclass, the Dependent instance is contained in the object. A Dependent subclass instance can be persistent only if it is contained in another persistent object. The life of a Dependent is the same as the life of its containing object. Dependents are never shared. Dependents are passed using copy semantics so that a client never works with the actual Dependent but rather with a copy. Dependent objects are always locked, accessed, stored, and committed in a transaction through their containing Entity, and Dependent objects do not have unique identities.

Command

The Command class is a specialization of the Dependent class. Command subclasses are used to encapsulate business logic for two reasons. One need is to provide a way to update a group of objects all at once while ensuring that, if any object in the group is not updated successfully, all the changes are reversed. Command classes used for this sole purpose are referred to as *edit* Commands. The business logic may span many business objects (classes), and that makes the placement of this logic within any of the objects impractical. In other words, the behavior represented by the Command class does not have a natural home on any business object represented in the application. The other use of Commands is to gain the advantage that by encapsulating the business logic within one object, the logic can change in the future without affecting its users. Commands are named with a *Cmd* suffix to distinguish them from Entities and Dependents (CallListGenerateCmd, for example). Commands can encapsulate other Commands, so a Command representing a business process could be composed of several Commands that represent tasks. Then either the task-level Commands can be executed individually, or the process-level Command can be executed in order to execute all its task Commands in a predetermined order.

Commands also have a unique characteristic that can dramatically benefit application performance. When executing a Command, the client can specify that the Command should execute locally or at the location of the objects the Command manipulates. If the Command executes locally, it may result in many remote method calls to the objects it manipulates in server processes. The second option allows *function shipping,* whereby the Command's business logic executes in the same server process as the objects it is accessing. A high-performance SanFrancisco application makes good use of Commands to ensure that it is taking advantage of this function shipping capability.

Localization

SanFrancisco has been designed with great attention paid to the issues related to internationalizing applications. There may be many business objects within an application that must be sensitive to internationalization. The Locale object is used in SanFrancisco as an identifier for a set of parameters that are specific to a cultural, geographical, or political region. Examples of locale-dependent information in an application are languages or text, date and time formats, and number formats. There are two ways to design your business objects within SanFrancisco to be locale-dependent. To support localization of business objects, two interfaces are provided: Describable and Translatable (see Figure 4-3).

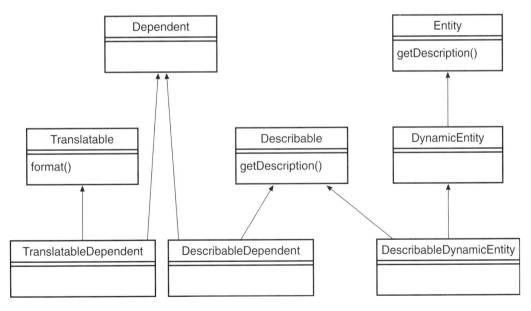

Figure 4-3. SanFrancisco Localization Support

You can see from the partial class diagram in Figure 4-3 that there are specializations of both Dependent and DynamicEntity that support the Describable interface: DescribableDependent and DescribableDynamicEntity. These classes contain a DescriptiveInformation object, which contains a collection of String descriptions that are keyed by locale. That allows the Describable object to hold multiple descriptions based on locale. The Describable classes support a getDescription() method that retrieves the correct description based on the currently active locale or a passed locale.

Translatable is a common interface for objects that provide locale-dependent String representations of themselves. The Translatable interface has two format() methods: one that gets the String representation of an object based on the active locale, and a second one that takes a specific locale as input. Examples of Translatable objects are the DTime and DDecimal classes provided by SanFrancisco. The DTime class is used to hold a timestamp that includes both date and time. When a DTime is represented as a String, the formatting should be based on locale so that the correct information can be displayed—for example, 03/08/98 1:00 PM (U.S. format) compared with 08.03.98 13:00 (European format). DDecimal, another concrete Translatable class supplied by SanFrancisco, is used to represent numeric values within the common business objects and core business processes. DDecimal implements an arbitrary-precision signed decimal providing a complete set of basic arithmetic operations. When a DDecimal is represented as a String, again the formatting should be based on locale—for example, 123,456.78 (U.S. format) versus 123.456,78 (European format).

Collections

Collections are a way to allow grouping of like objects and manipulation (accessing) of the elements within the collection. The SanFrancisco Foundation provides a set of concrete collection classes that can be used in several ways within an application. There are general scenarios in which it is helpful to group objects. You might use a Command, for example, that uses a collection of objects for its input. Another use is in implementing a one-to-many containment relationship to a business object within another business object. An AddressBook, for example, has a one-to-many relationship to Address. In the actual implementation of such a relationship, the containing business object holds a collection of the contained business object; the AddressBook holds a collection of Addresses. Another example is in the use of the query support in SanFrancisco. Results from a query are always returned as a collection of objects that match the query criteria. These concrete collections are fully implemented and can be used as is; you need not subclass them to use them.

There are several collection types, and they support various ways of accessing the elements. The Map collections, for example, support the retrieval of elements by a key value that is associated with each element. The List collections maintain the insertion order of the collection. The Set collections are unordered. A special type of collection, the EntityOwningExtent, has a special synergy with the underlying relational database datastore, allowing it to be scalable to huge numbers of elements. There is a group of collections that inherits from Entity and a group that inherits from Dependent. The collections that inherit from Entity have the same characteristics as Entities; they can be named, shared, persisted, and so on. The Entity collections are used in most situations except when you may have a small number of elements. They also support querying of the elements. The Dependent collections have the same characteristics as Dependents; they are lightweight and cannot be shared or persisted unless contained in a shared persistent object. The Dependent collections are recommended only for a small number of elements, and they do not support query. Figure 4-4 shows the various collections provided in SanFrancisco.

The EntityOwning prefix indicates that the elements of the collection are Entities and are owned by the collection; when the collection is deleted, all elements are deleted. Collection elements can be Strings, Entities, or Dependents. The Foundation provides a set of Dependent wrapper classes for the Java primitives to allow them to be elements within a collection.

An Iterator is an object that allows a client to access each element within a collection. An Iterator is created for a particular collection, and it maintains its position in the collection as the client uses it. So, for example, an Iterator has a method next() that accesses the next element in the collection. Iterator access is supported by all the collections. Accessing elements by key is also supported by some of the collections: the Map collections and the EntityOwningExtent. When you add an element to a Map collection, you must also specify a key value to assign to that element in the collection. Then you can access the elements by key; for example, there will be a method getElementBy(Key). An element in an EntityOwningExtent can have multiple keys that are actually defined by the return values from methods executed on the element.

Query, also supported in a subset of the SanFrancisco collections, allows a client to get a subset of objects based on some type of selection criteria. The result of a query on a particular collection is another collection—the Result collection—that contains a subset of the elements in the original collection that satisfy the query criteria. The query criteria are formatted as an SQL SELECT statement using an extension of SQL92—called OOSQL—that allows method navigation. Because the query is executed on objects, the selection criteria can be based on calls to methods on the elements in the collection. Query is discussed in more detail later in the context of a sample application.

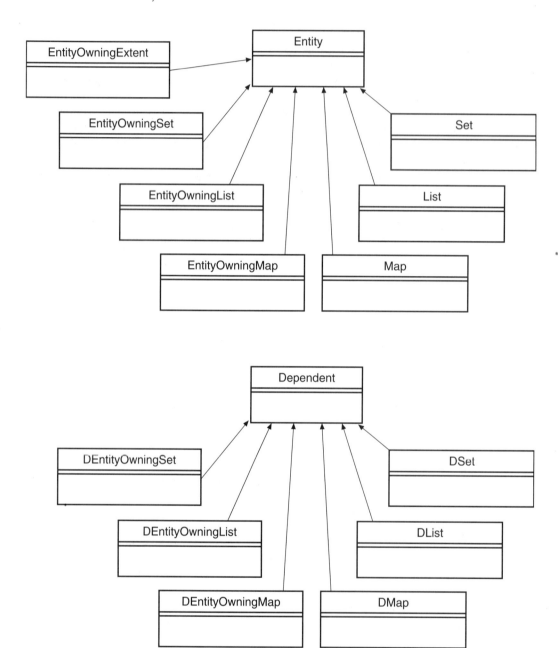

Figure 4-4. Collection Hierarchy

Summary

The SanFrancisco Foundation Object Model encapsulates the Foundation services and provides a set of base classes that are used and subclassed to implement new business objects. New business objects are ultimately subclasses of Entity, Dependent, or Command. Chapter 5 describes the SanFrancisco Programming Model: the rules to follow for extending the Foundation Object Model to build new business objects or for using existing business objects. The Foundation services used by a client application are also discussed, as are the Foundation utilities used for developing and deploying a SanFrancisco application.

5 Using the Foundation

Implementing an application using SanFrancisco involves using existing business objects provided by the framework. In some cases, you must define a new business object, not supplied by the framework, to satisfy your application requirements. The SanFrancisco Programming Model is a set of rules to follow in both cases. The programming model consists of two parts. The *Business Object Developer Programming Model* is a set of rules to be used for extending the SanFrancisco Foundation Object Model. These rules contain information on how to implement a subclass of an Entity, Dependent, or Command class, how to implement one-to-many relationships between classes, and so on. The *Client Programming Model* is a set of rules on how to use existing SanFrancisco business objects. It contains information on how to create instances of Entities, Dependents, and Commands, how to access existing instances, how to copy objects, and more. The programming models exist to ensure an application developer creates well behaved SanFrancisco objects and applications. Although the rules are numerous, several tools are provided within the product, such as code generators, to ensure adherence to the rules while easing the work of the programmer.

To explore the use of the Foundation and the programming model more closely, let's look at a sample application built on it. The application is built on both the SanFrancisco Foundation layer and the common business objects. In this chapter we focus on new business objects, which are introduced and implemented as Entities, Dependents, and Commands, to illustrate the use of the Developer Programming Model. We also look at how to access and use objects to illustrate the Client Programming Model. Administration and configuration functions of the Foundation are also discussed.

Chapter 8, Using the Common Business Objects, uses the same sample application but focuses on the use and extension of the common business objects.

Application Case Study

Get Physical Sports Equipment (GPSE), a fictional wholesale distributor of sports equipment, markets to schools, colleges, and sports clubs across America. GPSE maintains a large inventory of sports equipment at reasonable prices. GPSE is using a paper system to record and maintain order information and wants to upgrade to an automated order entry system. The following sample application built on SanFrancisco satisfies the requirements of the GPSE order entry application.

The SanFrancisco Application Development Roadmap is used as the development process for the application. The Roadmap defines a set of activities that should be executed during development. They are the typical activities in any development process: requirements gathering, analysis, design, implementation, and test. The Roadmap also suggests how to document your work products. An advantage of following the Roadmap is that the documentation you create is similar to the SanFrancisco documentation. This helps you to understand the product documentation better. The most important advantage, however, is the help the Roadmap gives you in the mapping stages. The Roadmap continually asks you to stop and map the application requirements, analysis, and design to the SanFrancisco requirements, analysis, and design. This step ensures that you are fully utilizing SanFrancisco and gaining the benefits of reuse discussed earlier. You can use this mapping process whether or not you follow the rest of the Roadmap. Because we are focusing on the simpler objects in the application here, we do not dwell on the requirements and analysis stages but move quickly to design. Chapter 8, Using the Common Business Objects, and Chapter 11, Using the Core Business Processes, focus on the requirements and analysis stages.

The main objects found during analysis of the GPSE application requirements are Order, Product, Product Group, and Customer. Figure 5-1 shows the analysis-level UML class diagram for the GPSE application.

Some of these objects map to existing objects in SanFrancisco. Examples are Address, BusinessPartner (Customer), and Company; these common business objects are discussed in Chapter 7, Common Business Object Categories. SanFrancisco provides a set of Order Management core business processes, but for sample purposes they are not used here. Therefore, Product, ProductGroup, OrderHeader, and OrderLine are the new business objects that must be designed and implemented.

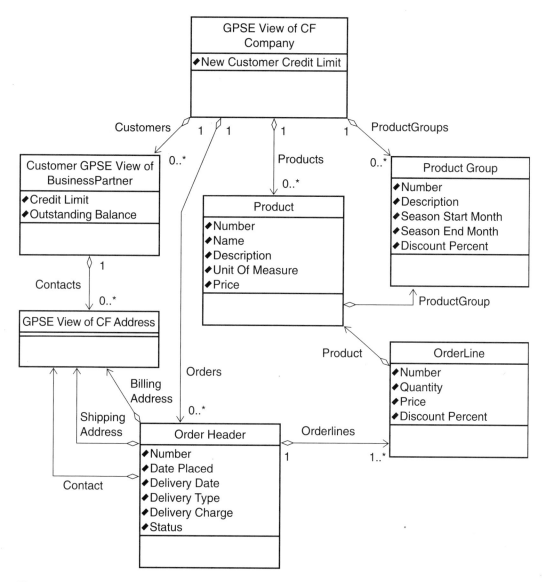

Figure 5-1. GPSE Analysis Class Diagram

Mapping Business Objects to SanFrancisco

The three basic classes in the SanFrancisco Foundation Object Model to which you will map your new business objects are Entity, Dependent, and Command. As described earlier, there are a couple of variations of Entity and Dependent to support localization, and they are used in many cases. Entities are used for business objects that must be shared and used concurrently within the application. Dependents are used for lightweight objects that do not need to be shared. Commands are used to encapsulate business logic.

In the sample GPSE application analysis, we have several new business objects that must be implemented: Product, ProductGroup, OrderHeader, and OrderLine. In the sample application the Product, ProductGroup, and Order-Header objects typically are shared and so are mapped to Entities. OrderLines, however, typically are not shared and usually make no sense unless associated with an OrderHeader. OrderLines are mapped to Dependent. Another object that is necessary at design time is DeliveryType, which encapsulates the delivery charge and the number of days necessary for shipping an order. Delivery-Types are lightweight objects, so they could be mapped to Dependent. But another aspect of Dependents is that they are contained by copy within an Entity. Because every Order has a DeliveryType and there are a small number of unique DeliveryType instances, they are mapped to Entity to avoid duplicating DeliveryType data in every order.

In Figure 5-2 you can see that OrderHeader actually maps to DynamicEntity, a specialized Entity. DynamicEntity has the Entity characteristics, with additional support for dynamically adding data, called properties, to an object instance at runtime. To remain flexible, most Entities really subclass from DynamicEntity. DescribableDynamicEntity has the additional capability to support a description of the object instance in multiple languages. Describable objects have a DescriptiveInformation object that holds multiple descriptions to support multiple languages. The descriptions can then be retrieved based on Locale. Because our Products, ProductGroups, and DeliveryTypes have descriptions associated with them, they are subclasses of DescribableDynamicEntity. Something not shown is how the one-to-many relationship between Order-Header and DOrderLine is designed. OrderHeader contains a collection of DOrderLines, a DMap keyed by the Product number for each order line.

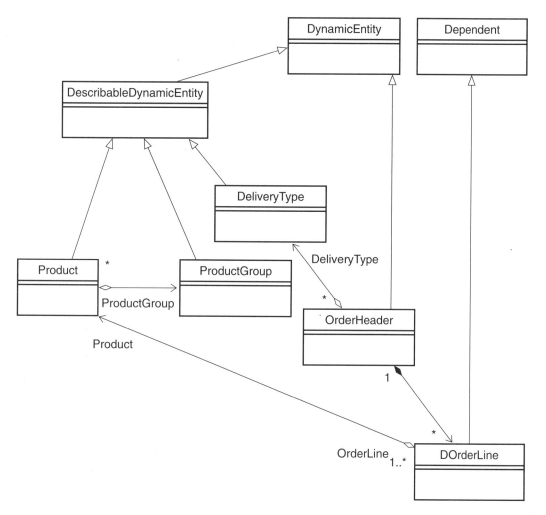

Figure 5-2. GPSE Design Class Diagram

Implementing SanFrancisco Business Objects

The SanFrancisco Programming Model is a set of rules to follow for implementing new SanFrancisco business objects or using existing business objects (see Figure 5-3). The Business Object Developer Programming Model is a set of rules for implementing new business objects on the SanFrancisco Foundation Object Model.

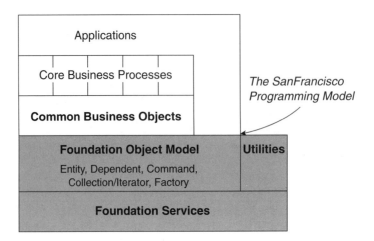

Figure 5-3. SanFrancisco Programming Model

Interfaces and Classes

One of the basic concepts that you must understand when implementing a new SanFrancisco business object is that each SanFrancisco class must provide both a Java interface and a Java class that implements the interface. This is necessary to support Java RMI, which is used to remotely invoke methods on object instances. Any method that can be called remotely must be defined in the interface. The *implementation class,* or *impl,* must implement the public interface methods and any other protected and private methods necessary. The *factory class* is used to instantiate an instance of the business object. SanFrancisco business objects are not created by calling constructors on the implementation class in a client program. Instead, they are created by calling a static create method in the business object's factory class. The factory class is necessary to support the Abstract Factory design pattern, allowing for class replacement at runtime. The relationships between the interface, impl, and factory are shown in Figure 5-4 using the GPSE Product object as an example.

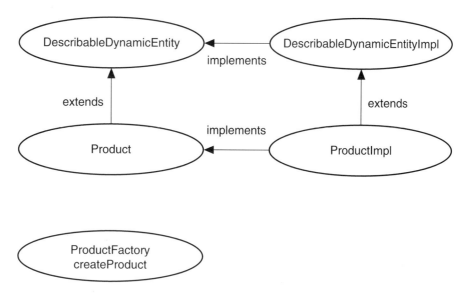

Figure 5-4. Relationships among the Interface, Impl, and Factory

For the GPSE Product object, the interface, impl, and factory are declared as follows:

Interface: Product.java

```
public interface Product extends DescribableDynamicEntity {
}
```

Impl: ProductImpl.java

```
public class ProductImpl extends DescribableDynamicEntityImpl
                         implements Product {
}
```

Factory: ProductFactory.java

```
public abstract class ProductFactory extends Object {
}
```

Creating an Entity Subclass

The Business Object Developer Programming Model describes the rules for implementing Entity subclasses. The programming model defines a set of methods that the subclass should support. The actual implementation of most of these methods can be generated with SanFrancisco supporting code genera-tors such as the one supplied with SanFrancisco. Each Entity subclass must conform to a set of rules described next.

Abstract Factory Create Methods

All concrete Entity subclasses must implement static create methods to support the Abstract Factory design pattern used in the Foundation. With this pattern, the class to instantiate is determined at runtime. An additional function of the design pattern in SanFrancisco is that the class to be instantiated is config-urable. Each subclass has a separate factory class that is used by the client to instantiate an instance of the business object (rather than using the Java new operation). The factory class implements create methods that delegate the actual creation of the class instance to the BaseFactory class based on a class name token. You can think of the *class name token* as a placeholder to indicate which class should be instantiated. It is the BaseFactory class that determines, from the configuration information and the class name token, which class to instantiate. The configuration of which class to instantiate allows you to replace an implementation class.

Two types of create methods are supported: tightly coupled and loosely coupled. The *tightly coupled* create method establishes ownership of the instance at create time, and the *loosely coupled* create method does not. The con-cept of *ownership* in SanFrancisco ties the life of an owning object to its owned objects. When the owning object is deleted, its owned objects are deleted. In the tightly coupled case, whether the Entity instance is persistent or transient is based on its owning object. If the owning object is persistent, the created Entity instance is persistent; otherwise, it is transient. In the loosely coupled case, the persistent or transient aspect of the object instance is determined by a location parameter specifying where to create the instance.

Following is an abbreviated example of a tightly coupled create method within the factory class for the GPSE Product:

```
1  public abstract class ProductFactory extends Object {
2    public final static Product createProduct(
                              ProductController owningController,
                              AccessMode accessMode,
                              String number,
                              String name,
                              DCurrencyValue price,
                              ProductGroup productGroup,
                              DescriptiveInformation description)
                              throws com.ibm.sf.gf.SFException {
3      boolean finished = false;
4      Product product = null;
```

```
5     ProductFactory factory =
        (ProductFactory) Global.factory().getSpecialFactory("GPSE.Product");
6     if (factory == null) {
7       Entity entity = Global.factory().createEntity(
                          "GPSE.Product",
                          accessMode,
                          owningController.getDirectlyOwnedProductsHdl(),
                          null);
8       Exception caughtException = null;
9       try {                 // Cast to the correct interface and initialize
10        product = (Product) entity;
11        product.initialize(owningController,number,name,price,
                          productGroup,description);
12        owningController.registerDirectlyOwnedProduct(product);
13        finished = true;
14      } catch (Exception exc1){
15        caughtException = exc1;
16      } finally {
17        if (!finished) {
18          entity.uninitialize();
19          Global.factory().deleteEntity(entity);
20        }
21      }
22    }
23    else {
        // Delegate to special factory
        ....
24    }

25    return (product);
26 }
```

The interesting things to note in this method are as follows:

- Line 1: This is the abstract factory class for Product. The naming convention for the factory classes is <class name>Factory.

- Line 2: Create methods are always named create<class name>. The parameters on the method include the owning object—the ProductController in this example—in the tightly coupled case and any information necessary to initialize the state of the instance.

- Line 5: Check to see whether a *special* factory has been configured for this class name token. The class name token, "GPSE.Product," follows the recommended naming convention of <package name>.<class name> and can be configured to specify the name of a special factory class that creation should be delegated to. You use a special factory to do something such as providing the correct key for putting an Entity in a legacy database. If a special factory exists, the create is delegated to its create method.

- Line 7: Use BaseFactory (obtained via the Global.factory() static method call) to create the Entity instance. Whether the Entity is persistent or transient is based on its owning object in this case. If the owning object is persistent, the created Entity instance is persistent; otherwise, it is transient. If this were a loosely coupled create method, the persistent or transient aspect of the object instance would be determined by a location parameter. The class name token is used to create the Entity. The class name token, "GPSE.Product," is configured to specify the real class name that should be used to instantiate the instance. This allows the real class name to change via configuration without affecting any code that uses the class token.

- Line 11: The Entity state is initialized. The createEntity() method will create the instance using the default constructor. The default constructor should not do initialization, which is done within the initialize() method if necessary. What is included in the initialize method is discussed later in this chapter.

- Line 12: Ownership of the instance with its owning object is established in the tightly coupled create method. In a loosely coupled create method implementation, this line would not exist.

You can see from the example that create methods follow a base set of rules. The benefit is that SanFrancisco code generators can completely and correctly generate these create methods in most cases, allowing the business object programmer to focus on implementing business logic.

Methods Always Recommended

For implementing an Entity subclass, the programming model defines a set of methods the subclass should always implement.

Override toString()

The toString() method should be implemented in the implementation class (the impl) to display useful information for debugging purposes. For application display of data, a format() method would be implemented to take localization into account. Following is an example of a toString() method from the GPSE Product class. In this example, toString() would return the result of calling toString() on the parent, concatenated with the Product number and name.

```
    public String toString() {
    try {
      String retVal = super.toString();
      retVal = retVal +
          " " +
        getNumber() +
          " " +
        getName();

      return (retVal);
    }
    catch (Exception ex) {
      String retVal = "Product::toString() - Unexpected exception: " + ex;
      return (retVal);
    }
}
```

Methods Required If Additional State Is Added to the Entity

For implementing an Entity subclass, the programming model defines a set of methods that should be implemented by the subclass if the subclass has added additional state. In most cases, these methods can be completely generated by a SanFrancisco code generator and need to be updated only if additional business processing is desired.

Provide Overloaded initialize()

The initialize method is needed to support the Abstract Factory design pattern that is implemented for all SanFrancisco business objects. The initialize() method is called from the object's create method to initialize the object state. Here is an abbreviated example of the GPSE. Product class initialize() method:

```
1   public void initialize(ProductController owningController,
                           String number,
                           String name,
                           DCurrencyValue price,
                           ProductGroup productGroup,
                           DescriptiveInformation description)
                 throws com.ibm.sf.gf.SFException {
2     super.initialize();

      // Set the descriptive information as owned by the product
3     setDescriptiveInformation(description, true);

      // Set the the discount selection policy
5     ivDiscountSelectionPolicy =
        DDiscountSelectionPolicyDefaultFactory.
          createDDiscountSelectionPolicyDefault();
```

```
      // Dependent and String objects should use the corresponding set
      // method to ensure that these objects are correctly allocated
      // and copied
6     setNumber(number);
7     setName(name);
8     setPrice(price);

      // entities can be set either with the corresponding set<entity>()
      // method or by calling setHandleToObject()
9     ivProductGroupHdl = setHandleToObject(ivProductGroupHdl,productGroup);
   }
```

The interesting things to note in this method are as follows:

- Line 2: The initialize() method always calls its superclass initialize() method to initialize the superclass state.

- Line 3: Because this is a DescribableDynamicEntity, it sets its DescriptiveInformation object as passed and indicates that it owns it. If the Entity owns its DescriptiveInformation, the DescriptiveInformation will be deleted when the Entity is deleted. In some cases the DescriptiveInformation is not owned, thereby allowing multiple class instances to share descriptions.

- Line 5: Not all initial state is passed in as parameters on the initialize() method. In this case, some initial data is actually being created.

- Lines 6, 7, and 8: The set methods are used to set Dependent and String attributes.

- Line 9: Entity attributes can be set using the set method. In this case, however, a helper method is used.

Provide get<attribute>() and set<attribute>()

A get and a set method should be provided for each attribute, including primitive and business object attributes. The get method should be public. The set method can be omitted if the attribute is read-only. The definitions of a get and a set method from the GPSE. Product class are as follows:

```
public String getNumber() throws com.ibm.sf.gf.SFException;
public void setNumber(String newNumber) throws com.ibm.sf.gf.SFException;
```

For contained Entity attributes that are owned, the ownership is reflected in the name of the method—for example, setOwnedAddress()—to highlight the ownership behavior of the method. The setOwnedAddress would first delete the current Address if it existed and then set the new one.

Override internalizeFromStream() and externalizeToStream()

These methods enhance the Java externalization support and are used whenever Entities must be flattened to a stream—for example, when they are persisted in POSIX files, when they are persisted to streamed columns in relational databases, and when they are copied between client and server. The implementation of these methods must read in and write out all of the object's persistent state, including both object and primitive instance variables.

Override destroy()

Whenever a business object is deleted, this method is called to delete any necessary contained objects. It should be implemented to delete all its contained object data.

Provide Collection Access Methods

Cases in which an Entity has a zero-to-many or one-to-many containment relationship to another class are typically implemented within the Entity as an attribute—in this case, a collection that contains the instances. The use of a collection is an implementation detail that should not be exposed to the client. Therefore, if you want the collection instances to be accessed from a client, you must provide collection access methods. The methods vary somewhat depending on the type of collection that is implemented. Collections with keys, for example, would expose an interface to allow the retrieval of an element by key. Collections with owned Entity elements would reflect the ownership in the naming of the collection access methods. An example of a containment relationship within the GPSE application is the OrderHeader, which has a one-to-many relationship with OrderLine. In this case, some of the methods available on OrderHeader to access OrderLines could be as follows:

```
// create iterator for collection of OrderLines
public Iterator createOrderLineIterator()
                throws com.ibm.sf.gf.SFException;


// get OrderLine at the next iterator position
public DOrderLine getNextOrderLine(Iterator position)
                throws com.ibm.sf.gf.SFException;


// determine if the collection includes this OrderLine
public boolean containsOrderLine(DOrderLine orderline)
                throws com.ibm.sf.gf.SFException;


// get the OrderLine at the specified iterator position
public DOrderLine getOrderLineAt(Iterator position)
                throws com.ibm.sf.gf.SFException;
```

```
// remove the OrderLine from the collection at the specified
// iterator position
public void removeOrderLineAt(Iterator position)
                throws com.ibm.sf.gf.SFException;

// remove the specified OrderLine from the collection
public void removeOrderLine(DOrderLine orderline)
                throws com.ibm.sf.gf.SFException;

// add the specified OrderLine to the collection
public void addOrderLine(DOrderLine orderLine)
                throws com.ibm.sf.gf.SFException;
```

Additionally, if the collection is an Entity collection, methods for querying the collection are exposed.

Instance Variables for Attributes

In general, the implementation class also declares instance variables for each attribute within the class. This may not be the case for primitive attributes that are computed; they are typically declared as protected. The naming convention for instance variables is iv<attribute name>. Primitives, Strings, and Dependents are contained by value, so the instance variable type is the primitive, String, or Dependent type. Entity attributes are held as Handle objects. Following are examples of some of the GPSE. OrderHeader class instance variables:

```
protected int ivStatus;                       // primitive int for order
                                                 status
protected DMap ivOrderLines;                  // a DMap collection of
                                                 OrderLines
protected Handle ivDeliveryTypeHdl;           // DeliveryType Entity held by
                                                 Handle
protected Handle ivCustomerHdl;               // Customer Entity held by
                                                 Handle
protected String ivNumber;                    // String order number
protected DTime ivDatePlaced;                 // Dependent DTime for date
                                                 order was placed
protected DTime ivDeliveryDate;               // Dependent DTime for delivery
                                                 date
protected DCurrencyValue ivDeliveryCharge;    // delivery charge for order
protected DCurrencyValue ivTotalAmount;       // total amount of order
protected int ivOrderLineNumber;              // order line count
```

Creating a Dependent Subclass

Creating a Dependent subclass is similar to creating an Entity subclass. The differences are listed here.

Abstract Static Create Methods

A factory class is also required for Dependent subclasses. The create methods are similar to those implemented for an Entity, but the code is simplified somewhat because special factories are not supported for Dependents and Dependents are always owned if contained in another business object. Class replacement is still supported via BaseFactory. In this case, the createDependent() method is used to create the Dependent subclass instance. In general, the factory class provides two create methods: one that creates a transient Dependent that is not contained within another object, and a second that creates a transient or persistent Dependent based on whether its containing object is transient or persistent.

Required Methods

For implementing a Dependent subclass, the programming model defines a set of methods that should be implemented by the subclass. Entity objects are considered equal if their Handles are equal. Because Dependents do not have Handles, they must implement the following methods. These methods are used, for example, when Dependents are contained within collections.

Override equals()

The equals() method should be overridden for Dependent subclasses to determine the equality of Dependent instances.

Override setEqual()

Similarly, the setEqual() method should be overridden to set one Dependent subclass instance equal to another.

Override hashCode()

Hash codes are integer values returned by the hashCode() method, which all Java objects support. Hash tables and collections use the hash code values to access elements. If the Dependent subclass does not inherit a suitable hash code implementation from its superclass, it should implement one.

Creating a Command Subclass

Command subclasses are specialized Dependents, so their implementation is similar to that of a Dependent subclass. As discussed in Chapter 4, Commands are implemented to encapsulate business logic and isolate it from other business objects, thereby allowing for easier future changes to that logic without affecting users. The typical client use of a Command is to create it and call a doAll() method to execute the business logic. Commands also support undo and redo operations. A Command subclass, therefore, must support these operations. So in addition to the Dependent subclass rules, Commands must implement the following:

Required Methods

For implementing a Command subclass, the programming model defines a set of methods that should be implemented by the subclass.

Override handleDo()

When a client calls the doAll() method, the Command subclass's handleDo() method is called. The handleDo implementation includes all the business logic encapsulated within the Command that will be executed.

Optional Methods

For implementing a Command subclass, the programming model defines a set of methods that may optionally be implemented by the subclass.

Override handleUndo() and handleRedo()

Another use of Commands is to encapsulate changes to persistent objects so that these changes can be easily undone and redone within a transaction. These Commands are normally used during user interaction, or editing, of object state and are referred to as edit Commands. Edit Commands implement the handleUndo() and handleRedo() methods, which are called by the undo() and redo() client methods. When a Command is created, it specifies whether it will allow undo operations.

Override handleReset()

Command objects can be implemented to be reusable. Reusable Commands allow the client to create the Command, execute the business logic, reset the Command, and execute it again. The handleReset() method should be implemented in a Command subclass if extra processing needs to be done when a Command is reset or if resetting of the Command is not allowed.

Within the GPSE application, Commands are used only to set up and initialize the application. These Commands are discussed in a later chapter.

Code Generation of SanFrancisco Business Objects

Although the SanFrancisco Business Object Developer Programming Model requires several method implementations in order to create a well-behaved object, most of these implementations can be defined with a set of code generation rules. In all cases described here (except for the business processing in Command subclasses and specialized hashcode() and toString() methods), the code can be completely generated by the SanFrancisco code generator. See Appendix A for information on the SanFrancisco code generator.

Using SanFrancisco Business Objects

Now that we've seen how to implement the business objects within the GPSE application, let's look at how they are used. A user of existing business objects in SanFrancisco is referred to as a *client*, so the SanFrancisco Client Programming Model describes the rules for using existing business objects. These rules include how to create object instances, how to access existing object instances, and how to update, copy, and destroy instances.

The Transaction Model

In general, every operation involving persistent objects in SanFrancisco should be done within a transaction. (The exception is the use of *no lock* copies of persistent objects, which is described later.) These transactions are managed through the BaseFactory class, which is the entry point to most services provided by the SanFrancisco Foundation layer. Each client process normally has one instance of BaseFactory. This instance can be accessed through a static factory() method on the Global class that is called at the start of a SanFrancisco application:

```
Global.factory()
```

This method returns the instance of BaseFactory for the local client process. If the instance doesn't yet exist, one is automatically created. BaseFactory provides methods to perform transaction control:

```
begin()   // start a transaction
commit()  // commit a transaction
rollback()// roll back a transaction
```

begin() is used to start a transaction. After changes are made to the business objects, commit() persists the changes to the datastore and releases any locks held. rollback() can be used in error situations to roll back any changes made to persistent objects and release any locks that were obtained during the transaction.

The AccessMode Class

The AccessMode class encapsulates all the parameters that can be used to control the way a shared, persistent Entity object is accessed. AccessMode determines how an object instance is locked and where the code is executed. Client programmers generally do not need to know the details of the various Access-Mode possibilities. Special static create methods exist on the AccessMode class that returns AccessMode objects suitable for most programming situations:

```
createNormal()      // use when an object is needed for reading
createPlusWrite()   // use when an object will be updated
```

What is returned by these methods can be customized so that the application uses the appropriate locking and access location.

Lock Modes

There are three main types of locking: optimistic, pessimistic, and no lock. *Pessimistic* locking in SanFrancisco uses the traditional read and write locks. When an object is locked with a pessimistic write lock, others cannot access the object in read or write mode. When an object is locked with a pessimistic read lock, others can access the same object to read but not to write. Generally, pessimistic locks should not be used for long-duration transactions when there is a high likelihood that someone else needs access to the same object. Pessimistic locking may be suitable when the likelihood of multiple users changing the same object is high, but there is no automatic recovery for transactions that fail because of the conflicting changes.

Two types of *optimistic* locking are provided. With a normal optimistic lock, the object is not locked for the duration of the transaction. A read lock is acquired in order to make a copy of the object and then is released. At commit time, any changed objects are checked for validity. If some other process has changed one of these objects during the transaction, the commit fails and an exception is thrown. The second type of optimistic locking, called *optimistic clean*, is similar to normal optimistic locking. The difference is that at commit time, all objects are checked for validity, including objects that were not changed within the transaction. Optimistic locking works well with transactions of short duration or that do not change the same objects as other tasks. Optimistic locking can improve system throughput by reducing contention among applications accessing the same objects.

When an object instance is accessed using the *no lock* mode, a local copy of the business object is made and no lock is held on the actual object. *No lock copies* work well for applications that use pessimistic locking; they let you get a snapshot of the object data to work with without excluding other tasks from working with the object. No lock copies of objects can be used across and outside transactions.

Access Location

Access location is also encapsulated within the AccessMode class. The access location specifies where the object methods will actually execute. If an object instance is accessed with *home access* location, methods are executed where the object exists; with home access, the client process is really working with a proxy, and methods are executed on the server. If an object instance is accessed with *local access* location, a copy of the instance is created on the client, and methods are executed on the copy. Local access is suitable when lots of methods are executed on an object and its data is not voluminous. Home access is suitable if a small number of methods are executed on an object and it has a large amount of data. Home access is not compatible with optimistic locking because optimistic locking is defined to work with local copies.

Creating Business Object Instances

A business object's class factory is always used by the client to create an object instance. The parameters on the create method determine whether a transient or a persistent instance is created and, if persistent, where the object is located. By "located," we mean which process will host the instance and which persistent store will be used. We discuss how this is determined, based on configuration information, later in this chapter. All persistent Entities should be created within a transaction. The Entity is not accessible by other processes until it is committed. Entity class factories may have tightly coupled and/or loosely coupled create methods. The tightly coupled create method requires an owning object, and the loosely coupled does not. Following are examples of creating a GPSE ProductGroup class instance. ProductGroups are always owned by a *controller* within the GPSE application, so no loosely coupled create method is supported. (For more information on controllers, see Chapter 8, Using the Common Business Objects.)

```
1 Global.factory().begin(); // start the transaction

  // create description, not shown here
  // get access to persistent owningObject, not shown here

  // create a persistent ProductGroup owned and located with its owner
2 ProductGroup productGroup = ProductGroupFactory.createProductGroup(
      owningObject,
      AccessMode.createPlusWrite(),
      "TNS001",
      "April",
      "September",
      tennisDescription);
```

```
    // create a persistent ProductGroup owned and located in its
    // default location
3   ProductGroup productGroup = ProductGroupFactory.createProductGroup(
        owningObject,
        Global.factory().getContainer(GPSE.ProductGroup), // default location
        AccessMode.createPlusWrite(),
        "BSK001",
        "September",
        "April",
        basketballDescription);


4   Global.factory().commit();

    // create a transient ProductGroup
5   ProductGroup productGroup = ProductGroupFactory.createProductGroup(
        transientOwningObject,
        null, // null for location handle, create transient
        AccessMode.createPlusWrite(),
        "TNS001",
        "April",
        "September",
        transientDescription);
```

The interesting things to note in this code example are as follows:

- Line 1: Starts a transaction because all persistent Entity instances should be created within a transaction.

- Line 2: This creates a persistent ProductGroup that is owned by the own-ingObject that is passed as the first parameter and is located in the same location as its owner.

- Line 3: A different create method that has an extra parameter is used here. This creates a persistent ProductGroup that is owned by the owning-Object passed as the first parameter. This ProductGroup, however, will be located based on the default configuration information for the Product-Group class, which is specified by calling the getContainer method.

- Line 5: A transient ProductGroup is created. Passing null for the location value creates a transient.

Creating Dependent instances is similar to creating Entities. Dependent sub-class instances are persistent only when contained in a persistent Entity object. Therefore, business object developers can create persistent Dependents but client programmers will always work with transient Dependents. The DOrder-Line class in the GPSE application is a Dependent subclass. An example of creating a DOrderLine instance is shown next. In this case, the DOrderLine is created as a transient and is then added to the persistent OrderHeader.

```
  // create initial order line
  DOrderLine orderLine = DOrderLineFactory.createDOrderLine(
    quantity, product);

  // add the order line to the order
  order.addOrderLineBy(orderLine, product.getNumber());
```

Accessing Existing Business Object Instances

SanFranciso persistent objects survive beyond the life of an application process. They are persisted to a datastore that is configurable. These Entity instances are not activated into memory on any server or client until requested. BaseFactory is used to activate existing persistent Entity instances into the server and/or client memory. Entities can be accessed by Handle or by a user alias. A Handle encapsulates an Entity's unique identity which the BaseFactory can use to locate the instance. Typically, a small number of core Entity instances within an application are assigned user aliases so that they can be accessed by name. Then other application Entities can be accessed via contained Handles. When using the common business objects, as you will later learn, most Entities are accessed via Company objects that contain them. Company objects in turn are stored in a CompanyController that has a known user alias. That is the case in the GPSE application. To illustrate this, let's first look at the GPSE Customer class, which contains another Entity instance, Address. An example of creating GPSE Customer with an Address is shown next. The Customer will then be assigned a user alias.

```
1 Global.factory().begin();

  // create billing address
2 Address billing = AddressFactory.createAddress(
      AccessMode.createPlusWrite(),
      Global.factory().getContainer("cf.Address"),
      countryController.getCountryBy(bCountry),
      bLocale);

  // set additional info in billing address
3 billing.setAddressee("John Doe");
4 billing.addAddressLineBy("123 Main St", "line1");
5 billing.setPostalCodeLocation("Menomonie");
6 billing.addAddressLineBy("WI", "state");
7 billing.setPostalCode("53471");

  // create shipping address - not shown
  // create contact address - not shown
```

```
 // create Customer
8 Customer customer = CustomerFactory.createCustomer(owningController,
     AccessMode.createNormal(),
     "University of Wisconsin - Stout",
     billing,
     contact,
     shipping);

9 Global.factory().addUserAlias("TestCustomer", customer.getHandle());

10Global.factory().commit();
```

The interesting things to note in this code example are as follows:

- Line 2: A persistent Address is created for the Customer's billing address.
- Line 8: A Customer is created, and the billing address is passed as a parameter. Within Customer's initialize() method a Handle to this Address would be assigned to an instance variable.
- Line 9: A user alias of "TestCustomer" is assigned to correspond to the Customer instance just created.

Now let's show how the top-level Entity—the Customer instance in this simple example—can be accessed via user alias; then the Address is retrieved by Handle.

```
Global.factory().begin();

// get customer assigned to the "TestCustomer" user alias
Customer customer = (Customer) Global.factory().getEntity(
    "TestCustomer",   // user alias
    AccessMode.createPlusWrite()); // access for update

// get the Customer's billing address
Address billingAddress = customer.getBillingAddress();

// update the billing address addressee
billingAddress.setAddressee("Jane Doe");
    ....
Global.factory.commit();
```

Notice that when the Entity is accessed, an AccessMode is again specified. Remember that this class specifies how the object is locked and where methods execute. In this case, the billing Address will be changed so the PlusWrite access mode is used. The billing Address is accessed by calling a get method on the Customer. The Customer contains a Handle to the Address. The Address's addressee is changed via the set method. And again, any access, other than no lock copies, on persistent Entities must be done within a transaction.

Existing persistent Dependent instances are always accessed via a get method on a persistent business object because a Dependent instance is persistent only if its containing object is persistent. What is returned from the get method is a copy of the Dependent instance. This means that if the "persistent" Dependent is changed, the set method must be called to actually persist the Dependent. The GPSE Customer class contains a Dependent DCurrencyValue for the Customer's credit limit. Here is an example of accessing the credit limit and changing it for the Customer instance created earlier.

```
Global.factory().begin();

// get customer assigned to the "TestCustomer" user alias
Customer customer = (Customer) Global.factory().getEntity(
    "TestCustomer",
    AccessMode.createPlusWrite());

// get a copy of the Customer's current credit limit
DCurrencyValue creditLimit = customer.getCreditLimit();

// create a DDecimal representing the new credit limit to be assigned
DDecimal newCreditLimitValue = DDecimalFactory.createDDecimal(1000.00);

// set the DDecimal value of the new credit limit in the copy
// previously retrieved
creditLimit.setValue(newCreditLimitValue);

// update the Customer with the new credit limit
customer.setCreditLimit(creditLimit);

Global.factory().commit();
```

Accessing and Querying Collections

Other common functions needed by the client programmer are the abilities to access and query a collection of objects. As discussed earlier, when a business object contains a collection of business object instances, it will have methods that allow the client to access the collection. The OrderHeader class, for example, includes methods to access its DOrderLines. A helper class, Iterator, is used to access each element in a collection. Here is an example that illustrates accessing each DOrderLine in an OrderHeader to print the order information to the screen.

```
// access the OrderHeader - not shown

1 System.out.println("The OrderHeader: ");
2 System.out.println("Id:   " + order.getNumber());
3 System.out.println("Order total with delivery:   " +
                         order.getTotalWithDelivery().format());
4 System.out.println("Order status:   " + order.getStatus());
5 System.out.println("Order lines:");

  // create an iterator to use to access each order line
6 Iterator it = order.createOrderLineIterator();

  // get the first order line, if none exist, null is returned
7 DOrderLine ol = order.getNextOrderLine(it);

  // continue to access each order line in the order
8 while (ol != null) {
9    System.out.println("       Order line number:   " + ol.getNumber());
10   System.out.println("       Product:   " +
                       ol.getProduct().getDescription());
11   System.out.println("       Quantity:   " + ol.getQuantity());
12   System.out.println("       UnitPrice:   " + ol.getUnitPrice().format());
13   System.out.println("       Discount:   " + ol.getDiscountPercent());
14   System.out.println("       Line total with discount:   " +
                       ol.getTotalAmount().format());

     // get the new order line in the order
15   ol = order.getNextOrderLine(it);
16}
```

The iteration and access of the DOrderLine objects are shown in lines 6–16. There are some other interesting things to point out in this code example. In line 3, the total for the order is displayed. The total is stored as DCurrency-Value, which supports the Translatable interface. Translatable is a common interface for objects that provide locale-dependent String representations of themselves. The Translatable interface has two format() methods: one that gets the String representation of an object based on the active locale, and a second one that takes a specific locale as input. So the order total in this example is displayed using the current active locale information for things such as the decimal symbol. In line 10, the Product description for an OrderLine is displayed. The Product object supports the Describable interface, which supports methods to get a language- or locale-dependent description of an object. In this example, the description of Product will be displayed based on the active locale.

Query, also supported on a subset of the SanFrancisco collections, allows a client to get a subset of objects based on some type of selection criteria. The result of a query on a particular collection is another collection—the result collection—that contains a subset of the elements in the original collection that satisfy the query criteria. For example, in the GPSE application you might want to find all orders for a particular Customer. The query criteria are formatted as an SQL SELECT statement using a subset of SQL92. Because the query is executed on objects, the selection criteria may be based on calling methods on the elements in the collection. In our example, there is a SELECT statement that calls the getCustomer method on each order in the collection.

```
select order from orderCollection order where order.getCustomer()..getId() =
'CUST002'
```

This query would then be executed on the orderCollection via queryElements, a method on the collection. Logically, when this query is executed each element in the order collection is accessed, the getCustomer() method is called on the order, the getId() method is called on the Customer, and then the return from that method is compared to 'CUST002.' If we look at that processing more closely, what also happens is that if the order elements are not active on the server where this query is executed, they must first be activated so that the get-Customer() method can be called; then if the Customer element is not active, it will also be activated so that the getId() method can be called on it. When objects are used to execute the query, it is referred to as *object query.* Because GPSE is a successful company, it will have large numbers of orders that will be processed for this query, and that could result in a long-running object query. To optimize queries, SanFrancisco also provides *query pushdown*, in which the object query is converted into a form that can be processed efficiently by the underlying datastore. In SanFrancisco, query pushdown is supported only for relational database persistence. In this case, an attempt can be made to convert the query to an SQL statement that can be processed directly by the relational database. Query pushdown is supported only on one SanFrancisco collection, EntityOwningExtent. The purpose of this collection is to support large-scale collections by tying them to the underlying datastore.

Collections are also sorted via query. Because most of the SanFrancisco collections are unordered (except for List collections), to sort them, you can use a query with an *order-by* clause to get the results in sorted order. To continue with the same example, suppose we want the list of orders for this particular customer returned sorted by the date the order was placed. The following statement would accomplish that:

```
select order from orderCollection order where order.getCustomer()..getId() =
'CUST002' order by order.getDatePlaced();
```

The SanFrancisco query support also includes host variable support. *Host variables* can be used as an alternative to hard-coding a value within the select statement, such as the earlier 'CUST002.' The value of the host variable can then be passed on the query. Following is an alternative query for our example that uses host variables:

```
// get access to the Customer using the customer number and get
// its Handle - not shown
select order from orderCollection order where order.getCustomerHdl() = :cust
order by order.getDatePlaced();
```

The customer Handle that should be substituted for the host variable (indicated with the ":") would then be passed on the query.

When a business object contains an Entity collection of business object instances, it has methods that allow the client to query the collection. To complete this example, here is the code necessary to execute the queries discussed earlier:

```
// access order controller that contains collection of orders

//
// execute query without host variables
//

// create query string
String queryString =
  "select order from orderCollection order" +
    "where order.getCustomer()..getId() = '" +
    customerId + "';";

// execute the query
Set result = (Set)orderController.queryOwnedOrderHeaders(
    queryString,
    "orderCollection",
    null, null, null, null, false);

//
// execute query with host variables
//

// access the customer controller that contains collection of
// customers - not shown

// get access to a Customer with a particular key value
Handle custHdl = customerController.getCustomerBy(
    customerKey).getHandle();
```

```
// execute the query indicating a host variable is used
String hostVars[] = {"hostVar"};
Object hostVals[] = {custHdl};
Set result = (Set)orderController.queryOwnedOrderHeaders(
    "select order from orderCollection order where order.getCustomerHdl()
      = :hostVar order by order.getDatePlaced();",
    "orderCollection",
    null, null, null, null, false,
    hostVars,
    hostVals);
```

Destroying Business Object Instances

Because many SanFrancisco business objects are persistent, they must explicitly be deleted when they are no longer needed. Client programmers use the BaseFactory deleteEntity() method to delete non-owned Entities. Because Dependent instances are persistent only if their containing object is persistent, all persistent Dependent instances are considered "owned" by their containing object. If an object is owned, its owning object has methods to allow deleting its owned objects if appropriate. If an object has an attribute that is a single object instance, you can use the setOwned<class name> method to delete the instance by passing null as the argument. If an object has a collection of owned objects, a remove<Owned><class name> method is available to delete one instance as well as a removeAll<Owned><class name>s to delete all instances.

Administering and Configuring a SanFrancisco Application

Deploying an application built on the SanFrancisco Foundation requires configuration and administration. For example, you must configure information about business object classes to determine where object instances should be created at runtime. To correctly persist your objects to a relational database you must specify which tables to persist class instances to. Configuration of the Logical SanFrancisco Network is also necessary to specify where business objects are allowed to reside. A Logical SanFrancisco Network (LSFN) consists of one or more processes, running on one or more systems, that provides services to one or more applications. LSFN is discussed in more detail later in this chapter. Administration consists of tasks such as creating user IDs and passwords for users of the system and specifying the resources users can access.

Class and Container Configuration

To understand class configuration in SanFrancisco, you must first understand the concept of *containers* as they are used within the Foundation. Containers are an abstraction of the persistent datastore that is used to persist your business objects. Containers are configured to a particular datastore, such as a relational database source. Classes, in turn, are configured to containers. The *class/container configuration* specifies those containers in which instances of a class can be created. As a result, the programmer need not code into an application any specifics of where persistent objects will exist. When a persistent Entity is created, the location of the Entity must be specified. In some cases, it is specified as the location of the owning object; the object is created in the same container as the owning object. In other cases, the location can be specified as the default container for that class. The only way containers are visible in the programming model is via the getContainer() method, which allows you to retrieve the default container Handle for a specified class name token. That Handle can then be used on a createEntity call to create the object in the correct container. An administrator can change container configuration at runtime to locate objects elsewhere within the network. Obviously, care must be taken in such cases to ensure that all objects are still accessible to the application.

Configuration information is stored in the SanFrancisco naming data. Class and container configuration can be done in two ways. The configuration can be specified in a text file that is input to a naming utility, or it can be entered through a graphical user interface, the Configuration utility.

Container Configuration

Configuring a container consists of configuring the datastore used for the container and the process that will host objects created in the container when they are active. Two types of containers are supported: POSIX and Rdb. *POSIX containers* use POSIX files to persist object instances. *Rdb containers* use a relational database to persist object instances. Several types of relational databases are supported. Rdb containers are the only type recommended for application deployment. POSIX containers can be useful during development and for demo purposes when a complete database system is not available.

The text file used as an option for SanFrancisco configuration contains several *stanzas*. Following are two examples of a stanza to configure a container for the GPSE application objects.

```
[CONTAINERS]

# configure an Rdb container
GPSEContainerRdb=*_SFBOProcess1,com.ibm.sf.gf.RdbContainer,ibmsf,DB2,
    Native,*,*,*

# configure a POSIX container
GPSEContainerPosix=*_SFBOProcess1,com.ibm.sf.gf.PosixContainer,*,*
```

The first stanza entry configures a container named GPSEContainerRdb that exists on process SFBOProcess1. The container is an Rdb container. The datasource name for the container is ibmsf, and it is a DB2 database. The database is accessed through its native interface.

The second stanza entry configures a container named GPSEContainerPosix that exists on process SFBOProcess1. The container is a POSIX container.

Class Configuration

Class configuration consists of several parts. First, the relationship between a class name token and a real class name must be configured. *Class tokens* are the String values that are used within a business object factory class when the BaseFactory create methods are called to create Entities, Dependents, and Commands. BaseFactory looks in the configuration data to determine the actual class to instantiate, so you must configure the real class name to instantiate when the class name token is used. Using a token instead of the actual instantiable class name allows the class to be replaced without source code modification. The same token passed during object creation can result in a different class being instantiated, based on the configuration data for the token. There are defined class tokens for every Entity, Dependent, and Command.

The *default container* for a class is also configured. This is the container that is returned when the BaseFactory getContainer() method is called. Classes can also be configured to allow instances to be created in other containers.

Here is an example of the class configuration for a few of the sample GPSE application classes.

```
[CONTAINERS]
GPSEContainer=*_SFBOProcess1,com.ibm.sf.gf.RdbContainer,ibmsf,DB2,
    Native,*,*,*

[ENTITY TOKENS]
GPSE.Product=GPSE.Product,GPSEContainer
GPSE.ProductGroup=GPSE.ProductGroup,GPSEContainer
GPSE.Customer=GPSE.Customer,GPSEContainer
GPSE.OrderHeader=GPSE.OrderHeader,GPSEContainer
GPSE.DeliveryType=GPSE.DeliveryType,GPSEContainer
```

```
[DEPENDENT TOKENS]
GPSE.DOrderLine=GPSE.DOrderLine

[COMMAND TOKENS]
GPSE.GPSESetupCmd=GPSE.GPSESetupCmd
```

In this example, the class name token is the same as the real class name. It is recommended that the class name token be the fully qualified package and class name because these tokens must be unique within the configuration.

The second identifier in the class configuration is the default container for the class. This allows instances of the class to be created in the container and is also the container returned on the BaseFactory getContainer() method. There are several ways to allow instances of a class to be created in multiple containers.

The Logical SanFrancisco Network

A Logical SanFrancisco Network includes any number of clients and servers (see Figure 5-5). The clients must be able to communicate with all the servers throughout the network because the servers typically contain the actual San-Francisco business objects the clients use. The servers must also communicate among themselves to access objects and SanFrancisco services.

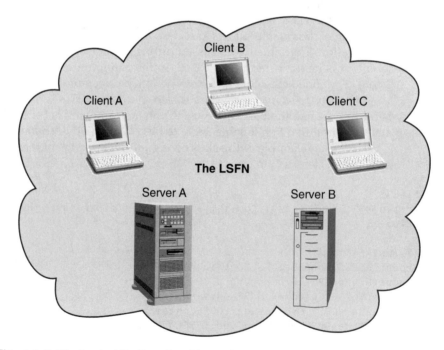

Figure 5-5. The Logical SanFrancisco Network

Configuration of the LSFN first requires defining the hosts in the network and specifying the processes that run on those hosts. TCP/IP is used to communicate between the various SanFrancisco processes. These processes are then assigned services that are supported in the network.

The central service in an LSFN is the *Global Server Manager* (GSM). The GSM can be configured for one process within the LSFN and coordinates all other processes and services in the network. The GSM process implicitly provides the naming service and security service. The naming service is responsible for managing the name space of the LSFN. This includes how to resolve user aliases and the class and container configuration information described earlier: which classes ultimately must be used to create instances of business objects, where those instances must be created, and what datastore to use. The security service manages authentication and authorization within the LSFN.

The remainder of the LSFN services are configured in *business object processes*, the processes where persistent business objects reside. These processes provide factory services and transaction services. They can also provide problem logging and conflict control services.

Let's try to tie the LSFN configuration with the container and class configuration described earlier. Figure 5-6 illustrates a sample LSFN for the GPSE application.

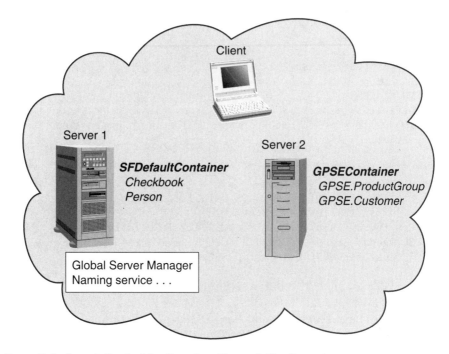

Figure 5-6. Sample Logical SanFrancisco Network Configuration

In this example, we configure Server1 to host the Global Server Manager. Server1 also holds any objects created in the SFDefaultContainer for which all the SanFrancisco sample classes are configured (including a CheckBook and a Person class). Server2 is the host for the GPSEContainer configured earlier. This means that Server2 must have a business object process with a factory and transaction service configured. Following is a sample text naming file that accomplishes all this configuration:

```
1    [HOSTS]
2    *=*,*,com.ibm.sf.gf.PosixContainer
3    Server2.ibm.com=NT,/home/applications/sf130,
        com.ibm.sf.gf.PosixContainer

4    [PROCESSES]
5    *_SFGSMProcess=
6    *_SFBOProcess1=
7    Server2_SFBOProcess2=

8    [FACTORY SERVICES]
9    *_SFGSMProcess=
10   *_SFBOProcess1=
11   Server2_SFBOProcess2=

12   [TRANSACTION SERVICES]
13   *_SFGSMProcess=
14   *_SFBOProcess1=
15   Server2_SFBOProcess2=

16   [CONTAINERS]
17   SFDefaultContainer=*_SFBOProcess1,com.ibm.sf.gf.PosixContainer,*,*
18   GPSEContainer=Server2_SFBOProcess2,com.ibm.sf.gf.RdbContainer,ibmsf,DB2,
        Native,*,*,*

19   [ENTITY TOKENS]
20   com.ibm.sf.samples.Person=
        com.ibm.sf.samples.Person,SFDefaultContainer
21   com.ibm.sf.samples.CheckBook=
        com.ibm.sf.samples.CheckBook,SFDefaultContainer
22   GPSE.ProductGroup=GPSE.ProductGroup,GPSEContainer
23   GPSE.Customer=GPSE.Customer,GPSEContainer
```

Let's examine this configuration.

- Line 2 configures the Server1 host. The * signifies that local configuration information can be used for the server name, platform type, and install directory.

- Line 3 configures Server2. The server name, platform type, and install directory are specified.

- Line 5 configures the GSM process for Server1 named SFGSMProcess.

- Line 6 configures a business object process for Server1 named SFBOProcess1.

- Line 7 configures a business object process for Server2 named SFBOProcess2.

- Lines 9–11 configure a factory service for each process.

- Lines 13–15 configure a transaction service for each process.

- Line 17 defines the SFDefaultContainer to exist in SFBOProcess1 (on Server1).

- Line 18 defines the GPSEContainer to exist in SFBOProcess2 (on Server2).

- Lines 20 and 21 define CheckBook and Person classes to exist in SFDefaultContainer (in SFBOProcess1 on Server1).

- Lines 22 and 23 define ProductGroup and Customer classes to exist in GPSEContainer (in SFBOProcess2 on Server2).

Now let's go back to an example introduced earlier to create a GPSE Product-Group class instance.

```
// create a persistent ProductGroup owned and located in its
// default location
ProductGroup productGroup = ProductGroupFactory.createProductGroup(
    owningObject,
    Global.factory().getContainer(GPSE.ProductGroup), // default location
    AccessMode.createPlusWrite(),
    "BSK001",
    "September",
    "April",
    basketballDescription);
```

By calling the Global.factory().getContainer("GPSE.ProductGroup") the GPSE-Container will be used to locate this instance (line 22 configures Product-Group's default container as GPSEContainer). Because this container is configured to be hosted by SFBOProcess2 on Server2 (line 18), the instance will be created there. Because GPSEContainer is an Rdb container, the instance will be persisted to the DB2 datasource, ibmsf, configured for the container. The ProductGroupFactory uses "GPSE.ProductGroup" as the class name token on the call to createEntity():

```
Entity entity = Global.factory().createEntity("GPSE.Product", ...)
```

So the real class name instantiated is GPSE.Product, as defined on line 22.

Schema Mapping

Schema mapping refers to the way objects are persisted to a relational database (see Figure 5-7). SanFrancisco supports two types of persistence through the use of containers: POSIX and relational database. Relational database, however, is the only persistent store recommended for deploying an application. So how do you get your class instances and their corresponding attributes stored to rows in a relational database table? That's where schema mapping comes in. Schema mapping is the task of mapping an *object schema*—classes, instances, and attributes—to the relational schema—tables, rows, and columns. Schema mapping plays a very important role if existing tables, sometimes referred to as *legacy* tables, must be accommodated. You can use the schema mapping support in SanFrancisco to use existing tables for persistence or when new tables are desired.

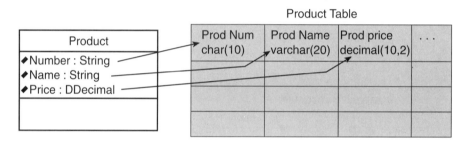

Figure 5-7. Schema Mapping

There is a great amount of flexibility in the support provided. If no special customization of tables is necessary or desired, there is literally no work to do. SanFrancisco provides a *default schema mapping* service that determines the schema mapping for a class the first time an instance is created based on a set of default mappings. The table names, column names, and data types for the columns are selected by the schema mapper. One table is created for each class. The default schema mapper need only be "turned on" simply by configuring the classes to an Rdb container, as in the configuration examples discussed earlier. The following configuration information would be enough to persist instances of ProductGroup to a relational database table, taking all the defaults provided by the default schema mapper:

```
[CONTAINERS]
GPSEContainer=*_SFBOProcess1,com.ibm.sf.gf.RdbContainer,ibmsf,DB2,
    Native,*,*,*

[ENTITY TOKENS]
GPSE.ProductGroup=GPSE.ProductGroup,GPSEContainer
```

In many cases, however, the default schema mapping may not be suitable. Even in the case of new tables, certain defaults are taken that do not result in optimal tables. For example, by default, String attributes are mapped to the VARCHAR(128) column data type. The default schema mapper has no information on what the maximum length of a String attribute can be. If within the application, however, the String is always limited to 10 characters, as in the GPSE application's Order numbers, there may be some performance and storage benefits to customizing the mapping for that attribute. Customizations are also typically needed to get more pushdown of queries. Another type of schema mapping, *extended schema mapping*, allows this customization.

Extended schema mapping provides the flexibility to map attributes to the desired table, column, and data type. The extended schema mapper uses a *schema mapping language* (SML) file to determine how to map the objects. The SML file is created by the provided *schema mapping tool*, which lets you customize the schema mapping for each attribute in a·class. Of course, in many cases, the default schema mapping is sufficient, and there is no requirement that every attribute be customized. The schema mapping tool uses a preference file, which can be defined by the user, to populate the default schema mapping, so only necessary attributes need to be customized. In our Order class, for example, we can choose to change the schema mapping only for the Order number attribute, changing the column type to CHAR(10). You can also map a class to multiple tables using extended schema mapping, and you can map one instance to multiple rows if necessary for very large objects. The tool also supports mapping subclasses and supports options such as mapping the parent attributes to one table and the subclass attributes to another table.

To use extended schema mapping, you need additional configuration to specify the SML file for a class. In the ProductGroup example, assuming that the SML file is named ProductGroup.sml, here is the required configuration:

```
[CONTAINERS]
GPSEContainer=*_SFBOProcess1,com.ibm.sf.gf.RdbContainer,ibmsf,DB2,
    Native,*,d:\sml,*

[ENTITY TOKENS]
GPSE.ProductGroup=GPSE.ProductGroup,GPSEContainer

[PERSISTENT ENTITY]
GPSE.ProductGroup=GPSE.ProductGroup,GPSEContainer,EXTENDED,ProductGroup
```

In this example, a directory is specified in the container configuration to define where the SML files can be found for classes configured for the container. A Persistent Entity stanza is also added. The entry in this stanza specifies that the GPSE.ProductGroup class will use extended schema mapping and that the SML file name is ProductGroup. The schema mapping service will then look for a ProductGroup.sml file in d:\sml when needed.

Extended schema mapping is necessary if existing tables are to be used for persistence of class instances. Keep in mind that SanFrancisco persistence requires that the table have a *primary key*, which is used to store the object's unique identity. As mentioned earlier, SanFrancisco Entities are assigned a unique identifier that is used to distinguish them within a Logical SanFrancisco Network. This identifier is ultimately encapsulated by SanFrancisco in the Handle to the instance. This identifier can be a generated object ID (automatically generated by the Foundation), or it can be user-specified. Every Entity instance contains its own unique identifier (its own Handle). This identifier is passed on the BaseFactory's createEntity method. If you are using the generated object ID, a null is passed as the key on the createEntity method, as shown in previous examples of class factory create methods. SanFrancisco must store this identifier in the persistent datastore. In the case of Rdb persistence, this identifier is stored in the table as the primary key.

If the object ID is used as the primary key, it is stored in a 16-byte OBJECTID column. Legacy databases are very unlikely to include such a column in their layout. The extended schema mapper allows you to map the unique identifier to a meaningful user-defined piece of information: the existing table's primary key. The primary key works well in this role because it is guaranteed to be unique and not null. When you're using a user-defined primary key, the OBJECTID column is no longer necessary in the database table, but the extended schema mapper must be used to define the primary key. The primary key value must also be wrapped in a Dependent subclass instance and must be passed on the createEntity method within a class factory. In this case, a special factory can be used.

Security Administration

The final configuration and administration associated with deploying an application is security. SanFrancisco provides both authentication and authorization security services. Authentication involves authenticating users of the system by means of a user ID and, optionally, a password. Authorization involves determining whether a specific user is authorized to use actions and resources of the system.

The security policy of the Logical SanFrancisco Network is configurable. You can configure whether user IDs and/or passwords are required, how long passwords are valid, when they expire, their maximum and minimum length, and so on. Both user groups and users can be defined using the User Administration utility. The Foundation provides a set of APIs that can be used to authenticate a user at runtime. An "all inclusive" API can be used to display a dialog box for the user ID and password and perform authentication based on the configured security policy. For example, if only user IDs are required, the userid field is required and the password field is optional. If passwords are required, the dialog box includes a button to allow changing a password, and so on. Here is an example of using the API:

```
LogonController.processLogon();
```

If "userids required" is not configured, this API does nothing. If security is enabled, it displays a logon dialog box. If the user is not authenticated (based on configured rules for how many attempts are allowed), an exception is thrown. If the user has already been authenticated, no logon dialog box is displayed. Using this API is convenient, but in some situations, such as when the user ID is not obtained from the user, it is not appropriate. In that case, a set of APIs, such as setUserid(), setPassword(), and validateUser(), allows the application programmer to process the authentication.

Secure task checking and server authorization are also configurable. *Secure tasks* are units of work within an application that the application programmer deems necessary to be secured. APIs are used to define these units of work. They can be small-scope tasks, such as changing an attribute, or large-scope tasks, such as executing a command. The secure tasks are named and given a description to allow them to be displayed with the Access Rights Administration utility. An *access right* consists of a user (or group), an action (or a secure task), and a resource (a company or none). In the GPSE application, we can have a user interface that allows someone to change a customer's credit limit. It can be an application requirement that only someone authorized to increase credit limits—someone from the credit department—be allowed to use that interface. We could create a secure task for changing credit limits as follows:

```
// create the secure task
SecureTask GPSETask = SecureTask.createSecureTask("ChangeCreditLimit",
    "Change a customer's credit limit");
GPSETask.setResourceType(SecureTask.RESOURCE_NONE);
// add the secure task to the com/gpse context
Global.security().addSecureTask(GPSETask, "com/gpse/oe");
```

This code defines the secure task to the system to allow access rights to be configured with it. We then configure the credit department users to this secure task. Within the application, this secure task is *activated* as follows:

```
try {
  // start of secure task
  Global.security().beginSecureTask("ChangeCreditLimit", "com/gpse/oe");
}
catch (NotAuthorizedException e) {
    // display message and exit
}
```

```
// get access to the customer - not shown

// set the credit limit
customer.setCreditLimit(creditLimit);

// end of the secure task
Global.security().endSecureTask("ChangeCreditLimit", "com/gpse/oe");
```

When the beginSecureTask() method is called, the security services determine whether the logged-on user has been authorized to execute this action. If not, an exception is thrown.

Server authorization is somewhat similar except that the user, rather than being authorized to a task, is authorized to a server process or a set of processes. In this way you could partition your data onto secure servers and limit access to the server processes through the server authorization mechanism.

Summary

This chapter uses a sample application as the context for discussing various aspects of the SanFrancisco Programming Model and also the tools for administering and configuring a SanFrancisco application. The programming model is the set of rules that must be followed when you implement new business objects or use existing business objects. Having a defined set of programming rules enables SanFrancisco supporting code generators to generate a considerable amount of a class's implementation. As a result, the business object developer can focus on the implementation of the unique business logic necessary to satisfy application requirements.

The discussion in this chapter really focuses on design, implementation, use, and deployment of new business objects within the GPSE Order Entry application. Chapter 8 continues with the GPSE sample, focusing on the use of the common business objects and design patterns within the application.

Part III

The Common Business Objects

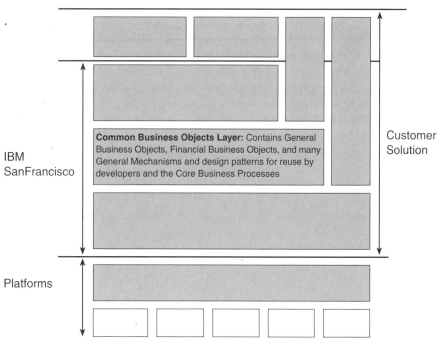

IBM SanFrancisco

Common Business Objects Layer: Contains General Business Objects, Financial Business Objects, and many General Mechanisms and design patterns for reuse by developers and the Core Business Processes

Customer Solution

Platforms

The Common Business Object layer

The Common Business Objects layer provides the processes and business objects that are common across more than one business application domain. This layer includes processes and business objects that are

- Readily identifiable by domain experts, such as those for supporting currencies
- Used for getting information into a financial application, such as a General Ledger
- Abstract solutions to recurring problems, called generalized mechanisms

The Common Business Objects layer lies between the Foundation layer and the Core Business Processes layer. By being built on the Foundation layer and following the SanFrancisco Programming Model, the Common Business Objects layer is isolated from the underlying technology.

The business objects and processes in the Common Business Objects layer are used by the core business processes or by a solution provider in two main ways. First, the business objects and processes can be used without modification. For example, the currency support is used without modification by the General Ledger and Accounts Receivable/Accounts Payable core business processes. Second, these objects and processes can be used by extending them. For example, the Order Management core business process extends the Business-Partner class to add information it needs so that a BusinessPartner class can be used as the customer or supplier on an order.

The common business objects are discussed in detail in the next three chapters: Chapter 6, An Introduction to the Common Business Objects, focuses on the key concepts and patterns in the Common Business Objects layer. Chapter 7, Common Business Object Categories, provides an overview of the contents of the Common Business Objects layer. Chapter 8, Using the Common Business Objects, shows an example of using the contents of the Common Business Objects layer.

6 An Introduction to the Common Business Objects

Contents of the Common Business Objects Layer

This chapter introduces the Common Business Objects layer of the SanFrancisco component framework, focusing on the key concepts and patterns. We provide an overview of the contents of this layer and explain how they are used.

The Common Business Objects layer, as well as the Core Business Processes layer, was populated by IBM working with a number of business partners. One group participated in developing the business objects, and another in validating them. To determine which business objects to initially provide as part of the Common Business Objects layer, IBM leveraged the experience of the business partners working with SanFrancisco. Because SanFrancisco could not provide all possible common business objects, early efforts were focused on those used by the core business processes. Then as the core business processes were being built, additional common business objects were identified and added. This layer will continue to grow as solution providers send feedback and more core business processes are developed.

The portion of the common business objects that is most recognizable to domain experts is the general business objects, which can be used to represent data and to perform common operations. For example, objects in the Business Partner category provide a means of representing the individuals and businesses (such as customers) that a business deals with. This includes the ability to represent the organization of the business partner. For example, if you do business with a company that has two divisions—Hardware and Software—you could represent this arrangement using a hierarchy consisting of a Business-Partner instance representing the company and two child BusinessPartner instances—one for each division. This hierarchy allows you to represent the fact that you have agreements with the company that affect your relationship with both divisions; you associate the agreements with the BusinessPartner instance representing the company. When the system is looking for agreements, first the division (child) is searched and then the company (parent). When a special agreement is reached with the Software division, the agreement can be associated with the Software division instance of BusinessPartner so that the special agreement is found before the more general one.

The Common Business Objects layer also contains a number of processes and business objects that financial domain experts will recognize, such as objects related to banking and bank accounts. The Common Business Objects layer also provides a means of getting financial information into a financial application: by applying the SanFrancisco *generic interface* pattern. Using a variation of the Facade pattern (from *Design Patterns*, the book mentioned in Chapter 2), you allow an outside application to use the financial application without having to know any details about the financial system or even whether one is present. Generic interfaces are currently provided for the General Ledger core business process (including some banking support) and the Accounts Receivable/Accounts Payable core business process.

The final piece of the Common Business Objects layer is the generalized mechanisms. These are solutions to recurring problems that have been made general enough (abstracted) to be used in many situations. These mechanisms come in the form of patterns that have been partially implemented and can be used as miniature frameworks. For example, the generalized mechanism Cached Balances is abstracted to the point that anything that can be aggregated (such as a numeric total) can be stored and maintained over any criteria. You use the Cached Balances to manage the product balances on each product. The criteria consist of things such as the warehouse and the stock type (normal, damaged, and so on). The balances that are stored and maintained are the total of the product for each combination of the criteria. This means that you can ask the product balances how much of the product in warehouse A is damaged and get the result immediately. Without the Cached Balances you would have to look at all the inventory records and sum up all those that affect the amount of damaged product in warehouse A.

Using the Contents of the Common Business Objects Layer

Depending on your needs, the business objects and processes in the Common Business Objects layer can be used without modification or can be extended. The core business processes, which are built on top of the Common Business Objects layer, use them in both ways.

When used without modification, business objects are tied together with each other and with any new business objects added by the application. For example, suppose you are creating an application that manages conversion of money from one currency to another (also called exchanging money). You must be able to calculate the equivalent value of money in one currency from an amount of money in another currency. For example, suppose you must calculate how many French francs to give for 10 U.S. dollars. The Common Business Objects layer supplies business objects to represent the various currencies and the exchange rates between them. It also supplies the processes for calculating the equivalent value. In addition, it supports the definition of multiple exchange rate tables, so the application could, for example, have one set of exchange rates to use if cash is exchanged and another set if traveler's checks are exchanged. You could build this application on top of the Common Business Objects layer without having to modify the supplied business objects. This includes not having to tie the business objects together because they already work together. The only function the application must add is the implementation of how they are used, which, in this case, could be done as part of the client programming phase.

On the other hand, at times the objects provided in the Common Business Objects layer are not quite what you need. A class might not have all the attributes your application needs, or a class might provide a process that is not suitable for your application. These situations are driven by your requirements and the business objects from the Common Business Objects layer you are using. For example, if your application must represent a customer, the Business Partner category objects provide a good starting point but probably must be extended for your needs. In this case, you usually extend BusinessPartner by wrapping it with a new Customer object you create and wiring methods through to the BusinessPartner class as appropriate. To help you determine the correct way to extend the Common Business Objects layer, SanFrancisco provides a manual called the Extension Guide. It describes the various extension techniques that can be used not only with the Common Business Objects layer but also with the core business processes. The Extension Guide also describes the trade-offs involved in each of the extension techniques.

This does not mean that you will always find what you need in the Common Business Objects layer. Determining what to use must be part of your application development process. SanFrancisco provides the Roadmap, a sample development process that can be used if you don't already have a development process or as an example for modifying your development process. The Roadmap guides you in periodically checking to see whether you can map to what SanFrancisco provides. The Roadmap is described in Chapter 1, An Overview of SanFrancisco Development.

Common Business Object Categories

How you use the Common Business Objects layer is tied to the needs of your application. The Common Business Objects layer is not just a class library but instead is a set of interrelated frameworks. When you decide to use a piece of the Common Business Objects layer, you use the piece you've chosen within the context of the other pieces it works with. That is, it provides not only the nuts and bolts but also preassembled units.

For example, to represent and work with exchange rates between two currencies, you can use the exchange rate support provided by SanFrancisco. Deciding to use the exchange rate support means that you are also deciding to use the context for the exchange rate support. In this case, the exchange rate support depends on the support for representing various currencies, so you must also use that. Usually, as in this case, the context is something you would have needed anyway.

To ease in identifying interactions among the pieces of the Common Business Objects layer, SanFrancisco groups the pieces into categories. A *category* contains business objects and processes that work closely together. Among other things, the Currency category contains support for the following:

- Representing currencies. For example, USD represents U.S. dollars; DEM represents German marks.

- Representing and working with a currency value, which is a combination of a value (DDecimal) with a Currency object (for example, 3.25 USD).

- Representing and working with exchange rates.

Although these objects are collected together because it is likely that using one will lead to your using the others, you can still use only pieces of a category. For example, the support for representing currencies is not dependent on any of the other support in the Currency category.

In addition to relationships within a category, there are relationships between the categories. For example, the relationship could represent the fact that one of the business objects in a lower level category is an attribute of one of the using category's business objects. Relationships between the categories are restricted to only one direction. This arrangement makes the categories more independent, allowing you to use the appropriate category and only the set of categories it depends on. This layered approach helps maximize reuse because without this restriction, use of one category would quickly require use of all the other categories as well.

The Company Category

All categories are assumed to have a dependency on the Company category because this category is used in two ways:

- To represent your company organization and structure
- As a context for your application, which causes the dependency

Representing Your Company Organization and Structure

The Company category provides two major business objects: Enterprise and Company. A company structure consists of one instance of Enterprise, which must be the start of any hierarchy, and any number of instances of Company, which make up the remainder of the hierarchy.

Figure 6-1 shows an example of one company hierarchy. In this example, the hierarchy represents four related companies. The Enterprise represents the main company, Games Inc. This company owns all the others. It directly owns the child companies Board Games Inc. and Electronic Games Inc. Electronic Games Inc. owns the child company Video Games Inc.

Figure 6-2 shows a company hierarchy representing the business units within a company. The Enterprise represents the overall company, which in our example is called Computer Stuff Inc. This company is divided into two divisions: Software and Hardware. The Hardware division has two pieces: one that resells computers and another that manufactures portable computers. The ability to build an arbitrary hierarchy of Company instances is flexible enough to allow definition of almost any organizational structure.

Using the Company as the Context for Your Application

The company hierarchy is also used as a context. This means that deciding which Company you are working with also determines which business rules, default values, and business objects can be seen and used in the application. The Company is the *owner* of business objects. It owns those business objects that a domain expert would expect it to own and those objects that are not owned by any other business object. For example, the definition of which currencies can

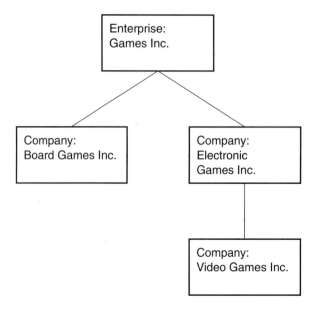

Figure 6-1. Company Hierarchy Example

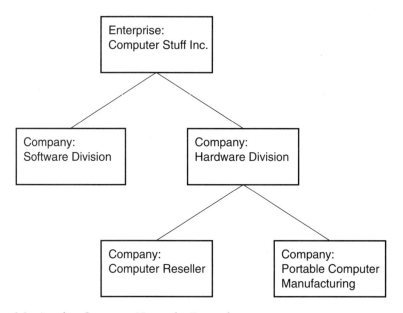

Figure 6-2. Another Company Hierarchy Example

be used with a particular company in the hierarchy either doesn't have an owner or is naturally owned by the company, depending on your perspective. This means that when you query the system about a particular company, you want to be able to ask whether a particular currency can be used with it. To be more concrete, using the sample company hierarchy in Figure 6-2, we need to be able to determine whether our computer reseller can invoice someone in French francs.

These business objects are managed by a special collection called a *controller.* The controller is an instance of the SanFrancisco Controller pattern (described later in this chapter). This pattern not only defines how the collection of business objects is managed but also allows for sharing of information across the company hierarchy. In other words, you can define the Currency controller on the Enterprise and have all child companies share the same definition. For example, because the enterprise Computer Stuff Inc. is based in the United States, it would require that all its related companies support U.S. dollars.

The controller behavior of sharing information across the company hierarchy depends on the underlying use of the Property Container pattern by the Company hierarchy. The hierarchy uses the ability to chain property containers (see Chapter 4, The Foundation Object Model for more information on property containers). Each company's property container is chained to the property container of its parent.

Suppose that a property is requested at the lowest level of the company hierarchy. That company's property container is checked, and, if the property is not found, the request is delegated to the company's parent company. This delegation continues until the property is found or the Enterprise level is reached. If the property is not on the Enterprise, the property does not exist. (Note that property containers let you either use the chaining or simply look at those properties that are "directly" on the Company.)

An example of this behavior is shown in Figure 6-3. In this example, the company wants to distinguish among the various parts of the company by having each one use a different color when presenting the company logo. So when this property is retrieved from the Enterprise, the color Blue is retrieved. When it is retrieved from the Software division, Green is returned, and from the Hardware division Yellow is returned. The Portable Computer Manufacturing company does not have the property, so when the property is retrieved from it, it delegates the request to the parent, which returns Yellow. On the other hand, the Computer Reseller company has the property and does not get it from the parent. Both of the Hardware division children handle the property correctly, but what happens if the division's color changes? The Portable Computer Manufacturing company will get the change automatically, and the Computer Reseller company will not get it until it is also changed (or the property is removed). Depending on the requirements for the particular property, this may or may not be the correct behavior.

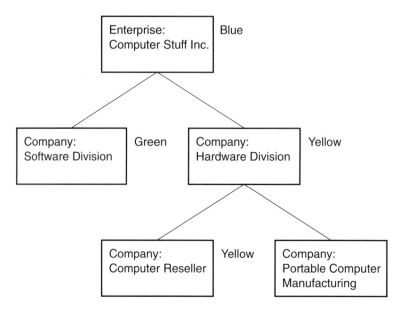

Figure 6-3. Example of Chained Properties in the Company Hierarchy

The controllers use this chained property behavior of the company hierarchy by associating the controller with a company as a property. Thus, if you want all companies to share the same set of currencies, the Currency controller is associated with the Enterprise. In that way, whenever the controller is requested from any of the companies by property, the one defined at the Enterprise will be found. See The Controller Pattern later in this chapter for more information on controllers.

The Active Company

To enable the locating of any persistent object, SanFrancisco recommends that all persistent objects be owned. This means that most Entities are owned by another Entity. However, there must be a starting point. Within SanFrancisco this starting point is the Enterprise, which is identified by using a user alias. (This is simply a way to name a particular persistent Entity; see Chapter 5 for more information on user aliases.) Although the Enterprise can be used to get to all other persistent business objects, it is not the most convenient place to start. A more natural place to start is with the company you want to work with because this defines what will be visible. This starting company is called the *active company* by SanFrancisco. The active company must be set because the framework code assumes that it can request the active company as part of its processing. For example, when trying to determine whether a particular currency, such as U.S. dollars, is supported, you would go to the active company, get the Currency controller (which may be on a parent), and then ask the Currency controller whether the currency (U.S. dollars) is supported.

Your company hierarchies may contain companies that should not be used as active companies. For example, it might be a *pseudo* company—one that was added as a parent to two other companies to define information to be used by the two companies. To support this, SanFrancisco allows you to indicate whether or not a company can be used as an active company.

Patterns

One way in which SanFrancisco makes it easier to use the Common Business Objects layer, and the layers that build on it, is by defining a set of solutions that are consistently used throughout these layers. These solutions are called patterns. More formally, a *pattern* is a solution to a recurring problem that is captured in a way that allows it to be repeatedly applied to similar problems, with each application being unique. These solutions are captured in a way that makes it clear when the pattern should and shouldn't be used. This means that as you are using SanFrancisco you will find that similar requirements have been filled in a consistent manner. For example, each time a balance must be maintained for quick retrieval, the Cached Balances generalized mechanism is used. And when you're developing on top of SanFrancisco, the patterns provide a library of potential solutions that you can use.

SanFrancisco has two kinds of patterns: cookie-cutter patterns and mini-framework patterns. *Cookie-cutter patterns* are like the design patterns described in the *Design Patterns* book by Gamma et al. These are patterns that must be implemented uniquely each time they are applied. Although these patterns are unique for each use, SanFrancisco provides code generation support for a number of them. This makes it easier to use them. On the other hand, in *mini-framework patterns* SanFrancisco provides a partial implementation of the pattern. Some of them are provided as part of the Foundation, but most of them are provided as part of the generalized mechanisms in the Common Business Objects layer.

The Controller Pattern

The Controller pattern is a cookie-cutter pattern that can be almost completely generated. *A controller* can be thought of as a special type of collection that interacts with the company hierarchy. This interaction allows sharing of information between companies. For example, a company can be made up of divisions that include many departments. To make the company run smoothly, certain information must be defined at the division level and must be consistently used by each of its departments.

There are three types of controllers that define what, if any, sharing is done: a root controller, an aggregating controller, and a hiding controller. A *root controller* does not look above it in the company hierarchy for shared business objects. It acts as if only its elements exist in its collection. An *aggregating controller* shares objects higher than it in the company hierarchy. It does this by asking its parent controller—the controller above it in the company hierarchy—for its elements and then adding its elements. This continues until a root controller is encountered. When an element is in an aggregating controller and this element already exists in a parent controller, the element added lowest in the hierarchy is the one used. This allows overriding behavior. A *hiding controller* is basically an aggregating controller with the added ability to identify elements to exclude after the total set of elements is determined. This ensures that no matter at what level the element is added, it is still hidden.

Figure 6-4 is an example of controllers within a company hierarchy. For each element of the Company hierarchy, the following is visible on the associated Currency controller:

- Computer Stuff Inc.: U.S. dollars and Canadian dollars.

- Software Division: Italian lire and U.S. dollars. Note that although this is a child of the Enterprise, because it has a root controller, it does not look beyond its own elements.

- Hardware Division: U.S. dollars, Canadian dollars, French francs, and Mexican nuevo pesos. This has an aggregating controller, so it gets the elements available on the parent and adds its own elements.

- Computer Reseller: U.S. dollars, Canadian dollars, French francs, and Mexican nuevo pesos. This is not the same list as that of the Hardware Division. First, the controller gets the parent's list of elements, and then it adds its own element, which in this case is French francs. Because French francs are already in the list, it is replaced. This might have been done in this case because the overriding currency object representing the French francs has some additional data associated with it that the Computer Reseller company needs. This can also be used to override attributes set on an object by a parent company.

- Portable Computer Manufacturing: U.S. dollars, Canadian dollars, French francs, and Mexican nuevo pesos. This company does not have a controller. When the controller is requested, to make the request for the elements, the controller on the parent is found and used. The controllers are associated with the company as properties, so the chained property behavior of companies was used to locate the controller.

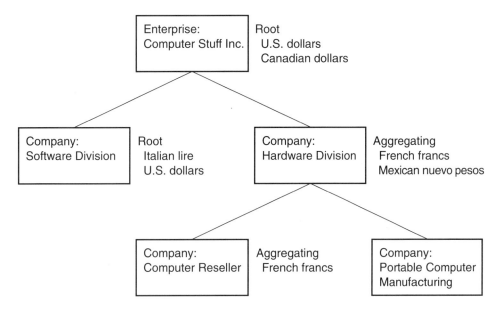

Figure 6-4. Example of Controllers in a Company Hierarchy

A key benefit of controllers is that they can be added, removed, or changed independently at any level of the organizational hierarchy without affecting other controllers. Controllers implement indirect links through the organizational hierarchy. This means that changing a controller does not necessitate that all child controllers update their links to the new parent controller (because the links are fixed by the organizational hierarchy). For example, in our company hierarchy, we add French francs and Mexican nuevo pesos to Computer Stuff Inc.'s controller and remove the aggregating controller on the Hardware division (without touching any of the other controllers). The only results that would change would be that two new entries—French francs and Mexican nuevo pesos—would be available on Computer Stuff Inc.

This pattern describes the interaction with the company hierarchy of each type of controller as well as the other collection functionality supported by the controller. Each controller is unique to what it controls; for example, Currency objects are controlled by a Currency controller, and Bank objects by a Bank controller. To ensure consistency across all uses of this key pattern, SanFrancisco provides almost total code generation for controllers. To generate a controller, you simply add the controller, its relationship to the item it controls, and a few directives defining the type of controller (and possibly options) to the design model; then you run the code generator against this model. The result is a fully working set of controller business objects.

The Policy Pattern

Another important cookie-cutter pattern is the Policy pattern, a variation of the Strategy pattern from the *Design Patterns* book by Gamma et al. This pattern is a way of capturing an algorithm or business policy so that it can be easily replaced. SanFrancisco adds the concept of scope. The three scopes are object, company, and application.

A policy that has *object scope* is identical to the Strategy pattern in that the policy is associated with the object using the policy. For example, a Business-Partner class could support a method checkCredit() that is supported by the CheckCreditPolicy policy class. BusinessPartner would have an instance of CheckCreditPolicy as an attribute. So when the checkCredit() method is called, BusinessPartner can retrieve the policy directly and delegate handling of the method to it.

A policy that has company scope is retrieved from the Company (as a property) rather than from the object itself. Thus, in the preceding example, when the checkCredit() method is called, CheckCreditPolicy is retrieved from Company. One thing to remember is that the Company is part of the company hierarchy, so when this property is retrieved, it may come directly from the Company it was requested from (typically the active company) or from one of its parent Companies.

The final scope that SanFrancisco adds is application scoped. In this case, the policy is not associated with a particular object but instead is created when it is needed. By using the class replacement support (Chapter 5) in the Foundation, you can change this policy for all uses within the application by class-replacing the policy class. For example, each time the checkCredit() method is called, BusinessPartner creates a CheckCreditPolicy and delegates handling of the method to it. When CheckCreditPolicy is class-replaced by MyCheckCredit-Policy (a subclass of CheckCreditPolicy), the creation now returns the new MyCheckCreditPolicy. Thus the BusinessPartner creates a MyCheckCreditPolicy and delegates handling of the method to it.

Whatever scope the policy has, the Policy pattern is a common extension point used in SanFrancisco. It is commonly used when the domain logic is likely to change, such as when the business environment changes, or when the algorithm varies among countries, companies, business domains, and so on.

SanFrancisco also provides two variations of the Policy pattern: Chain of Responsibility Driven Policy and Token Driven Policy. The Chain of Responsibility Driven Policy (discussed in Chapter 7) adds the ability for a number of participating objects to supply the Policy that should be used. The Token Driven Policy (see Chapter 7) allows different policies to be chosen based on the token passed.

Remaining Patterns

The Controller and Policy patterns are the two most important patterns used by SanFrancisco. A number of other patterns are also defined. The mini-framework patterns are described under Generalized Mechanisms in Chapter 7. The cookie-cutter patterns, depending on where they are first used by SanFrancisco, are described in Chapters 7 and 9 under Patterns. No matter where they are described, you can use all of them whether you are building your application on only the Common Business Objects layer or on the Core Business Processes layer.

Summary

The Common Business Objects layer is applicable to the most diverse set of business applications. It has been created and populated with this in mind. This layer introduces the concept of using the Company not only as a representation of your organization but also as the context for the application. Controllers allow business objects to be shared across the company hierarchy, and the Policy pattern is used to encapsulate business logic to enable easy customization.

Chapter 7 provides a high-level overview of what is provided by the Common Business Objects layer and discusses the additional patterns it uses.

7

Common Business Object Categories

This chapter gives you a high-level look at the contents of the Common Business Objects layer. The intent is for you to gain an understanding of what is provided by SanFrancisco. Depending on your role, you can then determine which pieces you need further information about. Domain experts can go to the Common Business Objects User Guide or the requirements and scenarios provided with SanFrancisco for more detail. Developers can look at the sample described in Chapter 8 and then refer to the Common Business Objects User Guide, the design model, the JavaDoc, or the source code provided with SanFrancisco for more details.

SanFrancisco provides a number of categories beyond the Company category described in Chapter 6. These categories can be discussed in many different ways. One way is to divide them into three major groups. The first group comprises general business objects. These categories contain business objects (business classes and processes) that are common across all domains. The second group is the financial business objects. These categories contain business objects commonly needed for dealing with financial domains. The third group, the generalized mechanisms, provides implemented solutions to common recurring problems.

General Business Objects

The general business objects group contains business objects and processes that most domains recognize, including the Company category and the Currency category. The categories are described here in alphabetical order.

Address

All applications keep track of how to contact a business or individual, usually by getting and maintaining an address. SanFrancisco provides the core pieces of an address, such as the phone number and e-mail address. In addition, it lets you add tagged information, called address lines, to an address. In this manner, a State line, which is applicable in the United States, can be added to addresses but omitted or replaced with something more appropriate for addresses outside the United States.

Figure 7-1 shows an example of an Address object with address lines for a U.S. address. These lines are the tagged information that can be added to the address. In this example, three lines are added: Line 1, City, and State.

In addition to the Address, this category lets you represent Areas and Countries. The Area represents any breakdown into areas you require. For example, you might divide the United States into three regions: the East Coast,

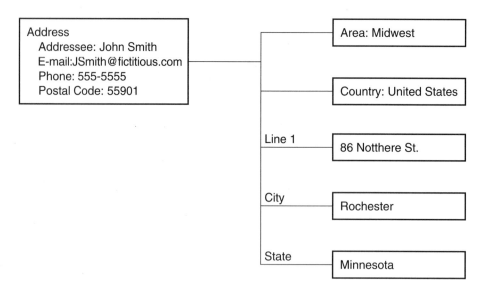

Figure 7-1. Example of a U.S. Address

the West Coast, and the Midwest. The Country, in this example, is United States. Note that although Area and Country are used to help classify Addresses, they can be used independently of the Address. For example, Country is used by the Bank object because Bank identifiers are guaranteed to be unique only within a particular Country.

Business Partner

The individuals your companies do business with are referred to by SanFrancisco as business partners (see Figure 7-2). For example, a business partner can be the customer for an order or the supplier for a purchase order. Like Company, the Business Partner category supports a BusinessPartner object hierarchy. This allows sharing of data from the parent BusinessPartner to the child BusinessPartner or for the child to override the data. For example, you might negotiate a set of payment terms—when and how to pay—with the parent BusinessPartner; all child BusinessPartners might use it, or one of the child

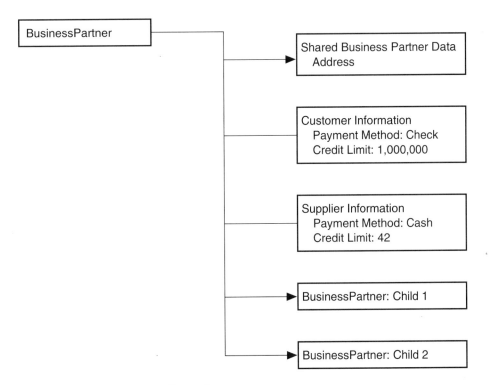

Figure 7-2. Business Partner Example

BusinessPartners might negotiate or might previously have negotiated payment terms.

The Business Partner category also supports having some of its data unique to a Company and some of it shared between all companies in the organization. For example, the business partner's address should be the same no matter whom it does business with. However, the credit limit (how much it can owe) is controlled by each individual company.

A business partner in SanFrancisco can be both a customer and a supplier at the same time. The common portion is pulled into the BusinessPartner class, and the unique customer or supplier attributes are added. The payment method is one of the attributes held in the customer or supplier information because the payment method differs depending on whether we are dealing with the business partner as a customer or supplier. On the other hand, whether the business partner is a customer or supplier (or both) has no impact on the business partner's hierarchy.

SanFrancisco also lets you associate and manage the amount a business partner owes a company and the amount the company owes a business partner. This category is called Business Partner Balances. This information is used for activities such as credit checking to determine whether a customer can place an order or an order can be shipped to a customer. To make these checks quickly, the criteria for what to include in the customer's outstanding balance can be cached (that is, calculated and then stored and maintained from that point on).

Company

Company is described in detail in Chapter 6.

Credit Checking

This category provides the support for establishing credit limits and for checking credit limits against the total owed by a business partner for shipped goods or the total owed and ordered by a business partner. For example, it can be used to confirm a sales order, issue credit notes, credit an account for a bonus, or prepare a customer order. The individual company determines when, and against which total credit balance, checking is performed.

SanFrancisco allows you to build your own policies for credit checking (see Figure 7-3). These policies can vary depending on many criteria. In particular, the policies can vary by business partner. The policies can vary based on whether they are being checked as a customer or as a supplier and depending on the process being performed. For example, you might want to have one pol-

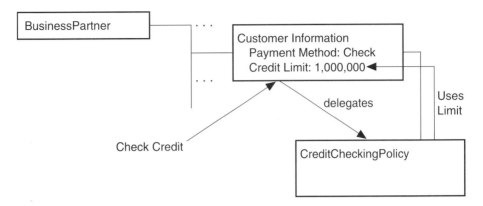

Figure 7-3. Performing a Credit Check

icy, when you are taking an order, that checks all outstanding orders against one limit, and another policy, when you are about to ship an order, that checks the amount of unpaid shipped orders against another lower limit.

After the policies are configured, the credit checking is performed using an operation on the customer- or supplier-specific part of the BusinessPartner. This part also has a credit limit that, depending on the policy, will be used during this checking.

Currency

This category supports working with money. It supports defining currencies and one or more exchange rate types (with their associated exchange rate factors) to be used by a company (or companies if they are shared).

The Currencies are typically defined to be the set of ISO standard three-character currency identifiers, such as USD for U.S. dollars and DEM for German deutsche marks. In addition to defining the currency identifier, things such as the smallest unit—the penny for USD and the pfennig for DEM—and information necessary to correctly format and display currencies are also part of the Currency.

Exchange rates, which define how to convert from one currency to another, are supported in a flexible way in SanFrancisco. Following are examples:

- Exchange rates can be based on dates or on the fiscal periods defined in the fiscal calendar. For example, an exchange rate can be defined from January 1, 1999, to February 2, 1999, or for the fiscal period 1st Quarter.

- Fixed exchange rates, starting from an effective date, can be defined. This capability supports the transition to the euro; the exchange rates between the euro and the first group of participating countries was fixed on January 1, 1999.

- You can create and use multiple tables of exchange rates—for example, having a special exchange rate table for tax purposes or for intercompany transactions.

- The use of exchange rates can be customized with respect to how the tables are used. For example, in the conversion from German deutsche marks to U.S. dollars, you can first convert from German deutsche marks to Japanese yen and then convert from Japanese yen to U.S. dollars.

- Full support for working with the euro, including properly handling the fixed exchange rates and applying the triangulation rules so that conversions from French francs to German deutsche marks properly uses the euro.

Building on top of this, this category supports associating a decimal value with a particular currency. SanFrancisco calls this a CurrencyValue. CurrencyValue supports all the standard mathematical functions as well as methods for converting them to a different currency.

A CurrencyValue is sufficient if you are working with only one currency, but when you begin to work with multiple currencies, you must keep track of not only the currency you use for your bookkeeping but also the currency in which the transaction occurred. SanFrancisco supports this with the TransactionValue (see Figure 7-4). The basic TransactionValue consists of two Currency-

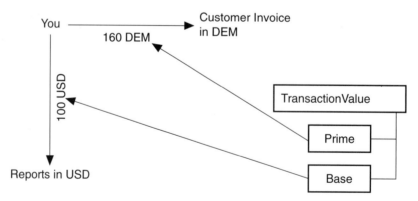

Figure 7-4. TransactionValue Example

Values: one for the currency of the transaction, called the *prime* value, and another for the currency used for bookkeeping, called the *base* value. For example, if you are a U.S. company billing a German company, you would bill it 160 DEM, which (assuming an exchange rate of 1.6 to 1) is 100 USD. Thus your TransactionValue would have a prime value of 160 DEM and a base value of 100 USD. The TransactionValue also supports many of the basic mathematical operations and supports using exchange rates to populate both values when only one is given.

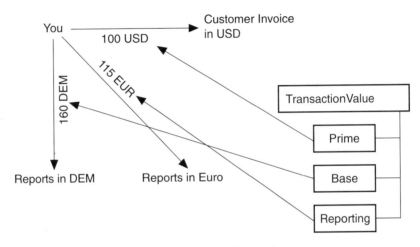

Figure 7-5. Transaction Value Supporting Euro Example

For countries that are transitioning to the euro as a base currency, a special extended transaction value is provided (see Figure 7-5). It adds a third currency value and the concept of having one currency value treated as the base currency and the other as the *reporting* currency. This allows the switch from the original currency to be gradual, first treating the euro as a reporting currency and then treating the original currency as the reporting currency.

Document Location

The Document Location category is used to define a set of possible locations, such as "Jeff's desk," "Document Archives," and "Invoice Approval." These locations are then used to indicate where an item, such as a supplier invoice, is located. The location does not have to be a physical location; it could be an electronic location, such as a uniform resource locator (URL).

The Document Location is useful for documents that, as part of their processing, must move throughout the company or may need to be located rapidly. The support provided by SanFrancisco lets you associate policies or special attributes with document locations as well as add new locations easily.

Fiscal Calendar

The Fiscal Calendar category is used to represent the accounting year and periods of the company. In some cases, these periods correspond to a working calendar (called a Natural Calendar by SanFrancisco), although they need not. For example, the fiscal year may consist of four quarters that cover the final one-fourth of one year and three-fourths of the next year. Or the fiscal periods can be defined to be four weeks long, giving each period a consistent length. The actual fiscal calendar definition corresponds to the financial periods used by a company.

The fiscal periods are used for recording transactions so that the costs and earnings are assigned the proper place in time. The fiscal periods are either dated or undated and have a particular type. *Dated* periods are used for normal accounting. *Undated* periods are either opening or closing periods at the start or end of a fiscal year, or adjustment periods. The latter are used to make accounting adjustments.

The fiscal calendar support is similar to the support provided by the Periodized Calendar category (discussed later). However, the Periodized Calendar supports only breaking the calendar into periods and is used in nonfinancial situations.

Figure 7-6 shows an example of a configured FiscalCalendar. This calendar consists of two years—1999 and 2000—each of which consists of five periods. They begin with an undated opening period, followed by two dated periods that together cover the entire year; then there is an adjustment period and a closing period. The opening and closing periods could be used to transfer balances between accounts, something that is often used to zero out an account at the end of the year. The adjustment periods could be used to let you close the dated periods and still book items into the fiscal year before closing it.

Initials

Initials can be used to identify roles of users of the system—for example, distinguishing supervisors from operators in an order entry system. Supervisors can approve high-value orders and can allow a customer to temporarily exceed the credit limit. An operator does not have these abilities. Because not all applications use initials in this way, SanFrancisco does not tie this to the security provided by the Foundation layer.

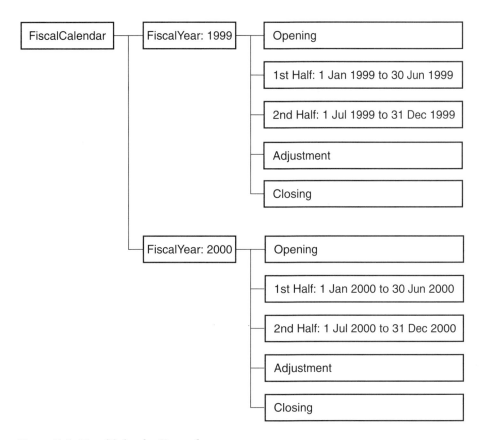

Figure 7-6. FiscalCalendar Example

Initials are also used to identify who did something—for example, who took an order or authorized a refund. In paper·systems, these actions would consist of having the person initial the document. With no hard-copy document to initial, the SanFrancisco Initials object can simply be associated with the object to record this information, along with the transaction, on the affected object.

The Initials and SignatoryAbility business objects provide this support. Signatory abilities are things that can or cannot be done, such as approving an expense account. An Initials object represents an individual and contains that individual's full name. An Initials object can be asked whether it supports a particular SignatoryAbility. In this way, you can determine whether someone can do something ahead of time or when the person tries to "initial" that something has been done.

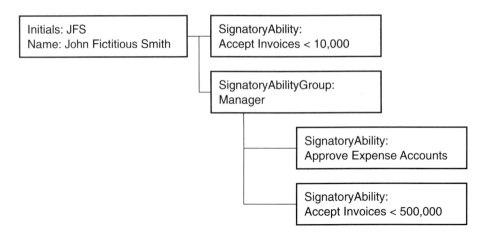

Figure 7-7. Initials Example

SanFrancisco also provides SignatoryAbility Groups, which let you group a set of signatory abilities and grant them at the same time. For example, you might want to provide a group for clerks (containing the things they are authorized to do) and another group for managers.

Figure 7-7 shows a case in which an Initials object is defined for John Fictitious Smith. When John joined the company he was given the SignatoryAbility to accept invoices for < 10,000, an ability given to everyone. When John was promoted to manager, the manager SignatoryAbilityGroup was added to his Initials, giving him two new signatory abilities. One was to approve expense accounts, and the other was to accept invoices < 500,000. Although these new abilities give John more ability than the signatory ability he already had, the existing one was not removed. It was left so that when he leaves management, the manager SignatoryAbilityGroup can simply be removed, leaving him the correct nonmanager abilities.

Natural Calendar

The Natural Calendar, also known as a working calendar, is used for the following purposes:

- Doing calculations related to working days. This allows you to determine which working day would be three working days from today or how many working days fall between two dates.

- Doing calculations related to working hours. This allows you to determine the date and time that are four working hours from a certain date and time.

- Associating information with a day of the week or a particular day.

Working Days

The NaturalCalendar supports working days by allowing you to indicate which days are working and which are nonworking. To reduce the number of days you must mark when configuring the NaturalCalendar, a week of default days is used to indicate the default values. This allows you to easily indicate that all weekend days are nonworking days. Then the information on individual dates can be changed to indicate the company holidays or partial work days.

Figure 7-8 shows an example of a NaturalCalendar. The seven default days (Sunday through Saturday) are shown on the right, and each day of the year is shown on the left. Each day is associated with a default day. For December 24

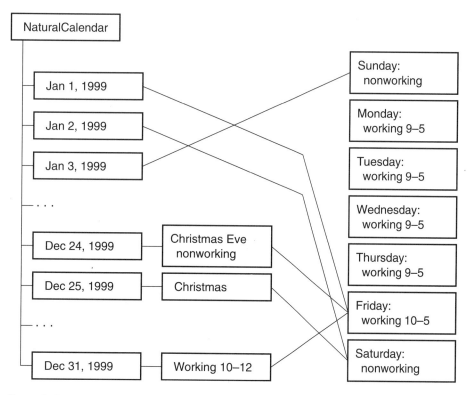

Figure 7-8. NaturalCalendar Example

we want to indicate that this is the Christmas Eve holiday, so we override the default day to add this description and to indicate it is nonworking. Note that the overriding day is still linked to the default day. This link is used to retrieve any information that has not been overridden. For example, December 25, Christmas, falls on a Saturday, so we need not indicate that it is a nonworking day because it links to Saturday, already a nonworking day.

Working Hours

The NaturalCalendar supports working hours by allowing work periods to be to be defined for working days. SanFrancisco lets you associate a single work period with a working day, but this can be customized if more than one work period is needed. Like the description, the work period can be overridden for a particular working day.

Figure 7-8, mentioned earlier, shows an example of a NaturalCalendar with work periods defined for the working days. Monday through Thursday the work period is from 9 AM to 5 PM. However, every Friday from 9 AM to 10 AM there is a mandatory companywide meeting. We do not consider that part of the working hours, so Friday's work period is defined to be from 10 AM to 5 PM. The December 31, 1999, work period has been overridden in the example to be from 10 AM to 12 noon because the company gives everyone that afternoon off.

When you query the system for the day and time that will occur a number of working hours from a certain day and time, the result can be adjusted based on your needs. For example, you could move a delivery that would be late on a Friday to early the next Monday or adjust a deadline that falls on a Monday morning back to the preceding Friday afternoon.

Associating Information with a Day of the Week or a Particular Day

The NaturalCalendar also supports adding information to one of the default days or a particular day. When information is added to a default day, it appears as if that information occurs on every date that is associated with the default day. For example, your application could always ask the NaturalCalendar for any reminders for that day and display them for you. If you then added a reminder to Thursday about the mandatory meeting on Fridays, you would get this reminder every Thursday. On the other hand, if you wanted the reminder on only one particular day, you could add it to that particular day.

Figure 7-9 shows an example of adding these reminders. The reminder "Meeting Tomorrow" was added to the default day for Thursday; when you ask for the reminder for December 30, 1999, because it is associated with the default day for Thursday, you will get back "Meeting Tomorrow." On the other hand, on December 31, 1999, when you ask for the reminder, you will get back "Half day today!" However, for January 1, 1999, when you ask for the reminder, you will get a message that there is no reminder for that date.

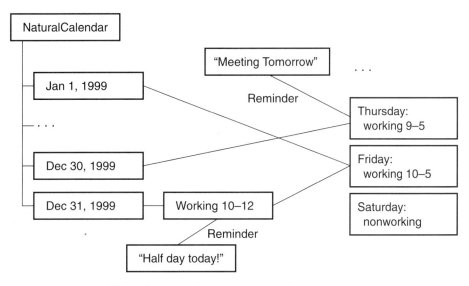

Figure 7-9. NaturalCalendar Example: Associating Information

Number Series

The Number Series category provides the support for generating numbers according to a specific numbering scheme, such as when you are assigning serial numbers or numbering invoices. The support includes deciding where to start and end, how to increment, and how to build the generated number. For example, you could decide to start at 1, end at 203, increment by 3, and have a prefix of "MyNumber" with the number padded, with zeros, to three digits. Thus the number series would generate "MyNumber001," "MyNumber004," and so on.

The NumberSeries category also supports the concept of subseries, which allows the definition of a group of generated numbers that have the same characteristics. This category is useful when the same characteristics are used from year to year but each year must start over with the same initial value.

One way that the number series can be used is to generate unique identifiers for business objects. As part of the Controller pattern, you can specify that the controlled item has a policy that generates the unique number for the controlled item. When SanFrancisco ships a sample identifier generation policy, SanFrancisco often uses a NumberSeries to generate the unique identifier.

Payment Method

The Payment Method category provides the means to define the way payments are made. This may be negotiated between the buyer and seller of a service or goods (or vice versa for credit situations). For example, cash, check, electronic transfer, and 30 days net are some of the payment methods that can be used. The Payment Method is extended in the core business processes to add special considerations such as bank information and general ledger accounts to use for each method.

Payment Terms

The Payment Terms category lets you define the terms of payment agreed upon between a buyer and a seller. This includes the information needed to calculate installment payments (or credits). It also holds the information necessary to calculate expiration dates and any discount amounts. This category also lets you take a *snapshot* of the payment terms so that after they are agreed to for a particular interaction, they do not get changed when the general agreement is renegotiated. Thus existing interactions continue with the previous agreement; new or future interactions use the new payment terms.

The Payment Terms category is broken into pieces that define the individual installment (or installments) that will make up the payment. Each piece consists of enough information to determine the date and the amount of the installment. However, one piece is always special. It represents what to do with the remainder after all other installments are subtracted from the payment. This means that it needs only the information to calculate the date of the installment because the amount is whatever is left.

Figure 7-10 shows an example of a payment terms definition. This example shows a set of terms in which 30% is due in one month, the next 30% in two months, and the remainder in three months. If it were to start on June 1, 1999, and the customer owed 100 USD, it would owe 30 USD on July 1, 30 USD more on August 1, and the remaining 40 USD on September 1.

PaymentTerms also provides many options for specifying when the installment is due. You can specify a particular day of the week or a particular day of the month as well as a relative number of days or, as shown in the example, a relative number of months.

This category also provides support for early payment discounts. For each installment definition, you can add the amount that should be taken off if a payment is made before a certain date.

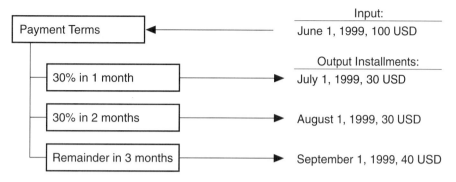

Figure 7-10. Payment Terms Example

Periodized Calendar

The Periodized Calendar is made up of PeriodizedYears, which are made up of CalendarPeriods. These periods can be dated or undated. The dated periods need not correlate to the Natural (or Working) Calendar. The Periodized Calendar category is similar to the Fiscal Calendar except that it is intended for non-financial use. It has only dated and undated periods and does not support the special period types.

For example, the PeriodizedCalendar could be used to manage the maintenance of a machine on a production line. You could break the year into a maintenance cycle, with periods when the machine is in operation and other ones when it is not in operation.

Figure 7-11 shows an example of using a PeriodizedCalendar to manage the production and maintenance cycles of a machine. In this example, the PeriodizedYears represent the tooling cycles of the machine. For example, suppose that a machine can produce parts for either bicycles or motorcycles depending on how it is configured. Reconfiguring the machine is called *retooling*. Each tooling cycle is represented by a periodized year. Within the tooling cycle, there is a period of retooling followed by alternating production periods and maintenance periods.

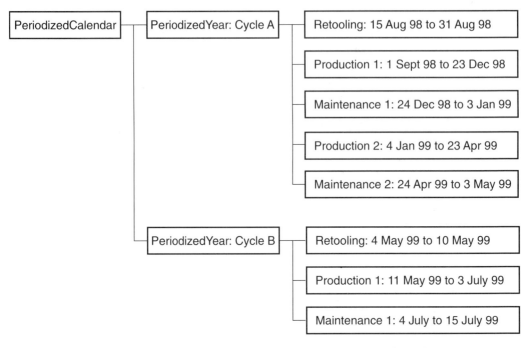

Figure 7-11. PeriodizedCalendar Example

Process Token

Most business tasks can be broken into individual processes. In some cases, you must be able to indicate which process you are executing. For example, suppose you are doing a credit check (see Figure 7-12). When the customer is ordering, you want to check one total and limit; when you are about to ship the order, you want to check another total (the value of what has shipped) and a lower limit. Ordering and Shipping would be two different processes and would be assigned different *process tokens*.

The process token is then passed as part of the processing and can be used to affect what is done in methods that are called from both processes. To allow the process token to affect the processing, a method that is passed this token can be written. In this way, the method can do different things depending on the value of the token.

The process token is used in the Token Driven Policy pattern. In this pattern, a policy map returns the correct policy to use for a given token. Thus the method does not need to know the details of what must be done for each token but instead simply uses it as a key to get the appropriate business logic for that task for that process.

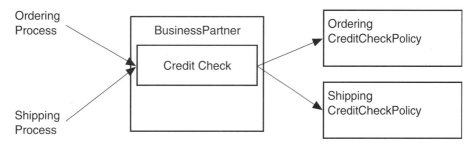

Figure 7-12. Process Token Example

Project

Often you organize the activities of your business into projects. This allows you to group various events, people, tasks, and costs associated with the project, giving you the opportunity to analyze the project's costs and activities to manage your business.

The Project category supports the definition of project identifiers, which vary by business. For example, if you are producing software, each application could have its own project identifier for each release.

Supplementary Charges

This category helps you add miscellaneous charges: the charges that are added to an agreed-on price for a business transaction, such as special handling charges or size of order. The supplementary charges are defined by each company as appropriate to its business.

Supplementary charges are tagged with a charge type. The type may be nothing more than an identifying tag. A fixed charge type supports fixed charges (that is, a flat fee). However, developers may extend SanFrancisco to add charge types that calculate charges based on a business object (such as the amount of an order or the total weight of the goods to be shipped). The charge types are set up when supplementary charges are configured.

Supplementary charges are commonly used on invoices. For example, shipping and handling charges would be added to an invoice.

Unit of Measure

This category supports working with dimensioned quantities such as 3 feet or 25 pounds. This category is important because if you simply use a number to represent a quantity, it is easy to make mistakes, such as trying to add 3 feet to 13 meters.

The first task in working with dimensioned quantities is to define the dimensions, called the unit of measure in SanFrancisco. Examples are case, pallet, and 6-pack. Then you associate them with a quantity to create a *Quantity-Unit*. Examples are 3 cases, 1 pallet, and 23 6-packs.

Sometimes you may deal with a customer in one unit of measure but keep track of the quantities in a consistent unit of measure internally. You do this by using a TransactionQuantity that contains two QuantityUnits: one for the amount in the unit of measure used with the customer (the prime quantity unit), and a second one for the internally used unit of measure (the base quantity unit). For example, we might sell our customer 1,000 kilograms of sugar but track it internally as 4 pallets of sugar (see Figure 7-13).

When you begin dealing with more than one unit of measure, you need the ability to convert from one unit of measure to another. This is supported by the UnitCategory. It allows you to define the association of 1,000 kilograms of sugar, 1,000 1-kilogram packs, and 4 pallets. SanFrancisco always represents the main unit of measure with a ratio of one and all other ratios in relation to it. Thus this definition becomes 1 kilogram of sugar, 1 1-kilogram pack and 0.004 pallets (see Figure 7-14).

The other aspect of dealing with physical items is that you must know their physical properties or dimensions to determine things such as how much space a 1-kilogram bag of sugar takes. This knowledge is especially important when you try to determine how much you can keep in a certain warehouse location

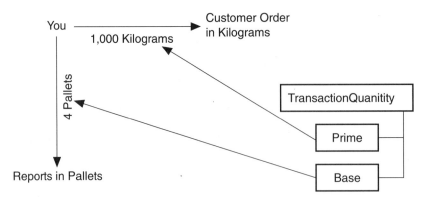

Figure 7-13. Transaction Quantity Example

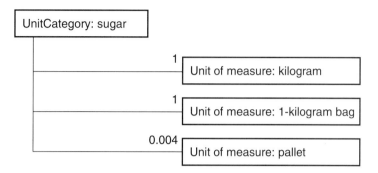

Figure 7-14. UnitCategory Example

or load onto a truck. SanFrancisco's measurement supports this capability. It also lets you record the net and gross values for the dimensions. As a result, you can do things such as specify that the length of an item is 3 meters but becomes 4 meters when the item is packaged.

Financial Business Objects

The financial business objects in the Common Business Objects layer are those financial objects that are generally applicable or required for sharing of information with the financial core business processes. More financial business objects are provided in the General Ledger core business process and the Accounts Receivable/Accounts Payable core business process.

Bank Accounts

To deal with your bank accounts and your business partner's bank accounts you need a way to represent them. SanFrancisco lets you represent the bank and two types of bank accounts: internal and external. InternalBankAccounts are your accounts with the bank. ExternalBankAccounts are your business partner's accounts at the bank. A single bank may have both kinds of accounts because you and your business partner may use the same bank.

These two types of accounts are treated separately because each type requires different information. When dealing with external (business partner) bank accounts, you need only enough information to communicate with the bank and identify the account. For example, it is common in Europe to transfer money using electronic transfer. This support allows you to include a pre-printed electronic transfer form when sending an invoice to a business partner.

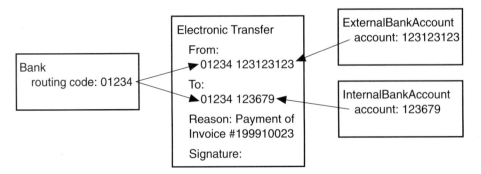

Figure 7-15. Bank Accounts Electronic Transfer Slip Example

Figure 7-15 shows an example of generating an electronic transfer slip. Both the external and internal bank accounts are with the same bank, so the "from" and "to" bank routing codes are the same, 01234. The ExternalBank-Account for the business partner we are billing contains the account number to use for the "transfer from" account. The InternalBankAccount to which we transfer the money has the account as one of its attributes. Thus an electronic transfer can be generated, and the customer need only check it for correctness and sign it before sending it to the bank.

On the other hand, when dealing with internal (your) bank accounts, you need to be able to do two things: identify your accounts and determine which general ledger account you should use when updating your financial status because of an interaction with your bank account, such as depositing money (see Figure 7-16).

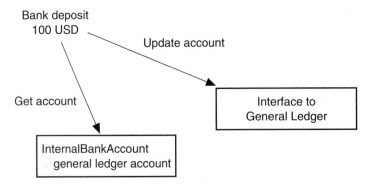

Figure 7-16. Bank Accounts Bank Deposit Example

Currency Gain/Loss Accounts

When you must deal with more than one currency, you must deal with exchange rate fluctuations. Usually, you handle it by using today's exchange rate and then, at a later date, recalculating the value using the new exchange rate and handling the change. This is known as currency revaluation.

Suppose, for example, that your business is owed money in a currency other than the currency you use to manage your business (that is, you record everything in equivalent USD so that you can get the total financial status for the company in USD). If you manage your business using USD, you are using USD as the *base currency* for your company. When you are owed 160 DEM, the equivalent 100 USD (assuming the exchange rate is 1.6) is recorded in your general ledger. When the bill is paid, you then take the new exchange rate—for example, 1.5—and calculate the new USD amount, 107 USD in this case. This means that although we were paid only the original 160 DEM, it is actually worth 7 USD more now than when we first recorded it in the General Ledger. This 7 USD is considered a currency gain and must be recorded in the General Ledger. Note that if the exchange rate had increased to 1.7, we would have had a 6 USD currency loss to record.

There are two types of currency gains or losses. The first is *realized*, as described in the earlier example. This type occurs when we know what the final exchange rate is—for example, because we have received the payment. The other kind of currency gain or loss is *unrealized*. This occurs when the exchange rate has changed, so we revalue, but we do not yet know the final exchange rate.

This category provides support for defining the General Ledger accounts to use for these different currency gains and losses. It is provided here so that the General Ledger, Accounts Receivable/Accounts Payable, or any other application calculating these currency gains and losses will record them in a consistent set of general ledger accounts.

Financial Batches

When working with the financial application, you may want to group your interactions with it based on criteria such as all work by an individual or all work for a particular session. After these interactions are grouped, you want to work with them as a unit, validating and then committing (*posting,* in financial terms) them. For this to work you must collect your interactions with the various financial subsystems to ensure that they are processed together in one financial batch.

This functionality is provided in the Common Business Objects layer so that you can include not only General Ledger and Accounts Receivable/Accounts Payable items but also the items from other applications. For example,

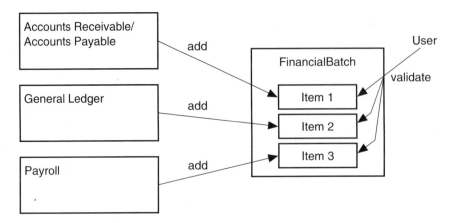

Figure 7-17. FinancialBatch Example

a payroll system might want to add paychecks to the FinancialBatch to ensure that they are processed as a group and that the appropriate general ledger accounts are processed at the same time.

Figure 7-17 shows an example in which each kind of financial item has been added to the FinancialBatch. When the user validates the FinancialBatch, it validates all the items that have been added to it.

Financial Calendar

When you're using a fiscal calendar for financial purposes, the support provided in the Fiscal Calendar category is not enough. You must be able to indicate the status of the periods and, if desired, the current (sometimes called the *default*) period. The status is used to indicate whether further transactions can be done for that period. SanFrancisco uses *closed* to indicate that transactions are no longer allowed, and *open* to indicate that they are allowed. The current period is used when the period is not specified. For example, when you create an entry into the General Ledger, the current period is retrieved and displayed as a default value for the period. The current period is limited to only date periods that are open. An example is shown in Figure 7-18.

One reason that this support is implemented as an addition to the Fiscal-Calendar, rather than being a part of the FiscalCalendar, is that any number of FinancialCalendars may be associated with a single FiscalCalendar. For example, there may be a FinancialCalendar for general ledger, a FinancialCalendar for accounts receivable, and a FinancialCalendar for accounts payable.

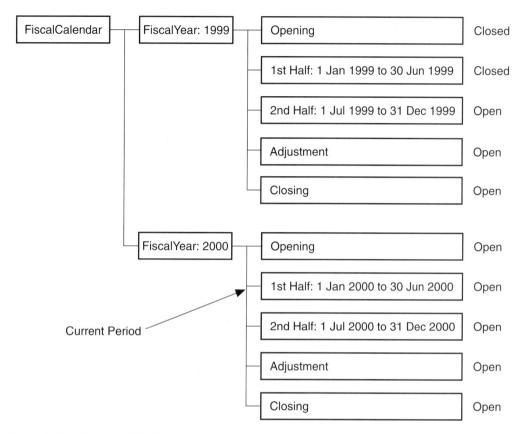

Figure 7-18. FinancialCalendar Example

Financial Integration

Working in a warehouse application, you work with things such as warehouses and products. Working in the general ledger you work with general ledger accounts. When your warehouse application affects the financial status of the company, it must notify the general ledger. The Financial Integration category lets you map from the things in the warehouse involved in the change in financial status into the appropriate general ledger account and lets you get the information into the general ledger.

By collecting the mapping knowledge in one place, the expert who knows how to do this mapping can capture that knowledge in financial integration. Then the warehouse users can use financial integration by working with the things they are used to, such as products and warehouses, without having to

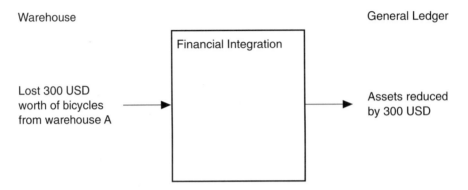

Figure 7-19. Financial Integration

know any of the details of the mapping. Figure 7-19 shows an example in which a process in the warehouse application must update the general ledger because 300 USD worth of bicycles have been lost from warehouse A. Financial integration can take bicycles, warehouse A, and the fact that they were lost and translate that to the appropriate posting to the asset account.

Although this support is discussed here in the context of a warehouse application, it is general enough that it can be used in any situation in which this type of mapping is needed.

Interface to Banks

When you make a bank deposit, you may collect a number of checks together into a single deposit slip, which the bank records as a single transaction. This single transaction is what shows up on your bank statement, so you must keep track of it to reconcile the bank statement when it comes. However, you must also keep track of the individual checks because they may be from different business partners and thus affect different General Ledger accounts (see Figure 7-20).

The ability to do this is provided by the Interface to Banks category. In the example, the deposit is represented by a GenericBankTransaction, and the individual checks by BankMovements. These abstract business objects allow you to represent any interaction with the bank.

A GenericBankTransaction and a BankMovement can go through a number of states during the interaction with the bank. For example, suppose that the deposit is in one currency, such as DEM, and the bank account is in USD. Until we know what exchange rate the bank used for the deposit, we do not know the actual amount of the GenericBankTransaction. The classes in this category support these states and the associated updating of the appropriate general ledger accounts.

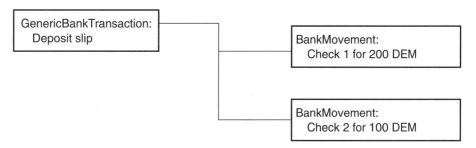

Figure 7-20. Deposit Example

The GenericBankTransaction follows the Generic Interface pattern. This means that the generic bank transaction support is not provided as part of the Common Business Objects layer. Instead, SanFrancisco provides support for it in the General Ledger core business process, which gives you the ability to work with bank transactions, such as reconciling them with bank statements.

Interface to General Ledger

In most businesses, whatever you do has an effect on the financial status of your business. It is crucial that applications outside the general ledger be able to get financial status changes into the general ledger. To do this, SanFrancisco provides a set of *facade* classes that allow an application outside the general ledger to get information into the general ledger. These facade classes are indicated by having *generic* as the first part of their class name.

There are two ways to work with the Interface to General Ledger category. It can be used directly, or it can be used through a set of commands it provides. The commands are the most convenient approach because they are guaranteed to complete successfully even if a General Ledger application supporting the facades does not exist. Figure 7-21 shows an example of the Interface to General Ledger category being used directly and indirectly. The AR/AP application uses the interface directly by interacting with the facade classes. On the other hand, the payroll application uses it indirectly by using the commands.

When the SanFrancisco General Ledger core business process is installed, the facade classes are replaced (via class replacement) by classes from the core business processes. On the other hand, another General Ledger application can do the same thing, replacing the facades with its own classes that correctly interface to it.

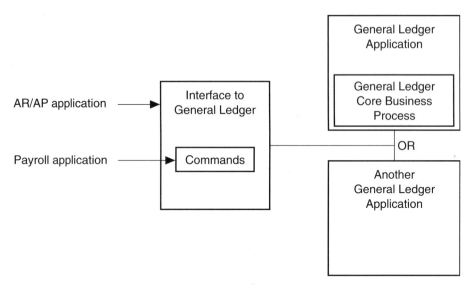

Figure 7-21. Interface to General Ledger

Interface to Accounts Receivable/Accounts Payable

In most businesses, you update your Accounts Receivable/Accounts Payable application whenever the status of an invoice or payment changes. SanFrancisco provides a set of facade classes that allow an application outside the Accounts Receivable/Accounts Payable to get information into the Accounts Receivable/Accounts Payable. These facade classes are indicated by having *generic* as the first part of their class name.

There are two ways to work with the Interface to Accounts Receivable/ Accounts Payable category. It can be used directly, or it can be used through a set of commands it provides. The commands are the most convenient approach because they are guaranteed to complete successfully even if an Accounts Receivable/Accounts Payable application supporting the facades does not exist.

Figure 7-22 shows an example of invoicing using the Interface to Accounts Receivable/Accounts Payable directly. Invoicing works directly with the facade classes.

When the SanFrancisco Accounts Receivable/Accounts Payable core business process is installed, the facade classes are replaced (via class replacement) with classes from the core business processes. On the other hand, another Accounts Receivable/Accounts Payable application can do the same thing, replacing the facades with its own classes that correctly interface to it.

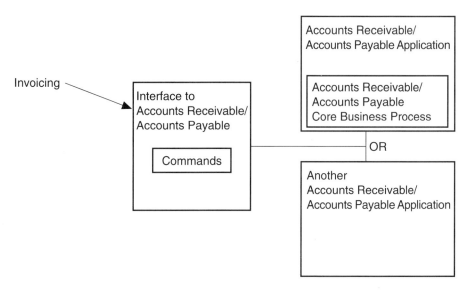

Figure 7-22. Interface to Accounts Receivable/Accounts Payable

Invoicing

At some point you may need to create an invoice to send to your customer (see Figure 7-23). SanFrancisco provides the underlying support for generating the data needed for the invoice. You can customize which items can be invoiced as well as what can be collected in a single invoice. Invoicing also notifies accounts receivable/accounts payable and the general ledger so that the accounts receivable/accounts payable can begin managing the money owed and the financial status is updated in the general ledger.

Currently, the Order Management core business process adds the ability to invoice the individual product orders and any supplemental charges, such as shipping charges. Another application might add services that can be included in the same invoices as the sales orders or are always kept on separate invoices. This customization is done via policies.

Invoicing support is flexible. It allows you to create a number of different invoices, including

- Sales order invoices for goods or services provided to a customer
- Credit notes for charges removed from an invoice or money returned to a customer
- Interest notes for additional charges against an invoice

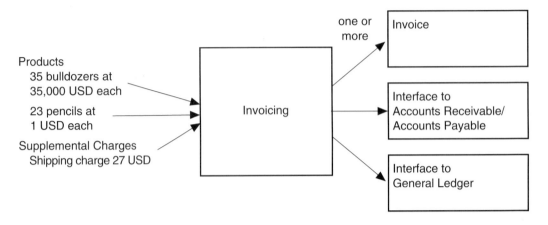

Figure 7-23. Invoicing

What goes into each invoice can be selected manually or automatically (using a policy that contains the criteria). After the pieces are selected, they can be processed individually or grouped into an invoice.

Generalized Mechanisms

Figure 7-24 shows the categories in the Generalized Mechanisms group that are currently available in the SanFrancisco Common Business Objects layer. Each of them is considered one of SanFrancisco's patterns and is covered in depth in the Extension Guide.

Although these categories can be used independently, the Hierarchy Level Information, LifeCycle, Hierarchical Extensible Item, and Extensible Item are discussed together under the LifeCycle heading.

Cached Balances

When you take an order, knowing immediately whether you have enough of the product to fill the order can make the difference between making and losing the order. You cannot afford to spend the time to add up all of the inventory. To make this check fast, you end up deciding what information you need. Then, rather than calculate the information each time, you calculate the information once; as the inventory changes, you update the information. This means that you take a little longer each time you change your inventory, but you can much more rapidly tell whether the product is available to fill the order.

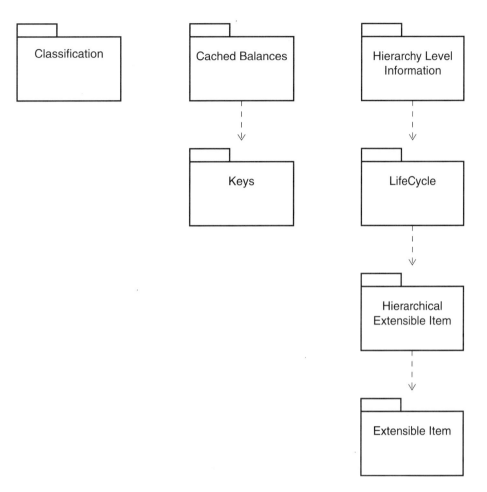

Figure 7-24. The Generalized Mechanism Categories

The information just discussed is usually referred to as the *product balances*. Product balances are kept for each product according to criteria such as the stock type (so that damaged stock can be excluded) and the warehouse that holds the product (because this affects the delivery time). This means that for each product you keep and maintain the balances for each stock type and warehouse combination. When it is discovered that a product in warehouse A is damaged, it is removed from the entry for the normal stock type in warehouse A and added to the entry for the damaged stock for warehouse A (see Figure 7-25).

There are similar requirements for General Ledger (getting account balances for reports) and for Business Partner (figuring out how much it currently

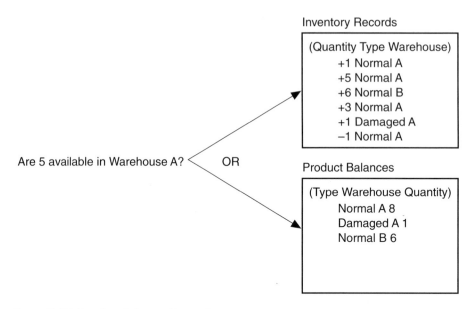

Figure 7-25. Product Balances Example

owes us for credit checking). Rather than solve this problem differently in each case, you can use a general solution called Cached Balances.

The Cached Balance support provides a mechanism for defining the information that must be available quickly and thus must be stored and maintained. This definition is based on the use of a Specification Key, described later, which, in this case, is used to indicate which criteria should be considered and which should be ignored. For example, if our criteria were the stock type and the warehouse, we could specify that we don't care about the warehouse and keep balances based only on the stock type. Although, in this case, this doesn't make sense from an application perspective, it makes sense in the other uses of cached balances.

The Cached Balances mechanism lets you get a single balance for a specific set of criteria. The criteria are encapsulated in an Access Key, described later. For example, the combination of Warehouse A and stock type Normal would define an Access Key (see Figure 7-26). We can also get a group of balances with their associated criteria (Access Keys) by using a set of criteria defined using a Specification Key. Thus we could ask for the balances for Warehouse A, all stock types. This would give us two balances: one for Warehouse A, stock type Normal, and a second one for Warehouse A, stock type Damaged.

One powerful feature of the Cached Balances support is the ability to fulfill requests for balances that the system has not been told explicitly to keep. The Cached Balances can take the balances it has and fulfill requests by calculating

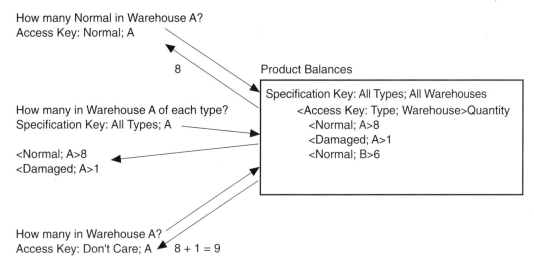

How many Normal in Warehouse A?
Access Key: Normal; A

8   Product Balances

How many in Warehouse A of each type?
Specification Key: All Types; A

<Normal; A>8
<Damaged; A>1

Specification Key: All Types; All Warehouses
<Access Key: Type; Warehouse>Quantity
<Normal; A>8
<Damaged; A>1
<Normal; B>6

How many in Warehouse A?
Access Key: Don't Care; A   8 + 1 = 9

Figure 7-26. Cached Balances Example

the result from what it has. In particular, it can fill any request that is for a subset of the balances it has been explicitly told to keep. For example, suppose that you request the balance, ignoring warehouse, for the Normal stock type. Rather than go back to the inventory data, Cached Balances adds the entries for the Normal stock type for each Warehouse to return the result (14, in our example).

The Cached Balances mechanism is designed so that each time it is used the user can decide what amount of it to expose. For example, in product balances, only individual balances can be requested. It is also designed so that each user can decide how to make the trade-off between speed and storage. The product balances and the general ledger balances leave this decision to the user.

Another powerful feature of Cached Balances is that anything that can be aggregated can be cached. In other words, you can cache not only the simple numeric totals but also the set of objects that would result from a query. In that case, you would not cache simply a number but rather a collection, and updating would add and remove from this collection.

Classification

When you are managing business information, you must often create classifications. That is, you define possible classifications, such as A, B, and C, and you manage items by classifying them according to these groupings. For example, if you classify the items as A, B, and C, you can ask to work with only those classified as B, or you can indicate that special processing should be done with those items classified as C. A concrete example is classifying products into A, B, and C. Many businesses use A to indicate that a product is a good seller and an important part of the product line. They use B to indicate a good product, and C to indicate a product that probably should no longer be sold. These classifications are then used in processing the products. When replenishing a product you take this classification into account, automatically ordering a large number of products classified A but requiring manual intervention to order any more products classified C.

When you identify the need for a classification during design, you usually handle it by using a variation of the Controller pattern called Dynamic Identifier. When using this pattern you define a specific class for the classification and for controlling the classification. For example, SanFrancisco provides DocumentLocation and PaymentMethod in the Common Business Objects layer; in the Warehouse core business processes, it provides the ABC Classification described earlier. However, some classification must be done dynamically. To support dynamic definition of classifications, SanFrancisco provides the Classification category.

The Classification category provides support for dynamically creating a Classification controller and for creating elements within it. One Classification controller is created for each new classification desired and is uniquely identified to associate it with the particular item it is classifying. The elements within this Classification controller represent each of the possible classifications.

For example, suppose that, to provide additional guidance for product replenishment (buying more when you run out), you want to classify the suppliers (see Figure 7-27). You create a classification controller associated with supplier quality and add the elements Gold, Silver, and Bronze. You then associate these classifications with each supplier and modify the replenishment algorithm to replenish using suppliers classified as Gold before those classified as Silver or Bronze.

Keys and Keyables

To consolidate information based on certain criteria, either you can write an algorithm that is tightly coupled to the criteria, or you can separate the criteria from the consolidation algorithm. For example, when you record financial status changes in the general ledger due to stock transactions (inventory changes) in the warehouse, you can collect all these transactions into one large transaction that contains many entries. In particular, each time stock is removed it causes the asset account to be decreased. Thus this transaction contains many entries that increase and decrease the asset account.

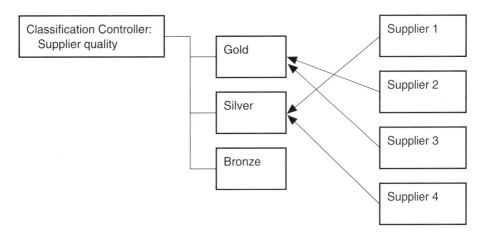

Figure 7-27. Classification Example

Figure 7-28 shows a sample set of the asset account transactions resulting from actions in the warehouse. We increased our assets by 100 because of a purchase, decreased our assets by 300 because of a sale, increased our assets by 600 because of a purchase, decreased our assets by 100 because a product was damaged, and decreased our assets by 200 because of a sale. These would not be the only transactions resulting from these events, but for this example we are focusing only on the transactions on the asset account.

One way to reduce the number of entries is to consolidate all the entries against the same account, in this case the asset account. Figure 7-29 shows the asset accounts being consolidated. The consolidation algorithm is hard-coded to check for the asset account and consolidate anything against that account. Note that the reason is lost in this case and is replaced by a generic Consolidated reason.

Unfortunately, this consolidation is not sufficient in many cases because you may need to keep the decreases due to damaged stock separate from the

(account, value, reason)

asset, +100, Purchase
asset, −300, Sale
asset, +600, Purchase
asset, −100, Damaged
asset, −200, Sale

Figure 7-28. Inventory Changes Example

(account, value, reason)

   asset, +100, Purchase
   asset, −300, Sale
   asset, +600, Purchase
   asset, −100, Damaged
   asset, −200, Sale

If asset account,
then consolidate

(account, value, reason)

   asset, +100, Consolidated

Figure 7-29. Consolidation by Asset Account

decreases due to sales. If you had written the algorithm to the original criteria, adding this new requirement could require rewriting the algorithm. Figure 7-30 shows the algorithm change and the changed results for our example.

However, if you separate the criteria from the algorithm, you can easily add the new criteria without affecting the consolidation algorithm. Figure 7-31 shows consolidation of the asset account using a key. A key containing the account type is created for each entry; if two entries have the same key, they are consolidated.

Figure 7-32 shows how this process would change if the additional criterion of the reason was added. Note that only the creation of the key changes; the algorithm that uses the key is untouched.

In this separation of the criteria from the algorithm, the key encapsulates a set of independent criteria and gives you an abstract way of dealing with it. In the consolidation example, you could use keys to encapsulate the consolidation criteria; thus your algorithm simply consolidates anything that has the same key associated with it.

This type of key, referred to as an Access Key, contains specific values for each of the criteria. When you access items by a set of criteria, you can hold them in a map, and the Access Key is the key to the map. Thus the Access Key is used to access items in a map based on a specific set of values for the criteria.

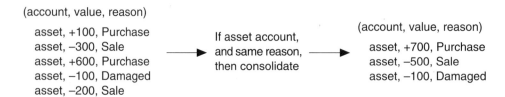

(account, value, reason)

   asset, +100, Purchase
   asset, −300, Sale
   asset, +600, Purchase
   asset, −100, Damaged
   asset, −200, Sale

If asset account,
and same reason,
then consolidate

(account, value, reason)

   asset, +700, Purchase
   asset, −500, Sale
   asset, −100, Damaged

Figure 7-30. Consolidation by Asset Account and Reason

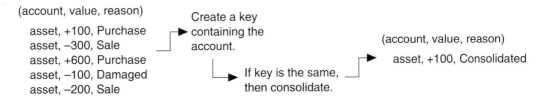

Figure 7-31. Consolidation Using a Key

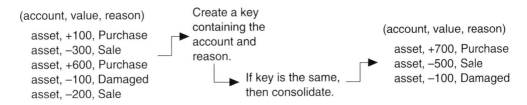

Figure 7-32. Consolidation Using a Key with More Criteria

Another key, called the Specification Key, allows you to specify the values that can be in an Access Key. This key is especially useful when you want to filter the criteria. Again, the algorithm that uses and filters the criteria does not need to know anything about what the actual criteria are.

An example of using a Specification Key is in the Cached Balances, described earlier. Balances for particular criteria, encapsulated in an Access Key, must be cached. You do not want to store all possible permutations of the criteria. Instead, you want to store only those balances associated with the criteria you are interested in. The Specification Key allows you to define the criteria to include. You can indicate that you want all values; that you want to act as if the criteria do not exist; that you want a set of criteria (such as A, B, or D); or that you want a range of criteria, such as 1 January 1999 through 3 March 1999.

Another powerful feature of Specification Keys is that you can use them abstractly with other Specification Keys. This is what allows you to ask Cached Balances for the balances associated with a Specification Key that is not cached and still have Cached Balances return the result. Cached Balances can look for balances cached with a Specification Key that is a superset of the request. The algorithm in Cached Balances knows nothing about the criteria, only that the required criteria are a subset of the criteria used for the cached balance. Cached Balances can then filter the existing balances and their associated Access Keys, using the new Specification Key, to get the desired result.

LifeCycle

A number of items are related to LifeCycle. Rather than talk about them independently, we discuss them together in this section. Their relationship to one another is shown in Figure 7-33. Although they are discussed together, they need not be used together; instead, a particular item and its dependencies could be used. For example, you could decide to use Hierarchical Extensible Item, which would imply you are using Extensible Item, and not use the other categories.

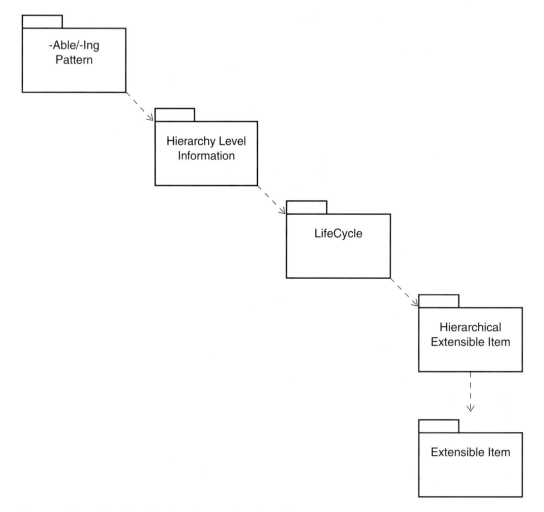

Figure 7-33. LifeCycle and Related Generalized Mechanisms

As you execute your business processes, some of the business objects go through states. Usually, a change in state is triggered by the process, such as an order taker confirming an order and thereby moving it into the confirmed state. The states of a business object can vary depending on a number of things. The states can vary depending on the business object—that is, each order type (purchase or sales) can have its own unique set of states and transitions—or the states can vary from Company to Company.

The LifeCycle pattern separates a business object's life cycle into a separate, dynamically configurable object. In this way, you can modify the business object's life cycle without changing the business object itself.

To process the changes in behavior as the business object transitions through its state machine, you break the business object into pieces that are dynamically added and removed. The state of the object, and what it can and cannot do, is defined at any point by the pieces that are associated with it. These pieces, called extensions, are supported by the Extensible Item generalized mechanism.

What the LifeCycle pattern adds to the Extensible Item is the ability to manage which extensions are available and when they are available and to determine what events cause them to be added and removed.

One aspect of the order example is that although the order can be thought of as a single business object going through a complex state machine, it can be broken into multiple pieces, each with its own state machine. For example, when the order is picked, some items may not be available and must be back-ordered. At this point, part of the order can be shipped and the other part must be back-ordered. Instead of creating a complex state machine that handles this compound state, you set up the Order object as a hierarchy of objects using the LifeCycle pattern; this hierarchy is called LifeCycle Managed Items. So instead of changing the state of the order, you add two new LifeCycle Managed Items: one to handle the back-ordered portion of the order, and a second one to handle the shippable part of the order.

To support this, the LifeCycle Managed Items must be aware of each other and must be able to work with each other. This support is added by the Hierarchical Extensible Item generalized mechanism, which adds the ability to put Extensible Items in a hierarchy and to communicate up and down the hierarchy.

The building of the hierarchy requires knowledge of what should be built in each case. This depends on the particular order type being processed and its life cycle. To encapsulate this knowledge, the Hierarchy Level Information generalized mechanism lets you define the hierarchy and helps control how children within the hierarchy are created—for example, identifying which Life-Cycle should be used for each level.

An associated pattern (not a generalized mechanism but rather a cookie-cutter pattern) is the -Able/-Ing pattern. This pattern lets you decompose the state machine into extensions that can more easily be used as interchangeable pieces in many different LifeCycles. The decomposition involves separating the information produced by the domain process (the -ing) from the information used to create the information (the -able). For example, a pick*able* extension would add the ability to pick, which would cause a pick*ing* extension to be added to indicate the results of picking.

Here's a summary, from the bottom up:

- Extensible Item lets you add and remove extensions, thereby adding, changing, or removing support for a particular set of operations.
- Hierarchical Extensible Item lets you put a number of Extensible Items into a hierarchy and communicate up and down the hierarchy.
- LifeCycle provides a way to control the events that cause extensions to be added and removed. It is separate from the Extensible Item so that it can be dynamically chosen for each instance of the Extensible Item.
- Hierarchy Level Information helps to define and control a hierarchy of LifeCycle-managed items and connects the LifeCycle to the LifeCycle-managed item.
- -Able/-Ing is a cookie-cutter pattern for decomposing the processes and data.

Figure 7-34 shows an example of a hierarchy of LifeCycle-managed items for an order. The OrderHeader contains the general information about the order. There would be one OrderDetail (order line) per product ordered. The Order-Detail contains, among other things, the amount the customer ordered and the warehouse from which we want to ship the product. When the pick method is called on the OrderDetail, a PickingDetail is added to the hierarchy as a child of the OrderDetail. A PickingDetail describes how much of the product to get from a particular location. In our example, only one PickingDetail is created, but we might have more than one—for example, when we need to pick the product from two different stock locations. When a PickingDetail is created, its quantity identified is subtracted from the quantity to be picked. When the quantity to be picked is zero, the pick method is removed. In this example, the Picking Detail is for the entire quantity to be picked, so the pick method is removed. The new Picking Detail provides a commit method.

Figure 7-35 shows an example of committing the PickingDetail. This is what happens when the product has been picked successfully—that is, the pick process has been completed and accepted. At that point the PickingDetail commit method is removed because it has been committed; a ship method is added because the order can now be shipped. Also, the quantity to ship is set to 10, and the quantity identified is set to zero. In this manner the quantities are propagated down the order hierarchy as they are processed.

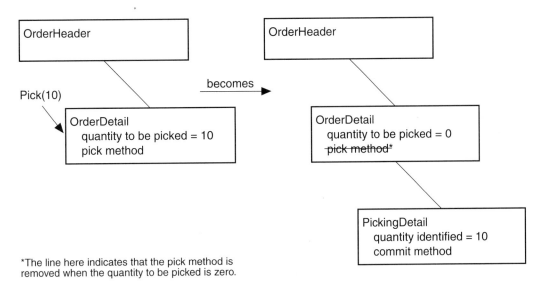

*The line here indicates that the pick method is
removed when the quantity to be picked is zero.

Figure 7-34. Creating a Pick List

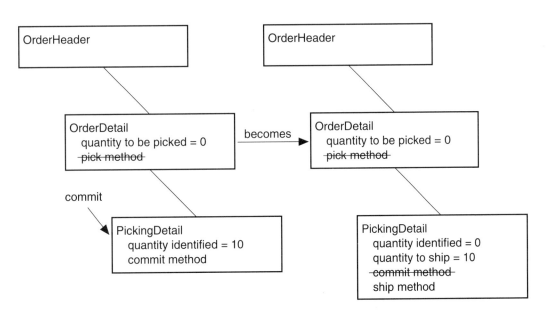

Figure 7-35. Committing a Pick List

In this example, each of the generalized mechanisms is used.

- The Extensible Item is used to control when the pick method is available. When the OrderDetail is created, an extension supporting the pick method is added; and when the PickingDetail is committed, the extension is removed.

- The Hierarchical Extensible item is used to notify the OrderDetail that picking is complete. When the PickingDetail is created, the PickingDetail notifies its parent in the hierarchy with the amount that has been assigned for picking in the future.

- The LifeCycle is used to control when the pick method is available. When the OrderDetail is notified that the total amount has been assigned for picking, the OrderDetail recognizes that all the requested amount has been assigned for picking and indicates that its state has changed. This state change causes the LifeCycle to then remove the extension supporting the pick method.

- The Hierarchy Level information is used to create the children in the order structure. When the pick method is called, the PickingDetail is created as a child in the hierarchy using the Hierarchy Level Information.

Patterns

The following patterns are used in the Common Business Objects layer. Note that patterns first used in the core business processes are discussed in Part IV, The Core Business Processes.

Controllers

This pattern is discussed in Chapter 6.

Generic Interface

The Generic Interface pattern defines how to allow the transfer of information into, and possibly out of, a domain, while requiring the least possible knowledge of the domain.

The key concept is that the target domain provides a set of generic business objects that act as a facade for the target domain. What is unique about these facades is that they use Class Replacement pattern to allow either the actual domain object or customized facades to replace the facades when an application in the target domain is provided.

See the earlier sections Interface to General Ledger and Interface to Accounts Receivable/Accounts Payable for examples of the Generic Interface pattern.

Token Driven Policy

In many cases, the business rules that must be applied within a process depend on what you are doing. For example, if you are checking a business partner's credit while taking an order, you want to look at everything the business partner currently owes you for shipped goods and also find out how much is currently on order but not shipped. However, when you are about to ship the order to the customer, you may want to check what you have already shipped to the customer. In each of these cases you would check against a different limit. You must be able to call the credit checking method and have it do the right thing depending on the process you are running.

This capability is supported by the Token Driven Policy pattern. In this pattern, the method implemented on a business object that is supported by the Token Driven Policy takes a process token (discussed earlier in this chapter). This token is used to get the appropriate policy from the policy map. Then the retrieved policy is used to do the processing.

Figure 7-36 shows an example of using a Token Driven Policy. The checkCredit method is called on the BusinessPartner, passing the process token OrderTaking. This method goes to the policy map to find the policy associated with the process token OrderTaking. In this case, the map returns the ShippedAndPending policy. The checkCredit method is then delegated to that policy.

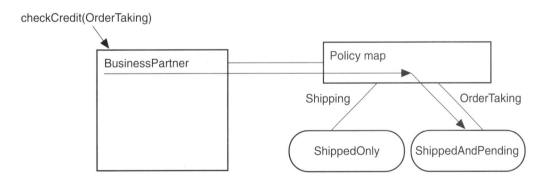

Figure 7-36. Token Driven Policy Example

Chain of Responsibility Driven Policy

When replenishing stock you normally define a set of rules for use by the entire company. These rules are usually simple, such as when there are fewer than 3, buy 100. But suppose one warehouse has a unique set of needs—for example, it has very restricted space. In this case you would like the simple rule to apply to all the warehouses except this one. For it, the rule might be when there are fewer than 2, buy 10. Moreover, one of your products is very expensive, so you would like to add another exception for it. This product's rule is when there are zero, buy 1.

These rules (replenishment rules, in this case) are encapsulated in policies. When the replenishment policy is needed, a chain of responsibility is followed to find the policy, and then the policy is used. The business objects involved in the chain of responsibility and the traversal of the chain of responsibility are encapsulated in a selection policy.

Figure 7-37 shows an example in which different replenishment policies would be necessary. An office supply company called Office Product Suppliers (OPS) is contracted to manage supply cabinets at its customer sites. It has decided to treat each site as a warehouse. OPS also has traditional warehouses where large quantities of products are stored. In this example, only one of each type of warehouse is shown. All the products are available in the Regional warehouse, and a subset (pens, pencils, and erasers) is available in the supply cabinets. OPS has three replenishment policies. The Normal policy, which everything should normally use, is that when the amount of product falls to less than 10, then 100 more should be ordered. For the supply cabinets, a different policy, the Cabinet policy, is used: When the product falls to less than 5, the amount needed to make the total in the cabinet 15 should be added. The final policy, the Backup policy, is for items, such as the copier, that are kept in the warehouse as a backup in case one of the copiers at a customer site breaks. This policy states that when the number falls below one, one should be added.

Figure 7-38 shows how these policies are related to the business objects. The Normal policy is associated with the Company object, the Cabinet policy with the Supply Cabinet warehouse, and the Backup Policy with the Copier. To see the replenishment selection policy's chain of responsibility, we divide the diagram into sections according to the order of the algorithm. These divisions are shown by a dashed line and are labeled on the left with the order of processing. The policy first looks on the Product, then the Warehouse, and finally the Company. For the Copier product, the Backup policy is found directly on the product. For the Erasers product, the policy used depends on which warehouse the product is in. When it is in the Supply Cabinet warehouse, the selection policy looks on the Product and does not find the policy; then it looks on the Warehouse and finds the Cabinet policy. On the other hand, if the Eraser product is in the Regional warehouse, the selection policy does not find the

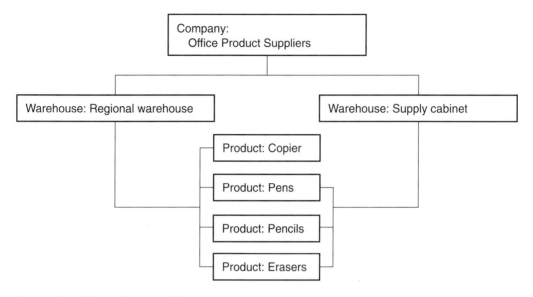

Figure 7-37. Chain of Responsibility Driven Policy

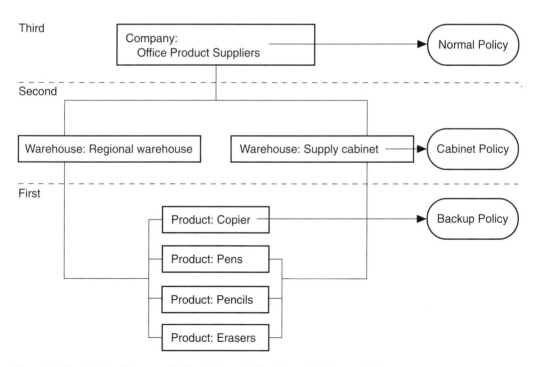

Figure 7-38. Chain of Responsibility Driven Policy Example, Expanded

policy on the Product or Warehouse. Instead, it finds the Normal policy on the Company.

If at a later date you need special handling for another product or another warehouse, you can add an appropriate replenishment policy that will automatically be found. You can also determine later that another business object needs to participate in the chain of responsibility by changing the selection policy. For example, after looking at the Product, you might want to look at a product group before going to the warehouse.

Summary

This chapter introduces each of the categories currently provided as part of the Common Business Objects layer. These categories are divided into three main groups:

- General business objects
- Financial business objects
- Generalized mechanisms

Each of these groups contains a number of business objects and processes or mechanisms that can be used in a wide variety of business applications.

This chapter also discusses the cookie-cutter patterns used by the Common Business Objects layer. Although all patterns can be used to build an application on the Common Business Objects layer, the remaining patterns are discussed in Part IV, The Core Business Processes, because the core business processes are the first place they are used in SanFrancisco.

Chapter 8 describes how you use the Common Business Objects layer by taking you through a sample application.

8 Using the Common Business Objects

Now that we have explored the functionality available in the SanFrancisco Common Business Objects layer, let's revisit the GPSE sample application (introduced in Chapter 5) to see some of the ways the SanFrancisco framework and extensions are used. The GPSE application takes advantage of several common business objects, such as Company and its inherent context hierarchy, BusinessPartner, Address, and Currency. Key patterns, such as controllers and policies, are also used.

When you view sample code in this chapter, notice that the rules and regulations established in the Foundation's programming model are applied. Additional programming model rules do not appear as layers of SanFrancisco are added; only reusable classes and patterns are added.

The GPSE Customer Classes

An example of the reuse of a common business object is the GPSE Customer class. At requirements time for the GPSE application, the following information was recorded:

Customer information is used in various parts of the business. Critical information must be collected for each new customer, including the customer name, contact information, and billing and shipping addresses. Each new customer should have a unique customer number, and each customer has an initial credit limit that changes as orders are made against the credit line.

The application requirements are mapped to the SanFrancisco processes as suggested in the SanFrancisco Application Development Roadmap. At requirements mapping time, the BusinessPartner requirements seemed to be a good match to the GPSE Customer class, as you can see in this excerpt from the BusinessPartner process description:

A business partner is usually a customer or a supplier. However, from a framework point of view, a business partner may be any person, organization, or legal entity depending on the specific application. Prospects or potential customers may be business partners in a marketing application, employees in a payroll application, patients in a health application, subscribers in a publishing application, banks in financial applications, and so on.

During analysis, more information is recorded to refine the application requirements, and an analysis-level object model is created. Figure 8-1 shows the GPSE model, indicating where common business objects are used.

You can see from the diagram that there are additional pieces of information—the credit limit and outstanding balance—that also must be contained in the Customer. Although the common business objects provide support for business partner balances and credit checking, to simplify this example those functions are not used. In this case, at analysis time, the decision was made to add the credit limit and outstanding balance to the existing BusinessPartner class as an extension.

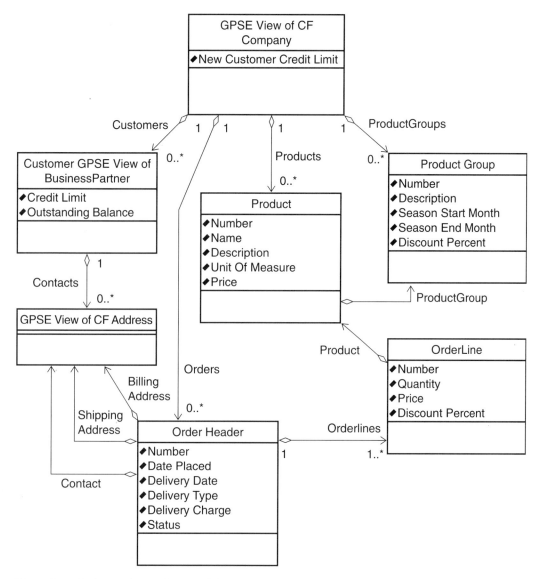

Figure 8-1. GPSE Analysis Class Model

Using the BusinessPartner Common Business Object and the Controller Pattern

It is during design that the decision is made on how to implement needed extensions. In the case of the GPSE Customer class, the choice was to create the Customer class as an aggregation of the BusinessPartner class. Aggregation implies that rather than subclass BusinessPartner, a new Customer class that contains a BusinessPartner instance is created. Any work that can be done by the BusinessPartner instance is delegated to it. After aggregation was chosen, the decision was made to hide the fact that the Customer contains a Business-Partner. Hiding the aggregated classes is called *hidden aggregation*. The opposite of hidden aggregation, *visible aggregation*, exposes BusinessPartner for direct manipulation through get and set methods. Hiding BusinessPartner, in this case, has many benefits. For example, the Customer class has all the necessary methods on it, and BusinessPartner should never need to be used directly by the client, simplifying the client interface. Hiding BusinessPartner from the end users also allows more freedom to alter implementation in the future.

Aggregation is a typical way that solution developers extend the common business objects. The advantage of extension using aggregation over subclassing is that it allows multiple solution developers to extend a common business object without having knowledge of each other's extensions. Because each extension is contained in the aggregating class, the common business object can be reused differently in different applications, even sharing the same common business object instances at an end user installation.

In addition to building the Customer itself, you must collect and maintain customers. The ownership decision—which class should own the customers—seems natural in this case: The Company must know all its customers, so it will own them. The Controller pattern discussed earlier gives applications a powerful way to collect and access customers on a company per company basis or even throughout the entire company hierarchy. In this case, controlling customers through the pattern is optimal. The class diagram in Figure 8-2 depicts the design use of BusinessPartner and the Controller pattern.

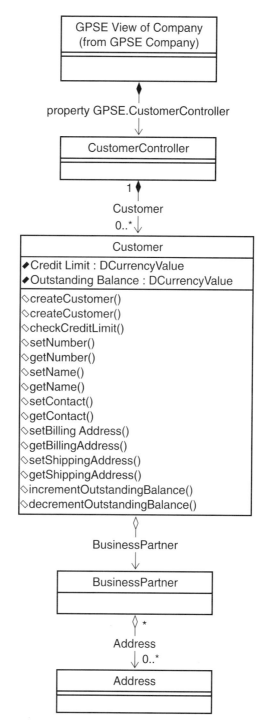

Figure 8-2. GPSE with BusinessPartner and Controller Pattern

The following methods in the design in Figure 8-2 are introduced on the Customer class but are delegated to BusinessPartner:

- getNumber()
- getName(), setName()
- getContact(), setContact()
- getBillingAddress(), setBillingAddress()
- getShippingAddress(), setShippingAddress()

You can use the SanFrancisco code generator to generate code for the Customer and CustomerController classes. The code generator takes care of building the necessary factories, interfaces, and implementations for the extensions. Except for the Customer class itself, the changes needed to get the classes compiled and running are fairly small. The Customer class takes more work in the implementation because of the choice of aggregation. There is more information about the SanFrancisco code generator in Appendix A, Tools.

The outer class scope for the Customer implementation class follows. This scope contains several instance variables that are used in the many pieces of code presented in this chapter. All this code is generated based on the class model presented earlier.

```
package GPSE;

import java.util.*;
import java.io.*;
import com.ibm.sf.gf.*;
import com.ibm.sf.cf.*;

public class CustomerImpl extends DynamicEntityImpl
                          implements Distinguishable, Customer {

  // method implementations - not shown

  // not owned and mandatory attribute
  // Handle for BusinessPartner Entity
  protected Handle ivBusinessPartnerHdl;

  // owned and optional attribute
  // the Dependent credit checking policy
  protected DCreditCheckPolicy ivCreditCheckPolicy;

  // owned and mandatory attribute
  // the Dependent credit limit value
  protected DCurrencyValue ivCreditLimit;
```

```
    // owned and mandatory attribute
    // the Dependent outstanding balance
    protected DCurrencyValue ivOutstandingBalance;

} // end of class CustomerImpl
```

Aggregation in the Customer class creates the bulk of the post-generation work. The work is to ensure that duplication of function is not created; basically, the BusinessPartner implementation should be used whenever possible. In general, there are two types of changes in the Customer class:

- Changes that require delegation of implementation to the contained BusinessPartner
- Initialization of the Customer (and BusinessPartner) instance

Remember that the BusinessPartner is an Entity and that Entities are contained within objects by their Handle. Each method that delegates to the Business-Partner must retrieve the object from its Handle. Although this may appear to add a large overhead to the method calls, many object caching mechanisms are in place to help performance. This technique also lets you delay the activation of a contained object until it is needed. The appropriate method is then called on the BusinessPartner. This process can be seen in the getName() and set-Name() method implementations in the Customer.

```java
public void setName(String name) throws com.ibm.sf.gf.SFException {

    // get access to the BusinessPartner instance referenced by the Handle
    BusinessPartner bp = (BusinessPartner)getObjectFromHandle(
        ivBusinessPartnerHdl,
        AccessMode.createPlusWrite());

    // set the name on the BusinessPartner
    bp.setLegalName(name);

}

public String getName() throws com.ibm.sf.gf.SFException {

    // get access to the BusinessPartner instance referenced by the Handle
    BusinessPartner bp = (BusinessPartner)getObjectFromHandle(
        ivBusinessPartnerHdl,
        AccessMode.createNormal());

    // return the name retrieved from the BusinessParnter
    return(bp.getLegalName());

}
```

The initialization of the Customer object may well be the most complex of the methods within the new Customer class. There are two initialization methods. One builds a BusinessPartner to base itself on and delegate to, and the other one takes a BusinessPartner as input, enabling GPSE to use existing Business-Partner instances. The create methods within the CustomerFactory call the correct initialize method. In a nutshell, the difference between the two methods, in addition to their signatures, is that the former creates a BusinessPartner, and the latter uses an existing BusinessPartner and can therefore omit much logic. Here, we present only the initialize method that does not use an existing BusinessPartner.

```
public void initialize(CustomerController owner,
    String name,
    Address billing,
    Address contact,
    Address shipping) throws com.ibm.sf.gf.SFException {

super.initialize();

// create BusinessPartner

// add associated data to the BusinessPartner

// create credit check policy
}
```

Before we get further into the code, another SanFrancisco decision must be illuminated. The BusinessPartner is split into two pieces, which can vary independently of each other. A large part of the data for a BusinessPartner is split into a BusinessPartnerSharedData object. The shared data is attached to companies and can be shared across them. Shared data is controlled and located by an ID. This decision allows some pieces of common BusinessPartner data—for example, the legal name—to be controlled at the Enterprise level, whereas other BusinessPartner data, such as a contact name, can vary at the individual Company level. This decision regarding shared data makes it easy for multiple business partners to use the same data; for multiple companies to create business partners that have the same data across companies; or for the system to have different representations of the same BusinessPartner in different companies. Because the shared data is a separate object, it must be created before the BusinessPartner itself is created.

Within the initialize() method, first the unique shared data object is created and stored in the Company's BusinessPartnerSharedDataController. After the shared data object is created, the BusinessPartner can be created in the company's BusinessPartnerController.

```
   // retrieve the company that the customer is stored in
 1 Company owningCompany = owner.getContainingCompany();

   // get the BusinessPartnerSharedDataController from the company
 2 BusinessPartnerSharedDataController bpsdController =
       (BusinessPartnerSharedDataController)(owningCompany.getPropertyBy(
         "cf.BusinessPartnerSharedDataController"));
 3 if (bpsdController == null) {
     // exception handling, throw exception to caller
 4 }

   // now create a shared data object stored in the controller
   // the name and billing address are part of the shared data
 5 BusinessPartnerSharedData bpsd =
       BusinessPartnerSharedDataFactory.createBusinessPartnerSharedData(
       bpsdController, AccessMode.createNormal(), null, name,
       billing, null, null, null, null, null);

   // retrieve the separate controller for the BusinessPartner
 6 BusinessPartnerController bpController =
       (BusinessPartnerController)(owningCompany.getPropertyBy(
         "cf.BusinessPartnerController"));
 7 if (bpController == null) {
     // exception handling, throw exception to caller
 8 }

   // create the business partner into the associated business
   // partner controller
 9 BusinessPartner bp = BusinessPartnerFactory.createBusinessPartner(
       bpController, AccessMode.createNormal(), bpsd.getId(),
       false, null, null);

   // store the handle to the entity, remember that entities themselves
   // are not stored
10 ivBusinessPartnerHdl = setHandleToObject(ivBusinessPartnerHdl, bp);
```

Following are some interesting things to note in the code:

- Line 1: A controller has a relationship to its owning Company. The CustomerController that will own the Customer is used to access the owning Company.

- Line 2: Controllers are attached as properties to a Company. To access the Controller, you use the getPropertyBy() method, passing a String key that indicates the name of the property. Execution follows the property chaining up the Company hierarchy until a match is found.

- Line 5: The Customer name and billing address are created as part of the BusinessPartnerSharedData. The billing address reuses the Address class, which is available as a common business object.
- Line 6: BusinessPartners are in a separate controller. This allows the company-level BusinessPartner data to vary from Company to Company.
- Line 9: To define the relationship to the shared data, the ID of the shared data is passed when the BusinessPartner is created.
- Line 10: Remember that the BusinessPartner that was created must be stored by its Handle.

With the BusinessPartner created, the initialize() method can set up the contact and shipping addresses. This data is attached to the BusinessPartner as one of the many addresses a BusinessPartner can keep. A key is attached to the addresses so that they can be retrieved independently of the order in which they are inserted.

```
// add the contact address
bp.addDirectlyOwnedAddressBy(contact, "Contact");  ·
// add the shipping address
bp.addDirectlyOwnedAddressBy(shipping, "ShippingAddress");
```

The remainder of the initialize() method sets up the financial data surrounding the customer. A default credit limit is attached to the current company by property. This default limit is retrieved and stored in the new Customer. Note that the credit limit value reuses another common business object, DCurrency-Value. Next, the default credit check policy is created and set appropriately.

```
// set initial credit limit
setCreditLimit((DCurrencyValue)owningCompany.getPropertyBy(
    "GPSE.NewCustomerCreditLimit"));

// set credit check policy
ivCreditCheckPolicy =
DCustomerCreditCheckPolicyDefaultFactory.
    createDCustomerCreditCheckPolicyDefault();
```

Finally, the current balance must be set. Remembering that an outstanding balance in a multinational corporation is more complex than simply a float, the application must go through several steps. First, we retrieve the Currency-Controller from the current company. Then we can retrieve the base currency type for the current company. By using the full Currency type, we can always adjust the balance to the various currency types that the company may be prepared to use.

```
// get the currency controller from the company
CurrencyController currController =
    (CurrencyController)(owningCompany.getPropertyBy(
      "cf.CurrencyController"));
if (currController == null) {
  // throw an exception to the caller
}

// create a decimal 0
DDecimal zero = DDecimalFactory.createDDecimal("0");
// and finally, set the outstanding balance in the current currency type
ivOutstandingBalance = DCurrencyValueFactory.
      createContainedDCurrencyValue(this,
        currController.getBaseCurrency(), zero);
```

One of the many things you should realize from the code surrounding this complex object is that much information is stored at a company level, and controllers are heavily used at this level. The Controller pattern is powerful when combined with the company context hierarchy. The controller allows different companies to have independent data optionally. For example, if a company has its own CurrencyController, it can have its own base currency, which subsequently is used in all the customers built for that particular company. On the other hand, if a company does not have its own CurrencyController, the first one encountered in the hierarchy is retrieved for use. In this manner, a parent company really sets the currency type for the customer. The implementation of the CustomerController in the GPSE application was generated completely by the code generator, with only minor modifications necessary.

The GPSE Product Classes

Let's explore two other GPSE classes—Product and ProductGroup—to see an example of the policy pattern (introduced in Chapter 6), another powerful and well-used pattern in SanFrancisco. It is used when it is desirable that the algorithm of an operation of an object be managed independently from the rest of the object. Discounting items within the GPSE application is implemented as policies to encapsulate the discount algorithms used. At requirements and analysis time, the GPSE Product and ProductGroup classes were defined. Although SanFrancisco provides a Product class in its Warehouse Management core business process, for sample purposes that class is not used in GPSE; rather, a new Entity subclass is created. In the analysis diagram shown earlier in Figure 8-1, you can see the relationships these two classes have. At requirements and analysis time, a set of rules for discounting products was defined.

- Verify whether a discount at the product level exists; if it does, use it.

- If a discount at the product level does not exist, verify the product group for a seasonal discount. If a seasonal discount exists in the product group, use it. The product group provides a season start month and season end month, which can be used to determine whether a specific request for a related product made at a particular time deserves a discount. If a product's request date falls outside the product group season start month and season end month, then a discount situation is determined.

- If no discount is available, return discount of 0.

To make the discounting as flexible as possible, it was decided that discounts could be defined for ProductGroups and Products, with a default discount also available at the company level. Discounts are applied to each line of an order. Only one discount is applied. The order for determining a discount is to use the discount on the Product if it's available; otherwise, use the discount for the appropriate ProductGroup if available; otherwise, use the discount on the Company.

Using the Policy Pattern

The discounting in the GPSE application is an example of a *Chain of Responsibility Policy*. Property containers, discussed earlier, support chaining through a getChainParent() method. If there is a *companywide policy* and a Company hierarchy has been implemented, the companywide policy can be attached to the Enterprise object and to some of the specific Company objects in the hierarchy. This is an example of a policy that is chained. From any Company you can retrieve the policy, either one that is directly attached to the Company or one that you get from the Enterprise by following the chain.

A Chain of Responsibility (COR)-driven policy is implemented differently. In COR-driven policies, multiple different chains can be established that are not limited to the Company hierarchy. The chain is set up in the policy itself rather than by using the chaining in property containers. This approach for chaining is much more flexible than implementing the chain directly in business objects; because the chain is isolated, you can easily replace it instead of having to modify multiple business objects to modify the chain. The reason for COR-driven policies is that some policies may apply to a group of different business classes. By contrast, simple policies are attached to one class of object; a customer credit check policy, for example, may be attached only to Customer object instances. The GPSE discount policy is more complex: It could apply to particular products as well as product groups. You might want the ability to discount some products deeply, if they are overstocked, or discount entire product groups to move them during their off-season. That's where COR-driven policies are useful. They have a policy class hierarchy similar to other types of policies—that is, a parent policy class is defined and then specialized by subclassing. They also have a policy that decides the order to use in looking for policies—for example, to look for the discount policy on a product first, a product group second, and so on.

Because the idea behind a policy is that it can be easily replaced, you never want to have client code call the policy method directly. Instead, the client code calls the visible method on the object that contains the policy; that method then calls the policy method on the contained policy object. In this way, the policy object can be replaced with an instance of a different subclass of the same policy without affecting the client code. In the GPSE example, a determine-Discount() method is part of the Product interface but is implemented via a policy. This means that the policy interface also has a determineDiscount() method. A policy is a Dependent and a subclass of DescribableDependent. An abstract policy declares an interface common to all the supported algorithms and may define utility methods. Concrete policies are subclassed from the abstract policy to define the specific behavior of the algorithms. A default concrete policy is a policy that is called if no other policy is provided.

The COR policy class hierarchy looks like a normal policy hierarchy. There is an abstract policy class that has one or more concrete subclasses to implement various policy algorithms. Here you may see multiple default policies, however, because the COR-driven policy can apply to different classes of objects and each one may need a default policy. Also, there is always a default policy for the Company. This is because the COR-driven policy must have a defined end point that is the Company. Figure 8-3 is the DiscountPolicy hierarchy for the GPSE application. You can see that there is an abstract class with a

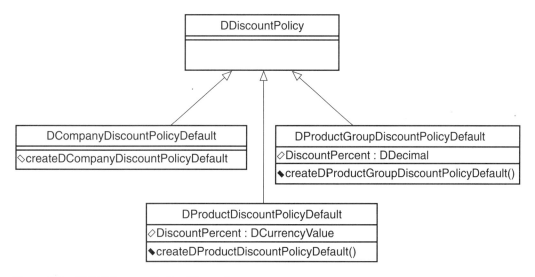

Figure 8-3. GPSE DiscountPolicy Hierarchy

concrete default policy for Company, Product, and ProductGroup—the three classes that are used in the chain of responsibility.

When implementing a COR policy, you define a *selection hierarchy* that follows a form similar to that of the policy class hierarchy. Again, there is an abstract selection policy with concrete subclasses (see Figure 8-4). In this case, the algorithm implemented by the concrete subclasses is actually an algorithm to select which policy class will be used. The "algorithm" walks through a defined chain of responsibility. The selection policy is held as an attribute on the domain class. In the GPSE application, it's the Product class's determineDiscount() method that is used to determine the discounting, so the selection policy is an attribute of Product.

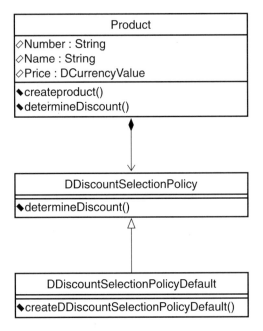

Figure 8-4. GPSE Selection Policy

All the policies that implement the domain algorithms are held as properties on the appropriate class—Products, ProductGroup, and Company in this example. Figure 8-5 shows the complete discounting hierarchy created for GPSE.

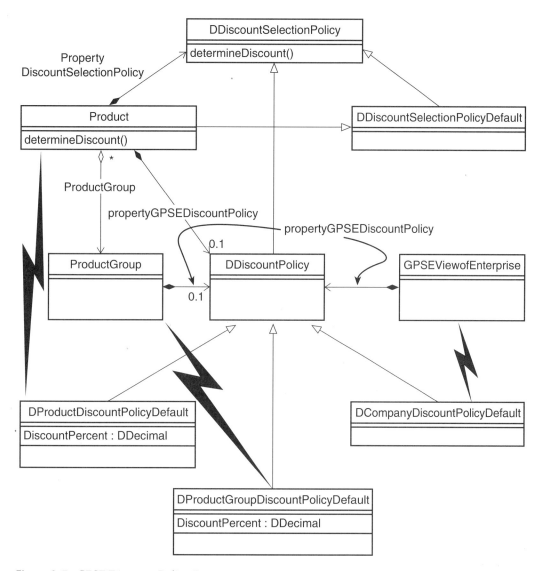

Figure 8-5. GPSE Discount Policy Design

To understand how this chain of responsibility works, let's look at the implementation. First, the Product class has a determineDiscount() method that is called when an order line for that product is created for an order. Its implementation follows:

```
public DDecimal determineDiscount(DDecimal quantity, DTime date)
    throws com.ibm.sf.gf.SFException {

  return (getDiscountSelectionPolicy().determineDiscount(
      this, quantity, date));

}
```

The default selection policy is an attribute of Product. The determineDiscount() method simply calls the determineDiscount() method on the selection policy.

The DDiscountSelectionPolicyDefault is the first concrete class in this COR policy implementation. The selection policy implements the chain of responsibility. Here is its determineDiscount() implementation:

```
public DDecimal determineDiscount(Product aProduct,
    DDecimal quantity, DTime date) throws com.ibm.sf.gf.SFException {

  // validate parameters - not shown

1   DDiscountPolicy discountPolicy = null;

  // check for discount policy on this Product
2   discountPolicy = (DDiscountPolicy)aProduct.
      getPropertyBy("GPSE.DiscountPolicy");

  // if product discount policy exists, return its discount
3   if (discountPolicy != null)
4     return (((DProductDiscountPolicyDefault)discountPolicy).
      determineDiscount(aProduct, quantity, date));

  // check for discount policy on the Product's ProductGroup
5   discountPolicy = (DDiscountPolicy)aProduct.getProductGroup().
      getPropertyBy("GPSE.DiscountPolicy");

  // if product group discount policy exists, return its discount
6   if (discountPolicy != null)
7     return (((DProductGroupDiscountPolicyDefault)discountPolicy).
      determineDiscount(aProduct, quantity, date));

  // check for discount policy on the Company
8   discountPolicy = (DDiscountPolicy)CompanyContext.getActiveCompany().
      getPropertyBy("GPSE.DiscountPolicy");
```

```
      // if company discount policy exists, return its discount
 9    if (discountPolicy != null)
10      return (((DCompanyDiscountPolicyDefault)discountPolicy).
          determineDiscount(aProduct, quantity, date));

11    else {
      // Severe error, no discount policy set for company.
      // Create exception - not shown
12    }
13}
```

Following are some interesting things to note from the preceding code:

- Lines 2 through 4: Check for a discount policy on the Product by property. If it exists, call the determineDiscount() method and return the discount value.

- Lines 5 through 7: Check for a discount policy on the Product's Product-Group by property. If it exists, call the determineDiscount() method and return the discount value.

- Lines 8 through 10: Check for a discount policy on the active Company. If it exists, call the determineDiscount() method and return the discount value.

The Product, ProductGroup, and Company discount policy determine-Discount() methods are then implemented to return a calculated discount. With this complete chain of responsibility policy implementation, discounts can be added to and removed from some, but not necessarily all, Products and ProductGroups as the business rules determine they are necessary.

Summary

Common business objects provided by SanFrancisco give the solution developer another level of reuse beyond that of the Foundation. The common business objects are large-grained objects with prebuilt data and functionality. From the example in this chapter, you can see that even if a common business object does not meet the exact needs of the application requirements, it can be and is usually meant to be extended and customized.

The example also shows how to take advantage of the patterns defined in SanFrancisco. Controllers, for example, are a key to storing and retrieving information. Controllers are used to collect information and attach it to the Company hierarchy. Dynamic property containment is used to extend the Company with default information and controllers. Dealing with these added attributes requires no change to the Company. Policies are used to encapsulate business logic and thereby minimize the impact of changes based on business requirements. For solution developers, another advantage of the use of the SanFrancisco patterns comes with consistent implementation within the application extensions and, as you'll see later, in the core business processes. Repeated use of the patterns simplifies the task of extending SanFrancisco and also helps you understand the core business processes and extensions made by others.

Part IV

The Core Business Processes

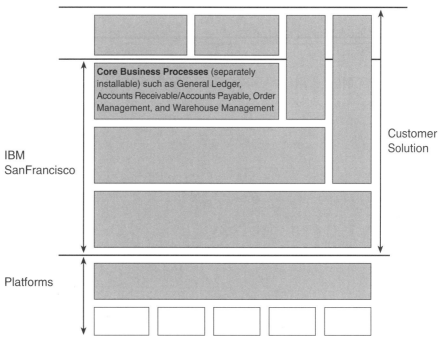

IBM SanFrancisco

Core Business Processes (separately installable) such as General Ledger, Accounts Receivable/Accounts Payable, Order Management, and Warehouse Management

Customer Solution

Platforms

The Core Business Processes

SanFrancisco's Core Business Processes layer provides the business objects and processes for specific business application domains (see figure on page 173). Currently, SanFrancisco provides four core business processes: Accounts Receivable/Accounts Payable (AR/AP), General Ledger (GL), Order Management (OM), and Warehouse Management (WM). Each domain is supported by its own unique business objects and processes.

Each core business process contains the business objects and processes used by all business applications in that domain. For example, any warehouse management application must have the ability to represent products and warehouses.

The core business processes are the focus of the next three chapters. Chapter 9, An Introduction to the Core Business Processes, gives an introduction to the core business processes, focusing on the key concepts and patterns. Chapter 10, Core Business Process Domains, provides an overview of the contents of the core business processes layer. Each domain is described, and then the support provided by SanFrancisco is explained. Chapter 11, Using the Core Business Processes, shows an example of using the contents of the Warehouse management core business process to build part of a business application.

An Introduction to the Core Business Processes

9

This chapter introduces the Core Business Processes layer of the SanFrancisco component framework. We describe the contents of this layer and give an overview of how they are used. We also define the application domains whose business activities are encapsulated in the business objects and processes in this layer.

Contents of the Core Business Processes

A domain expert will recognize the business objects and processes in the core business process devoted to his or her domain. But because IBM's goal was to create a component framework that would be universally applicable, those objects and processes may be packaged somewhat differently than expected. For example, any General Ledger (GL) core business process must support an account. However, you will not find a class called "Account" in the GL. Instead, the class is called a *posting combination*. The reason is that what an account is varies depending on the accounting principles you follow, the country you are operating in, and the way you do business. In some cases, the posting combination matches exactly what would be considered an account, and in other cases, what would be considered an account is only one piece of the posting combination. The posting combination is flexible enough that it can support many concepts of "account." The posting combination is an extreme case, however, because SanFrancisco tries to use common terms whenever it can. To alleviate terminology differences, SanFrancisco provides User Guides that describe the core business processes in familiar terms and maps them to the SanFrancisco terms. Also, SanFrancisco provides a glossary in which commonly used terms are mapped to the terms used in SanFrancisco.

The core business processes constitute the top layer provided by SanFrancisco. They use the common business objects, are built on the Foundation layer, and follow the SanFrancisco Programming Model. The core business processes use the business objects and processes provided in the Common Business Objects (CBO) layer in two ways: with and without modification. When a business object from the Common Business Objects layer is used without modification, the core business process normally uses it as an attribute. For example, the general ledger Journal class, which records financial transactions, uses a *TransactionValue*. The TransactionValue allows the general ledger to keep track of both the prime currency (the currency the transaction occurred in) and the base currency (the currency we keep track of our business in). On the other hand, when you modify or *extend* the CBO business objects, you usually do not use class replacement; instead, either you add properties to the CBO business object or you *wrap* it in a new business object (via aggregation). For example, the BusinessPartner class does not fulfill all the requirements that the Order Management core business process has for customers and suppliers. The Order Management core business process provides an OrderPartner, which wraps (aggregates) the CBO BusinessPartner and adds what is needed to fulfill its requirements. You do not create a completely independent BusinessPartner because the Order Management core business process may share the wrapped BusinessPartner with other applications running on SanFrancisco.

IBM determined which business objects and processes to provide in each core business process in a manner similar to the approach it used for the Common Business Objects layer. Two groups of experts in each domain worked with IBM to develop each core business process. One group was directly involved in developing the core business process, and the other had the responsibility for validation. These domain experts helped identify not only the business objects and processes that went into each core business process but also those that were not included and those that went instead into the Common Business Objects layer.

IBM is no longer actively adding new business objects and processes to the existing core business processes. However, it continues to maintain them, improve documentation, and address new requirements. For example, IBM has modified the core business processes to add support for the requirements associated with dealing with the transition to the new European euro currency. IBM is also working on new core business processes.

Using the Core Business Processes

When developing applications using the core business processes, you use an object-oriented development process. At certain points you will stop and map to SanFrancisco. For example, after you have captured your requirements, you can look at the requirements for the components SanFrancisco provides to see what you can reuse. If you are familiar with the components SanFrancisco provides, you might make the mapping easier by defining your requirements in light of them. When mapping, you map not only to the core business processes but also to the common business objects and, especially at the design level, to the Foundation layer. A number of the business objects in the Common Business Objects layer were extracted from the Core Business Processes layer when the objects were being developed. So if you do not find an object in the core business processes, you may find it in the Common Business Objects layer. Also, when you map the design, you also map to the generalized mechanisms provided by the Common Business Objects layer and things such as the collection support in the Foundation. One important factor you should take into consideration when mapping is that SanFrancisco provides all the analysis and design models and documentation as part of the product. This documentation is what allows you to map from each level of your development process, especially the requirements level. Chapter 1 of this book provides more details on incorporating SanFrancisco into your development process.

Although SanFrancisco provides many of the pieces, there isn't always something to map to. In these cases, you develop the business objects and processes you need. In other cases, SanFrancisco provides exactly what you need; after you map to it, you can reuse it as is. In most cases, when you map to San-Francisco it does not provide exactly what you need. The developers of SanFrancisco have identified common places where customization is needed. These customization points are called *extension points* and are usually implemented using patterns.

Often, you need only modify these extension points to fulfill your requirements. For example, suppose your warehouse application has the requirement to replenish stock—that is, buy more when (or just before) it runs out. Your requirements define the business rules for when you should replenish, how much you should buy, and how you should decide from whom to buy. This rule may be as simple as using fixed values, such as always buying ten when there are fewer than two, or it may be as complex as taking into account the price, delivery time, and sales characteristics of the product when deciding how much or even whether to replenish. The replenishment requirement is supported by the use of policies. When you map your requirements, you may find that SanFrancisco fulfills your requirement for replenishment except that you must modify a policy to have it use your business rules. You must also provide the mechanisms for selecting which products should be evaluated for replenishment and when they should be evaluated (for example, monthly, quarterly, when stock quantities reach a certain level, and so on). This is a good example of the building blocks SanFrancisco provides to let you create complex business processes. You can modify a building block via its built-in extension points, and you can also build complex processes to tie together multiple building blocks. For example, you can convert replenishment suggestions into purchase orders or into stock transfers between warehouses.

A number of the extension points provided by SanFrancisco let you perform customizations at an end user location. For example, suppose your requirement is that replenishment must be customized for each end user. SanFrancisco's use of policies means that you can decide whether and how much to expose a customization point to your end user. For example, you might decide to support three ways of doing replenishment and allow the end user to customize your application by picking one of the three.

There are also cases when SanFrancisco does not provide an extension point. This does not mean that you cannot use SanFrancisco. Rather, you can use one of the other extension methods described in the SanFrancisco Extension Guide. For example, you can extend a business object by creating a subclass of it and then specifying that the business object be class-replaced. In other words, you tell the factory to create your subclass instead of the original business object whenever the class is created. This technique allows you to add attributes and modify methods on the business object. The advantage of this approach (compared with creating a subclass and simply using it in your code) is that by using class replacement you are guaranteed that all instances of the business object will be the new subclass—even business objects created by existing framework code. The SanFrancisco Extension Guide describes various extension techniques and explains when and why they should and shouldn't be used.

Core Business Process Domains

The core business processes provide the business objects and processes for a particular application domain, but in some cases they have dependencies on one another. Figure 9-1 shows the direct relationships between the core business processes by showing a CBP on top of the thing it depends on.

The only direct dependency between the core business processes is from Order Management to Warehouse Management. This direct dependency means that Order Management is built on top of Warehouse Management and directly uses the business objects provided by Warehouse Management. For example, Order Management extends the product from Warehouse Management so that the product can be used to represent the individual items on the

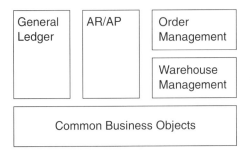

Figure 9-1. Core Business Process Relationships

order. This dependency is in one direction only—that is, Order Management is completely aware of Warehouse Management and its contents, but Warehouse Management has no knowledge of Order Management. This means that when you build an order management application (or combined order management and warehouse management application), you will use the Order Management CBP and the Warehouse Management CBP. However, when creating a warehouse application (or a non-order application based on Warehouse Management), you use only the Warehouse Management CBP.

There are a number of indirect dependencies among the core business processes. These dependencies are not obvious from the diagram because they occur on the interface categories provided as part of the financial business objects in the Common Business Objects layer. Figure 9-2 explicitly shows the indirect relationships. These indirect relationships provide a higher level of isolation between the CBPs and applications, on the one hand, and, on the other hand, the target CBP on which they are indirectly dependent. The support for the target CBP is always available as part of the Common Business Objects layer and always acts appropriately even if an actual target domain is a legacy system or is not even present.

When an order is invoiced, the AR/AP and the general ledger must be updated to reflect the invoice. As shown in Figure 9-2, order management updates the status in the AR/AP and general ledger using the Interface to AR/AP category and Interface to General Ledger category, respectively. In this case, order management uses two categories in the Common Business Objects layer—the Invoicing category and the Financial Integration category—to make sending information to the AR/AP and General Ledger easier. If a general ledger is not present, the Interface to the general ledger (via Financial Integration) accepts the information and, from the order management's perspective, acts as if the general ledger was updated even though the interface may actually discard the information.

Warehouse management can also cause the general ledger to be updated. This update occurs during a stock take (also called physical inventory) when

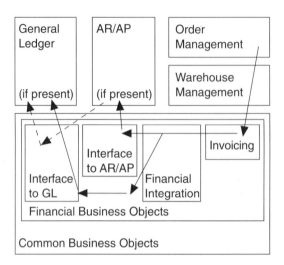

Figure 9-2. Indirect Relationships among the Core Business Processes

the number of products present does not match the expected number. This discrepancy causes a reduction or increase in stock, which means a reduction or increase in assets that must be reflected in the general ledger. This situation is not shown in the figure.

Another indirect dependency occurs between the AR/AP and the general ledger. As shown in Figure 9-2, the AR/AP directly uses the Interface to General Ledger category in the Common Business Objects layer. As payments for invoices are processed, for example, the AR/AP must update the general ledger to correctly reflect the effect of the payment on the financial status of the company. In some cases the general ledger has an account for each business partner, and it must be updated to reflect the application of the payment to the balance currently owed by that business partner.

Patterns

Although a number of new patterns are first used in the Core Business Processes layer, they can be used in any application built on SanFrancisco. All these patterns are cookie-cutter patterns. Each pattern must be applied each time it is used; no reusable portion is provided.

Keyed Attribute Retrieval

The determination of the price to charge for a product can involve a wide variety of factors, such as when it is purchased and the quantity purchased. These factors vary from application to application and are one of the ways an application can differentiate itself from other applications.

The Keyed Attribute Retrieval pattern involves using *keys*, one of the generalized mechanisms from the Common Business Objects layer (see Chapter 7). The key is used to encapsulate the factors (when a product is purchased and the quantity purchased). The key is then used to map from the factors to the item associated with them (in this case, price). This map is usually a controller. In this case, a Specification Key is used as an advanced Access Key. The Specification Key allows a price to be associated with a set of criteria—in this case, a date range. This pattern defines a series of lookups to find a particular item. For example, we would first look for the price of the product associated with a specific date and customer discount group; if that is not found, then we look for the price associated with only the customer discount group. This series of lookups is usually encapsulated in a policy so that it can be customized.

Figure 9-3 shows an example of a Price Definition controller and two requests for a price. The Price Definition controller has three entries. The bottom entry specifies that pens are on sale during July. Anyone in customer group A purchasing pens during July will get a price of 4 USD each. The middle entry defines the price when a customer in group A purchases a pen at any time. The top entry defines the price when a customer in group B purchases a pen at any time. So when you request the purchase price on July 23, 1999, by a customer in group B, first the Price Definition controller looks for a specific entry that covers this date. When it does not find one, it looks for an entry that is applicable for all dates. It finds this and returns the price of 3 USD each. The second request is for the price on July 23, 1999, for a purchase by a customer in group A.

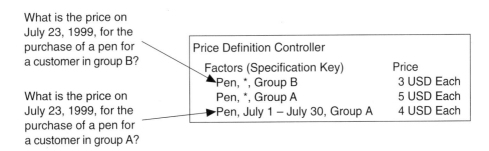

Figure 9-3. Keyed Attribute Retrieval Example

In this case, the Price Definition controller finds a specific entry and returns 4 USD each. One simplification in this example is that the Price Definition controller would normally have entries for each of the different products sold.

The advantage of using the Specification Key is that you can change the factors used in defining the price without affecting the algorithm that does the lookup in the Price controller. For example, if you wanted to take a specific customer into account when determining the price, you would extend the key by replacing the customer group with the specific customer.

List Generation

In many cases you must generate a list of items, such as a pick list. A *pick list* is used by the person (or machine, in the case of an automated warehouse) who actually goes into the warehouse and retrieves the products to send to a customer for a particular order. This list may include the products needed for one order, or it may be a combination of many orders. To generate the pick list, a set of orders ready for picking (that is, having picking details) is used. When picking is complete, either all the needed products will have been retrieved or only some of them (possibly none). The results of picking must be fed back to the item included on the pick list (the picking detail in this case) so that the proper handling can be done. For example, if only a part of the order was picked, you can wait for the remaining pieces before shipping the order, or you can ship a partial order and back-order the missing pieces.

Figure 9-4 shows an example of creating a pick list. Two orders' picking details are included in the pick list. One is for 13 pencils and 12 erasers, and the other is for 6 pencils. The generated pick list is for 19 pencils (13 + 6) and 12 erasers. The items in the pick list are associated with the items in the picking detail that make them up.

Figure 9-5 shows what happens when the pick list is confirmed. In this example, all 19 pencils were picked and that portion of each order is now shippable. Because all the items in order 2 are now shippable, that order can be shipped. On the other hand, order 1 still needs erasers. When the eraser picking was confirmed, only 10 of the requested 12 were available. The order is notified and can decide whether a partial order should be shipped (and a back-order initiated) or the order held.

The List Generation pattern encompasses the creation, control, and processing of the list (and reflects that processing back to the items used to build the list). Depending on the application, policies can be used in a number of places, allowing customization by the application provider when the pattern is used by a core business process.

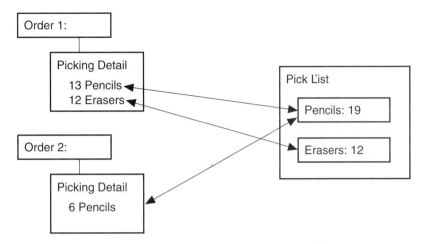

Figure 9-4. Generating a Pick List Using the List Generation Pattern

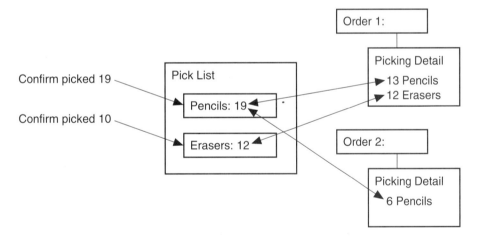

Figure 9-5. Confirming the Pick List

Summary

This chapter describes the core business processes and explains how to use them. It describes dependencies among the core business processes and discusses how these dependencies are implemented and managed. The patterns that are first used by the core business processes are also introduced. Chapter 10 gives an overview of the domains supported by the core business processes.

10 ***Core Business Process Domains***

The core business processes provided by SanFrancisco are the business objects and processes that provide the core for an application in a particular business domain. Each core business process was developed in cooperation with solution providers who are experienced in developing applications in the target domain. This expertise allowed IBM to identify business objects and processes that can be used as the basis for many types of applications within the domain. For example, a number of the domain experts had experience building international applications, which must work with more than one currency. This experience shows up in the core business processes as very robust support for multiple currencies that do not unduly complicate those applications that work with a single currency. The solution providers working on SanFrancisco also used their experience to help identify locations where customization points (extension points) needed to be added to each core business process. For example, whenever solution providers recognized that application users would need to change business rules easily for a particular application, policies of some form were placed in the core business process.

Currently, SanFrancisco provides the following core business processes:

- General Ledger (GL)
- Accounts Receivable/Accounts Payable (AR/AP)
- Warehouse Management (WM)
- Order Management (OM)

An in-depth description of each core business process is not only outside the scope of this book but also would require familiarity with each business domain. The following sections give a high-level overview of each of the core business processes. Each overview consists of the following:

- Domain description: A brief overview of the CBP's domain. This is not intended to be a complete coverage of the particular domain but instead focuses on the knowledge you need to understand what SanFrancisco provides.
- Core business process overview: A brief overview of the core business process. This is not a complete description of the CBP but instead focuses on the major business objects (structure) and business processes provided by SanFrancisco.

Each section is written to stand alone. However, because the Order Management CBP is built on top of the Warehouse Management CBP, it would be beneficial to read the Warehouse Management section before you read the Order Management section.

Detailed information on each of the core business processes is provided by its respective User Guide, Requirements, and Scenarios, all of which are included in SanFrancisco.

The General Ledger Core Business Process

The General Ledger (GL) core business process provides the core business objects and processes for an application that records and reports the financial status of your company. It is here that changes to the financial status of the company are processed. These financial status changes are produced by various subsystems, ledgers (such as those built on the AR/AP CBP), and the other applications of your company.

The main purpose of a general ledger application is to allow analysis of the flow of money in your company. This analysis is used to manage your business, to report to your investors, and to fulfill legal requirements.

The Domain

There are two major types of accounting systems: double entry and single entry. In *double entry* systems, all entries are made into two accounts. This system allows the books to be easily checked for correctness because two identical errors must be made for a mistake to be missed. In *single entry* systems, only one entry is made. Although there are still some single entry systems, double entry systems are more common. Also, a double entry system can be made to appear as a single entry system by presenting a single entry user interface that makes the other entries automatically. For these reasons, SanFrancisco supports double entry systems.

Chart of Accounts

At the heart of any general ledger is the *chart of accounts*, which defines the accounting structure used by your company. This accounting structure defines the information to be kept in your general ledger and its level of granularity. The accounting structure is defined by the legal requirements of the country (or countries) you are dealing with, the accounting principles you follow, and the way you run your business.

The key part of a chart of accounts is the *account* and its associated attributes. However, because the chart of accounts differs among countries and businesses, it can contain a wide variety of accounts. For example, financial status could be analyzed by major code, department, and personnel. The *major code* is an identifier, traditionally numeric, that is associated with the type of account. The major code could be numbers for cash, accounts payable, owner's equity, office supplies, and so on. The major code is usually used for standard analysis or reporting (discussed later). The *departments* are the departments within your company, designated by numbers such as 100, 200, and so on. These numbers are used to analyze how particular departments are doing. This allows you to answer questions such as "How much did department 100 spend on office supplies?" The *personnel* accounts are used to analyze individual employees—for example, comparing a salesperson's expenses to the revenue he or she brought in.

Figure 10-1 shows how the concept of an account varies by country. For a U.S. company, the major code, department, and personnel elements together define the account. One value for each element must be specified for a valid account. When such an element is not applicable, an additional entry is needed. For example, in the case of personnel a "Not associated with Personnel" value is defined. Other countries define the major code as the account and allow the other pieces to be optionally specified. The French system, for example, has two pieces that define the account. One piece is mandated by the government and must be used in all reports. However, these mandated accounts are not sufficient for the internal management of a business. Thus a second piece is defined for internal accounts. The combination of the government account piece and the internal account piece is the "account." One or the other must be specified. All other pieces are optional.

The key factors driving the account definition are government regulations, the type of business you are in, and the way you run your business.

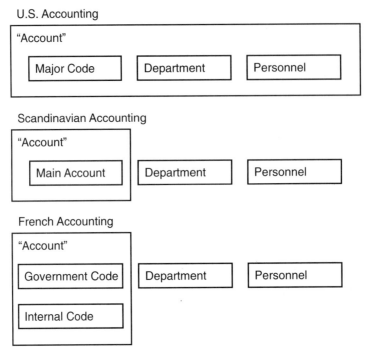

Figure 10-1. What Is an Account?

Journals and Dissections

The next important thing supported by a general ledger application is the recording of financial transactions against the accounts; transactions are created, worked with, and finalized. A *transaction* consists of a number of pairings of an account with an amount. These pairings, called *dissections* by SanFrancisco, are sometimes called *journal entries* in U.S. accounting. The collection of dissections is called a *journal*. A journal is kept for a particular fiscal period. Usually, a journal's credits and debits (from its dissections) balance.

Figure 10-2 shows an example of the journal that would result from paying rent. One dissection affects the rent account (debit), and the other one affects the bank account (credit). The journal balances because the total credits equal the total debits. This example is based on double entry bookkeeping. (Double entry bookkeeping and the concept of credit versus debit are not covered here. They are covered in detail in introductory accounting books.)

The dissection cannot simply hold on to a decimal number but instead must hold on to a transaction value (see Chapter 7). In this way, you can record financial interactions in which the interaction is in a currency (prime currency)

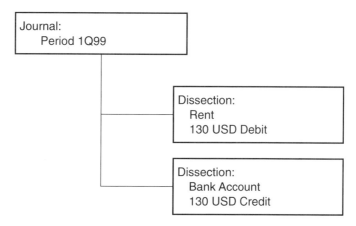

Figure 10-2. Journal Example

that is different from the currency you manage your business in (base currency). For example, if you keep your books in U.S. dollars (base currency) but you pay the rent in German deutsche marks (prime currency), you would want to keep track of the fact that you paid 208 DEM, which at the time was equivalent to 130 USD.

Another consideration is that in some cases two base currencies are needed—for example, when a company in one country is owned by a company in a different country. Usually the parent company consolidates the books of the two companies to get an overall view of how the combination of the companies is doing. This can be done in a number of ways. One is to calculate totals in one currency, convert them to the other, and use those figures. In some cases, this level of granularity is not enough, and, instead, each dissection must contain the prime currency and both base currencies. One special example is the transition to the euro, in which the countries transitioning to the euro want to temporarily have two base currencies. This approach allows a gradual transition to the euro and then the complete removal of the original currency.

Quantity Dissections

In some cases, you must record quantities in your general ledger. For example, you may want to record not only a value but also the quantity associated with it. If you were to purchase chickens, you might want to record how much you spent and how many chickens you bought. This support allows you to perform analysis related to quantities. For example, suppose that you allocate a rental space expense to each department depending on how much space it is using. You can use the quantity to record the amount of space used for that allocation. In this way, you can analyze how much floor space is used by a department and calculate the cost of increasing the space.

Budget Journals

Budgets are prepared in a similar way to journals. The big difference is that budgets do not normally balance. Usually, you create a budget for a reason, such as preparing the budget for the first quarter, and then you perform an analysis to see how the business is doing with respect to that budget. Budgets require the same processes used by the other journals.

Journal Processing

Journals are usually created, worked with, and then posted. *Posting* a journal involves ensuring that it is valid and then committing it. Normally, after a journal is posted, it can no longer be changed, but in some countries a journal can be *unposted* and changed. In this case, there is usually another indicator that defines whether the journal can be unposted. For example, in Italy a journal can be unposted until it is included in a report sent to the Italian government. What makes a journal valid depends on government regulations, the type of business you are in, and the way you run your business.

Reports and Balances

To manage the flow of money and to report the company's financial status to its owners, reports must be generated. Two common reports are the *balance sheet*, which shows assets and liabilities, and the *profit and loss statement* (or *income statement*), which shows the revenue and costs. These reports are generated by using the accounts and their attributes from the chart of accounts. For example, we could generate a report of all sales commissions by salespeople. These reports can either be printed (such as an annual report) or electronic (during analysis). The latter allows examination of the details of the entries.

Year-end Processing

Often, special processing is done at the end of the year—for example, closing out accounts or generating reports.

Revaluation

An international general ledger application supports revaluation of accounts that are held in a currency other than the base currency of your company—for example, when you have a Japanese bank account that is in yen but you manage your business in U.S. dollars. You periodically determine the current value of the account's balance in your base currency—in the example, the equivalent U.S. dollars for the Japanese yen balance of the account. This revaluation normally results in a currency gain or loss. Only general ledger accounts are revaluated in the general ledger. Other revaluation is done in the other ledgers, which then update the general ledger. For example, the AR/AP provides support for revaluing log items and ledger items, such as invoices.

Banks

A general ledger application (or a separate application) provides support for dealing with bank transactions, including recording your financial interactions with the bank, representing the bank statement, and reconciling the bank statement. This support includes appropriately updating the correct accounts—for example, when you deposit in a currency other than the bank currency and a currency gain or loss is realized because the bank uses a different exchange rate.

The Core Business Process

Now let's look at each of the accounting elements just discussed in terms of how it is implemented in SanFrancisco.

Chart of Accounts

As discussed earlier, the definition of an account in the chart of accounts varies quite a bit. To support any definition of an account, SanFrancisco uses the concept of a *PostingCombination* business object. A PostingCombination is made up of *AnalysisGroups*, which define the pieces of the PostingCombination, such as major code, department, or personnel. Each AnalysisGroup consists of a set of valid values called AnalysisCodes. So to define a particular account, a Posting-Combination containing a set of AnalysisCodes is created.

Figure 10-3 shows the relationship of the SanFrancisco approach to U.S. accounting. In this case, an entry for each of the AnalysisGroups must be present for the PostingCombination to be valid. Figure 10-4 shows an example of a valid PostingCombination.

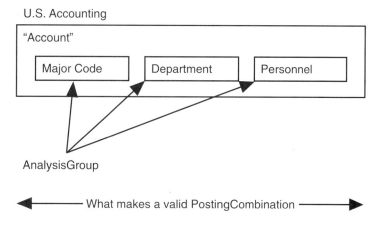

Figure 10-3. PostingCombination

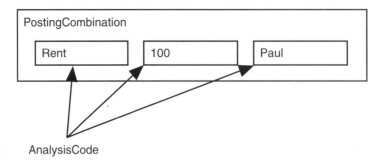

Figure 10-4. Valid PostingCombination Example

The posting combination, along with the ability to define what makes a valid posting combination, lets you customize the GL to support almost any chart of accounts.

For example, to support a Scandinavian chart of accounts you would create a Main Account AnalysisGroup and then customize the policy to require that an AnalysisCode from the Main Account AnalysisGroup must be present for the PostingCombination to be valid.

In addition to defining the pieces and valid combination of the pieces of the account, you must identify the type of account. GL provides support for identifying whether the account is a balance account (keeping track of assets and liabilities on the balance sheet) or a profit and loss account (keeping track of revenue and cost as part of the profit and loss statement). Other attributes are associated with particular combinations, and others can be added as part of customization. You can define these attributes (and the type) so they apply to more than one combination. For example, suppose that department 100 has been disbanded. You can say that all posting combinations that contain the analysis code 100 from the analysis group Department can no longer be used (post inhibited).

Journals and Dissections

GL provides business objects for Journal and Dissection that are identical to those described earlier. GL adds the ability to identify the type of the Journal—for example, identifying a bank journal—which can be used to drive special processing or display of the Journal. You can also identify the source of the Journal and the Dissections and thereby prohibit the changing of a Journal or Dissection outside the process that created it. For example, a Journal and the Dissection created by a bank transaction (interaction with the bank) should be changed only by changing the bank transaction, not manually.

SanFrancisco does not provide full dual base currency support, although an application developer could customize the GL to support it. SanFrancisco does, however, provide support for companies transitioning to the euro as their base currency.

Quantity Dissections

The GL supports quantities by associating a QuantityDissection business object with a Dissection. The use of quantities is completely optional, but if they are added to a Dissection, one or more can be added to a single Dissection. We could have one Dissection with an amount paid that has two associated QuantityDissections: one for the number of chickens, and the other for the number of pounds of chickens. A value is not required in a Dissection if it has one or more associated QuantityDissections; you can record the quantities alone.

Budget Journals

GL handles budget journals in the same way that it handles regular journals. To create a budget journal, you create a regular Journal and add a BudgetProfile to it. A *BudgetProfile* is an identifier of the budget this Journal is associated with. For example, "1st Quarter 1999 budget" could be a Budget profile.

Using a regular Journal allows all the processes that support regular Journals to be used with the budget journals. Budget journals do not usually have to balance. The journal validation policy checks whether the Journal being validated is a budget journal and, if it is, skips checking whether the Journal balances. If this arrangement differs from your requirements, it can be customized.

GL Business Processes

Now let's look at how the General Ledger core business process supports the related day-to-day business processes that companies typically carry out.

Journal Processing

A journal can be created, suspended, validated, and posted. The GL lets you customize the definition of what makes a journal valid. This validation is broken into

- Validation of the PostingCombination, which is defined by your chart of accounts
- Validation of each Dissection
- Validation of the Journal itself

For example, to validate a Dissection you might check that when a specific currency is required for a Dissection's PostingCombination, it matches the prime currency of the Dissection. Journal validation involves things such as ensuring that the Dissections balance and that the Journal's fiscal period allows posting (is open). These policies can be customized to meet your application requirements.

By default, GL Journals cannot be unposted, but they can easily be customized to allow unposting.

Reports and Balances

GL does not provide any reports; instead, it supports building reports by letting you retrieve the balances based on an extensive and flexible set of criteria. For example, you can request the balances for all profit and loss accounts in periods 1 through 4. These criteria are specified using a key, one of the generalized mechanisms in the CBO layer (see Chapter 7). This allows your application to customize the criteria on which balances can be retrieved. Balances that are needed often or quickly can be cached for quick retrieval using support based on the Cached Balances generalized mechanism from the CBO layer (also discussed in Chapter 7).

Year-end Processing

An example of year-end processing is supplied with GL. You can customize this example to do whatever processing your application needs to do.

Revaluation

Revaluation of general ledger accounts is supported by the GL. You can perform revaluation in two stages or combine it into one stage. The first stage is to determine the revalued values for a specific set of criteria, such as only bank accounts. The second stage is to apply the revaluation, creating the appropriate dissections to revalue the bank accounts.

Banks

The GL provides two kinds of support for working with banks. One type is for recording and managing interactions with the banks in the form of BankTransaction business objects. The other is to reconcile the BankTransactions with the statements from the bank.

The BankTransaction lets you record and manage many different interactions with the bank. For example, the BankTransaction could represent a deposit slip that contains multiple checks (as *BankMovements*; see Chapter 7). The processing of the BankTransaction depends on what it represents. In the case of a deposit slip, the deposit could be in a currency other than the currency used by the bank. In this case, the deposit must be reflected in the general ledger at the time of the deposit and again when the actual exchange rate used by the bank is known. The currency gain (or loss) is reflected in the general ledger.

The GL supports a BankStatement business object that represents the statement from the bank. Its entries can be reconciled with BankTransactions. Because determining which BankTransaction to reconcile with depends heavily on how a particular business and a particular bank operate, it is not provided by the GL. For example, if your bank lets you use a memo field that shows up on the statement, you could use that for reconciliation.

The Accounts Receivable/Accounts Payable Core Business Process

The Accounts Receivable/Accounts Payable (AR/AP) core business process, as the name implies, supports handling accounts receivable (money owed to you) and accounts payable (money you owe). Although the core business process supports accounts receivable and accounts payable in a combined manner, they are usually thought of as separate.

The Domain: Accounts Receivable

An accounts receivable application supports handling the invoices you send to customers and the payments you receive from customers. The goal is to manage this relationship so that you are assured that you get the money you are owed and that you correctly handle the money you are paid. For example, you want to take action when someone has not paid a 1,000 USD invoice on time. However, it would be a mistake to contact the customer and then find out that the payment was made but not handled correctly on your part. In some cases an invoice involves only one payment, but it can have payment terms associated with it, such as terms of 30% due in one month, an additional 30% due in two months, and the remaining 40% due in three months. (See Chapter 7 for more information on payment terms.) Payment terms break the invoice into installments. In the example shown in Figure 10-5, a 100 USD invoice issued on July 1 would have three installments: 30 USD due on August 1; 30 USD due on September 1; and 40 USD (the remainder) due on October 1. An invoice that involves only one payment would have only a single installment.

An accounts receivable application must support things such as allocating payments to installments, handling overdue invoices, managing payment

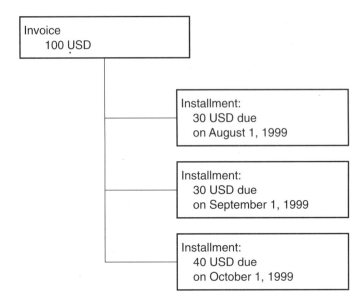

Figure 10-5. Accounts Receivable Invoice Example

forms that have a life cycle, and, for international companies, handling invoices and payments in a variety of currencies.

Allocating payments to installments involves determining which installment, or installments, is being paid by a payment. For example, if we receive a 60 USD payment, we can allocate it to the first two 30 USD installments in the example. Allocation can be as simple as matching a payment to a single installment or matching a payment with installments and making adjustments. Adjustments include a discount for an early payment or the writing off of a small discrepancy. A common situation involves writing off a difference between the payment and the total of the installments when it is less than some amount. If the payment in the example had been 59.50 USD instead of 60.00 USD, a 0.50 USD adjustment could be made so that the payment could be fully allocated to the two installments of 30 USD.

Figure 10-6 shows an example of allocating a payment to the installments of an invoice. In this example, the invoice has been paid in full even though it did not have to be. In this case the payment of 100 USD is allocated to three installments: 30 USD to the first and second to cover them completely, and 40 USD to the last installment.

Managing payments that have a life cycle involves determining when you can finally consider the money yours. If you are paid in cash, it is yours immediately, but some other forms of payment involve a period of time during which you cannot assume the money will remain yours, such as when you

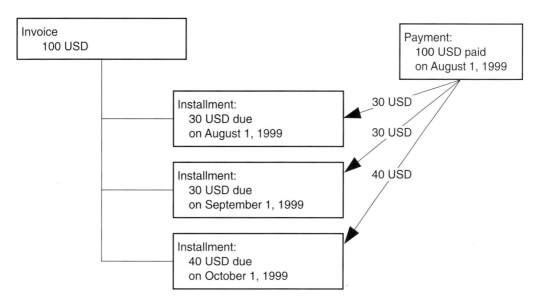

Figure 10-6. Accounts Receivable Allocation Example

receive a promissory note as a payment. In some countries, a promissory note can be treated in a special way. You can deposit the promissory note at the bank, but for a period of time the note might be rejected by the customer. You can then either resubmit the note or contact the customer for resolution.

Figure 10-7 shows an example of one possible life cycle for a promissory note. First, the note is received and at some point is deposited at the bank. The note is then either rejected immediately or, after 90 days, is considered finalized. If the note is rejected, it can either be resubmitted or written off, in which case the note is considered bad. There are a number of variations. One is that the note is sold to a collection agency.

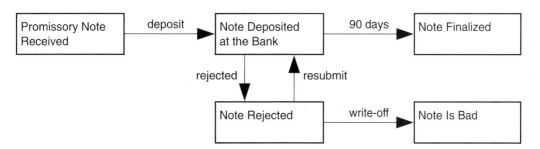

Figure 10-7. Accounts Receivable Promissory Note Life Cycle

For international companies, invoices and payments often occur in currencies other than the currency in which the business is managed. This means that you can allocate transactions in either the prime or the base currency. It also means that until the invoice is paid, the actual base currency value is not known. However, if your company uses the accrual method of accounting, you cannot wait until the invoice is paid to reflect it in the financial status of your company or the business partner account. For example, if an invoice is issued for 160 DEM when the exchange rate is 1.6 DEM/1.0 USD, the base currency value is 100 USD. However, suppose that when the payment comes in for 160 DEM, the exchange rate is 1.7 DEM/1.0 USD, the base currency value is now 96.97 USD. This means that the value of the payment is 3.03 USD less than you assumed when the invoice was issued. This difference is a realized currency loss. It is realized because you now know the final exchange rate. Unrealized gains or losses occur when you revalue the invoices to update your assumptions about the exchange rate to a more recent exchange rate. This is especially important when the exchange rate is very volatile because the assumption about the exchange rate is invalidated very quickly.

The Domain: Accounts Payable

An accounts payable application helps you manage what you owe your suppliers. This involves handling the invoices sent to you and your payment of them. The goal is to manage this relationship so that you pay the correct invoices at the correct time. What is correct varies from application to application and business to business. For example, your application may require that an incoming invoice be approved before it is eligible to be paid, thereby reducing the likelihood that you will pay an incorrect invoice. The invoice may involve only one payment, or it may have payment terms that define a set of installments. An invoice that involves only one payment has a single installment.

Figure 10-5, presented earlier, shows an accounts receivable invoice; the same information is needed for an accounts payable invoice. The only difference is whether we are owed the money or we owe the money.

An accounts payable application must support things such as determining when to pay each installment and allocating the payments to the installments. Determining when to pay each installment can be simple or complex. Suppose that your company does not have a cash flow problem and is able to pay all its installments on time. You need only pick the installments that are due and pay them. However, suppose that your competitor has serious cash flow problems and has only a certain amount available to pay toward its installments each month. He must carefully choose whom to pay and whom to put off paying. Usually, this process is a combination of automatic and manual processes. The automatic process, called a *payment run*, gathers the installments according to a particular set of criteria, such as those due before a certain date. The generated list can then be modified manually, possibly excluding some payments or including others. The criteria you use to generate the list and the changes you make to it manually are tied closely to how you do business. For example, in deciding whether to pay a particular installment, some businesses compare the late charge to what could be made on the same amount if it were invested.

After the installments have been chosen, the payments are allocated to record which installments were paid. Figure 10-6, presented earlier, shows allocation for accounts receivable; for accounts payable, this same picture is reversed. You are providing the payment to your supplier's invoice rather than handling a customer payment.

As with accounts receivable, for international companies invoices and payments occur in currencies other than the currency in which the business is managed. This means that amounts can be allocated in either the prime or the base currency. It also means that until you pay the invoice, the actual base currency value is not known. However, you cannot wait until the invoice is paid to reflect it in the financial status of your company or the business partner account. For example, if an invoice is issued for 550 FF when the exchange rate is 5.5 FF/1.0 USD, the base currency value is 100 USD. However, suppose that when we make the payment for 550 FF, the exchange rate is 5.0 FF/1.0 USD, so the base currency value is 110 USD. This means that the value of the invoice is now 10 USD more than we assumed when the invoice was received. This difference is a realized currency loss. It is realized because we now know the final exchange rate. Unrealized gains or losses occur when we revalue the invoices to update our assumptions about the exchange rate to a more recent exchange rate. This is especially important when the exchange rate is very volatile because the assumption about the exchange rate is invalidated very quickly.

Other Business Ledgers

The AR/AP name for the core business process tells only part of the story. The CBP can support other types of business ledgers that do processing similar to the accounts receivable and accounts payable. For example, an employee payroll application could be written that handles all the different items that go into a paycheck. For example, if employees pay for part of their medical benefits, a fixed amount comes out of each paycheck. You could handle this by creating an invoice (or something like it) with installments for each paycheck in the fixed amount.

Updating the General Ledger

All changes to the financial status of the company must be reflected in the general ledger. The accounts receivable application updates the general ledger when an invoice is created and when it is paid. When a payment has a life cycle, each portion of the life cycle that affects the financial status is reflected in the general ledger. An accounts payable application updates the general ledger when an invoice is received and when it is paid. The same principle applies to other business ledgers.

The Core Business Process

The developers of SanFrancisco, working with domain experts, noticed similarities between all accounts receivable, accounts payable, and general business ledgers. This observation led them to create generalizations of the common application elements that can be used to build any of the applications described earlier.

Ledger Item

The key generalization identified by the developers of SanFrancisco was the *LedgerItem* business object. A LedgerItem can be used to represent an invoice, payment, or any other item in a ledger that has a value. Each LedgerItem consists of one or more Installment business objects, with a payment being represented by a LedgerItem with a single Installment.

Figure 10-8 shows the invoice described earlier represented by a Ledger-Item. As before, the LedgerItem consists of three Installments.

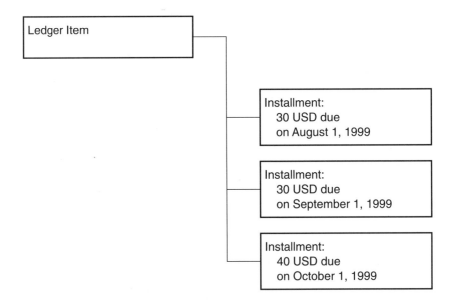

Figure 10-8. Ledger Item for an Invoice

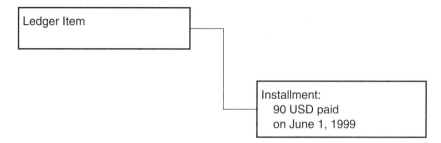

Figure 10-9. Ledger Item for a Payment

Figure 10-9 shows an example of a payment represented by a LedgerItem. The difference is that an Installment is used to hold the value of the payment. Note that the difference between the two LedgerItems is that one is a credit and the other is a debit.

AR/AP's LedgerItem provides a flexible way to support whatever you want in your application. For example, one thing that can occur in both accounts receivable and accounts payable applications is a credit note. A *credit note* is issued when the customer has overpaid and you must refund money or when you have returned items and should be refunded money. A credit note can easily be represented by a LedgerItem. The difference is that a credit note you issue is a debit and a credit note issued to you is a credit.

Log Items

Within the accounts payable application you may need to treat an item specially until it is approved. For this purpose SanFrancisco provides the more general LogItem business object. A LogItem allows you to represent an unapproved item and, when it is approved, to change it into a LedgerItem. A LogItem is very similar to a LedgerItem. It, too, is made up of Installments.

A LogItem is also flexible. You can use it in your application for anything that must be approved. For example, in an accounts receivable application you could add the ability to approve payments before they are applied.

Ledger Account

Another generalization is the *LedgerAccount* business object, which is used to represent the account with which the LogItems and LedgerItems are associated. In the case of an accounts receivable application, the customers are the LedgerAccounts. In the case of an accounts payable application, the LedgerAccounts are the suppliers. For a payroll business ledger, the LedgerAccounts would be the employees.

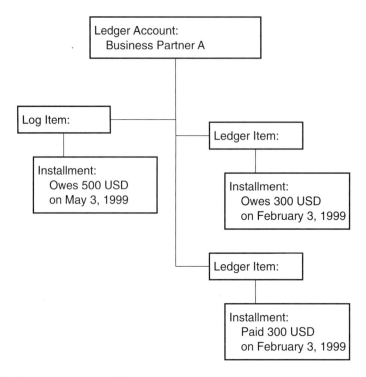

Figure 10-10. Ledger Account Example

Figure 10-10 shows an example of an accounts payable application's LedgerAccount. The LedgerAccount is for business partner A, which is a customer. Currently, there are two LedgerItems. One is an invoice for 300 USD, and the other is a payment for 300 USD. There is also a LogItem: an invoice for 500 USD that is waiting to be approved.

The use of a LedgerAccount with LedgerItems and LogItems allows you to define whatever you need as LedgerAccounts. For example, in a payroll application you would have LedgerAccounts for employees.

AR/AP Processes

Now let's look at how the AR/AP core business process supports the related day-to-day business processes that companies typically carry out.

Allocation

Allocation is a process performed between installments on LedgerItems for the same LedgerAccount. For example, in an accounts receivable application, this would be the invoices, payments, and credit notes (LedgerItems) of a customer (LedgerAccount). This generalization of allocation lets you allocate any LedgerItems with any other as long as the credits and debits match. You make adjustments by creating new LedgerItems containing an Installment for the adjustment; thus an adjustment is simply another LedgerItem involved in the allocation.

Figure 10-11 shows the equivalent allocation of a ledger item Installment to the allocation shown earlier in Figure 10-6. You make the allocation by making the "debits equal the credits." In this case, this means that the payment (100) equals the three amounts due (30 + 30 + 40 = 100).

AR/AP's support for allocation is flexible, allowing you to control which allocations are valid in which situations and providing some customizable automatic processing for things such as handling write-offs, discounts, and currency revaluations. You can also handle allocation between LedgerItems from different LedgerAccounts. This is necessary when a customer's parent

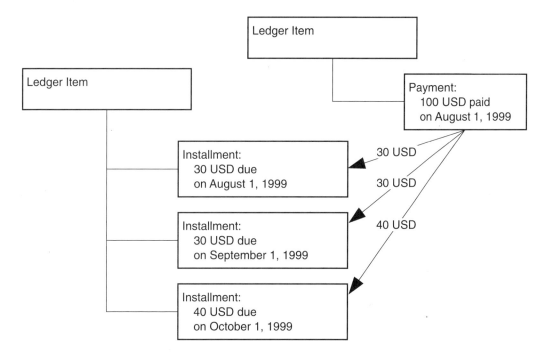

Figure 10-11. Allocation Example

company pays all the invoices for all its subcompanies. The invoice will be for the subcompany, and the payment for the parent company.

AR/AP also supports *deallocation*. If an error is made in allocating, it can be deallocated and reallocated correctly—for example, if a parent company payment was accidentally attributed to the wrong subcompany.

Payment Runs

SanFrancisco does not support deciding which installments to pay, but it supports processing the accounts payable installments to pay, called *payment runs*. You can customize your application to generate the payments in accordance with your requirements. For example, in accounts receivable, you could decide to return overpayments only after 30 days and only after the overpayment is applied to any outstanding amount the customer owes. This support works with LedgerAccounts and LedgerItems, so it can also be used by an accounts receivable application to handle credit notes that need to be paid.

Collection Documents

SanFrancisco's *CollectionDocument* business object allows an application to provide any special processing required for a payment. The collection document support uses the LifeCycle pattern (see Chapter 7) to allow customization of the collection document processing. For example, in Figure 10-7, you could add a statement for sending the promissory note to a collection agency.

Currency Revaluation

AR/AP supports the currency revaluation processing of LogItems and LedgerItems. If you have a LogItem or LedgerItem in a currency other than the currency you manage your business in, you can revalue it to account for exchange rate fluctuations. This support is for unrealized gains or losses. Realized gains and losses are handled during allocation.

Updating the General Ledger

In most cases, AR/AP automatically handles the processing of updates to the general ledger. The AR/AP does this through the Interface to General Ledger category in the Common Business Objects layer. For example, in an accounts receivable application, when you allocate a payment you also update the general ledger's account for the financial status associated with the business partner for the invoice. The AR/AP allows the application developer to customize the point at which the updates are made to the general ledger.

The Warehouse Management Core Business Process

The Warehouse Management (WM) core business processes provides the core business objects and processes for an application that defines and manages products sold or manufactured by a business.

The Domain

The key things that a warehouse application deals with are products, warehouses, and inventory. It tracks the products as they are received, stored, retrieved, and shipped.

The application must know which products are available in which warehouse. Some products may require special handling; for example, some parts have their own unique serial numbers. The application must allow for tracking those items by their serial numbers while they are in inventory and when they are shipped to a customer. Products may have special requirements—such as size, storage needs, handling considerations, and frequency of picking—that affect how and where they are stocked in the warehouse.

The warehouse manages space and the limitations of that space. Managing the space involves organizing the warehouse, possibly dividing it into multiple zones and locations. The limitations on the space may be its physical dimensions or some other attribute, such as whether it can handle frozen food.

Inventory is the amount of the product in each warehouse. Inventory is especially important when you analyze the inventory levels—for example, when you forecast to determine whether, and how much of, a product should be purchased. It is also important when you determine whether a requested amount of product is available—for example, during an availability check during order entry. Inventory of a particular product is often sorted by characteristics such as quality (for example, first quality versus second quality or damaged goods) or the type of processing it is undergoing (for example, goods in quality control).

Figure 10-12 shows an example of two warehouses that contain the products pen, model train, and ice cream. Warehouse 1 does not have zones or locations. Warehouse 1's inventory is 35 pens, 119 model trains, and 345 boxes of ice cream. Warehouse 2, on the other hand, has two zones—A and B—and one location in zone B, the freezer. In this warehouse the inventory is 23 pens in zone A, 2,004 model trains—with 4 in zone A and 2,000 in zone B—and 67 boxes of ice cream in zone B in the freezer location.

One process in warehouse management is replenishment, which involves ordering more of a product when the inventory falls below a certain level. Many factors determine how and from where you replenish. What you can use as replenishment sources and how you pick the sources vary from business to business.

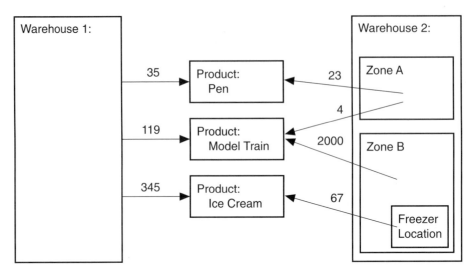

Figure 10-12. Warehouse Example

When a product is delivered to the receiving dock of the company, it is the responsibility of the warehouse personnel to verify the product with the associated document (such as a purchase order) and to prepare the products to be put into inventory. Upon receipt, the product may be applied to back orders instead of being moved into stock. Products can also be diverted to quality inspection. The rest of the products go into the inventory of that warehouse.

Removing a product from the warehouse is called picking. In this process a list of products and the quantity to retrieve are given to a person, called a picker, or a machine to retrieve. This pick list may include the specific location and zone from which the product should be picked. In the example in Figure 10-12, the pick list would indicate whether model trains should be picked from zone A or zone B.

Picked products are often bundled in varying ways—for example, to pull all goods for a particular customer—or to take advantage of numerous orders going to the same city by grouping them on a pallet for shipment by truck.

An important periodic process is a physical inventory (also called a stock take). This involves counting the product in the warehouse and verifying that it matches the inventory. The time interval varies among businesses. Some businesses make a count of inventory of high-value items every month and of low-value items every six months. Other businesses count inventory for a particular stock location only when the expected count for that location should equal zero. The handling of discrepancies between the count and the book inventory also varies. For example, you might handle the discrepancy by first doing a recount and then, if there is still a discrepancy, having a supervisor look into it and decide what should be done.

Quality control is another activity that must be supported by the warehouse. Quality control is performed when the product is received at the warehouse. A product that is currently in quality control must be managed separately from the normal inventory because it is not available to be picked.

Products can be moved between stock locations or even warehouses. For example, the stock may be consolidated to make it easier to manage. The request, movement, and receiving of the stock in the other location (or warehouse) must be documented and inventory updated.

Figure 10-13 shows a sample flow of products in the warehouse. Products come into reception and go into the warehouse, to quality control, or to fill a sales order (back order). Products are picked from specific warehouse zones (and locations), and the picked product is sent to quality control or to fill sales orders. When quality control is finished with a product, it returns the product to the warehouse. (Another business might allow products to go straight from quality control to fill sales orders). A stock movement moves a product between zone A and zone B.

Updating the General Ledger

The inventory represents an asset of the company, and, when inventory changes, the change in financial status must be reflected in the general ledger.

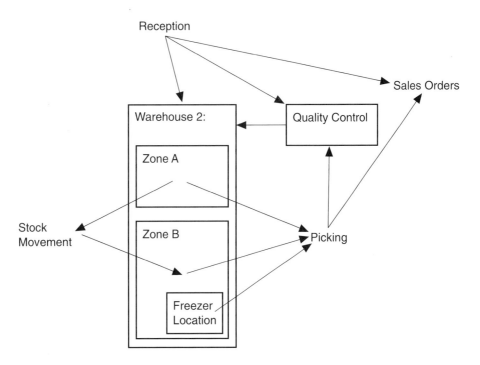

Figure 10-13. Warehouse Processing

For example, when a product is moved from warehouse 1 to warehouse 2, the value of the assets in warehouse 1 must be diminished and that of warehouse 2 increased.

The financial status also must be updated when a product is sold. This requires that the cost of the product be available so that the cost of goods sold can be updated. Costing is done differently by different businesses. There are a number of standard ways to do costing. For example, in the FIFO (first in, first out) method, you behave as if the product that has been in the warehouse the longest is the one that has been sold. Usually, you choose one way of calculating costs (sometimes because of legal requirements) and use the other ways of calculating cost for "what if" analysis.

The Core Business Process

The WM core business process provides the core structure and processes for a warehouse application. The core business objects it provides are Product, Warehouse, and Inventory. WM also provides a number of core processes so that they can be customized to the requirements of an application.

Product

The Product is the main business object in WM. It allows you to describe the products the warehouses will deal with. Along with the basic information about a product, you can manage products by lot or by serial number. A product is lot-controlled when you must identify which products were manufactured together. For example, consider the textiles business. Bolts of material from different lots are not exactly the same color. When you manufacture a garment, the material used to produce it must come from the same lot. You typically use serial number control, on the other hand, when you identify a specific product, such as a car. Serial numbers can be assigned before a product is received in the warehouse, or they can be added at the warehouse, depending on the business.

You can also identify the units a product can be stocked in. For example, for soda, you might use bottle, six-pack, and pallet. After these units are defined, they can be selectively enabled—for example, allowing only six-packs and pallets to be stocked. This definition of units can be used to convert stock between units. This means that a request for six bottles could be filled by a single six-pack.

You can also define a *single-level kit*, one that is made up of kit components in which the kit components cannot themselves be kits. A product can be defined as a kit, a kit component, or neither. For example, if we have the products pens, pencils, and erasers, we could define a "writing kit" product. The "writing kit" would consist of one pen, one pencil, and one eraser. We cannot, however, define a "deluxe writing kit" that contains a "writing kit" and a pad of paper.

Warehouse

The Warehouse business object allows you to represent the layout of the warehouse. The warehouse can be divided into locations, and the locations grouped into stock zones. For example, you could divide your warehouse into locations 1, 2, and 3, and locations 1 and 3 could be a frozen food zone. Defining locations and stock zones allows you to specify their physical limitations, such as the height limitation of the shelves in a location.

You can define which products can go in which warehouses, thereby allowing warehouses to specialize in certain products or product families.

Inventory

WM provides the ability to control inventory. Goods in stock, product reservations (stock that has been set aside to fill specific orders), and future receptions (stock you are planning to receive) are all represented. Inventory is managed at the product granularity; that is, if the product is lot-controlled, inventory is managed at the lot level. The goods in stock can be classified by stock type. This is used to distinguish normal stock from damaged stock, allowing you to ensure that you use only the normal stock when picking or checking the availability of a product. WM supports the updating and maintenance of product balances, which allow you quickly to determine how much of a product is available. Balances that include future receptions and reservations are also available.

Stock transactions are created every time inventory is modified and are maintained on a per product basis. These stock transactions are the basis on which sophisticated data warehousing and analysis tools can be built by applications. An example is the capability to look at the rate at which a product is being sold to determine which replenishment policy should be used for it.

WM Business Processes

WM provides many of the core processes used by a warehouse application. Many of the processes defined by WM serve a wide, diverse market (for example, distribution and manufacturing applications). These processes are designed to be completed by the application (or CBP) using WM. They are introduced in WM so that generic processing can occur in the warehouse application regardless of the source domain of the process. For example, you can merge picking details generated by both distribution and manufacturing processes into a single consolidated pick list at the warehouse management level. This approach also defines a common base for customization in various domains. For example, you might extend various processes differently when implementing a manufacturing application than when doing order entry.

Manual Stock Transactions

A manual stock transaction is used when the inventory is manually increased or decreased. These are cases that are beyond normal system-created stock transactions (such as picking). For example, the discovery of a damaged product requires that the warehouse application be notified so that the product is not included in normal processing, such as product availability checking. This process changes inventory, so the appropriate update to the general ledger is made.

Product Reservations

Product reservations capability allows a specific quantity of products to be reserved in one or more warehouses or locations. This customizable process is used to ensure that the inventory that has been allocated to a particular use is not allocated to another use (unless the first use frees it). For example, when an order is planned, the inventory needed to fill that order can be reserved to ensure that it is not used to plan another order (or for checking product availability).

Costing

Costing provides a means of determining the cost of each product sold. You need this information when determining the cost of goods sold for updating the general ledger and for determining how much profit is made on each item.

Five common ways of calculating costs are provided with WM. It provides the following two transaction-based costing algorithms:

- LIFO: The actual cost of the last goods received is used first.
- FIFO: The actual cost of the first goods received is used first.

It provides three nontransaction-based costing algorithms.

- Average: The cost of goods is defined as the average of all goods received.
- Standard: A cost that is to be used for all stock handled during a particular period is specified, regardless of the actual cost incurred for specific stock being received.
- Latest inbound: The cost of goods is based on the actual cost of the last goods received.

Although these methods are the most common, you can customize your costing method for other costing algorithms.

Normally, you choose one way of calculating costs and use it exclusively for updating the general ledger. This is because changing the costing calculation can make it difficult to analyze the company's financial status and may give misleading results. Also, in many countries, it is illegal to change your costing method during a fiscal year. For example, assuming that the cost of the product is increasing over time, if costs are calculated using LIFO, the highest-cost product is used. If FIFO is used, the lowest-cost product is used. So switching from LIFO to FIFO would make it appear that the company was suddenly more profitable, when only the means of calculating costs was changed. This restriction applies only to the updates to the general ledger. It is common that the other ways of calculating cost are used in "what if" analysis.

Replenishment

The replenishment process in SanFrancisco is used to evaluate inventory with respect to the reorder point (the quantity that should trigger an order) and makes recommendations for orders from a replenishment source (usually a supplier or another warehouse). Replenishment can be customized to a particular application's needs. This includes the ability to define replenishment sources for each product or for each combination of a product and a warehouse.

Availability Checking

Checking the availability of a product is an often-used process. The factors included in this check vary from application to application, so this is a process that can be customized. (It also varies based on the using process; for example, order entry has looser requirements than picking.) Availability checking often takes into account future receptions and reservations. For example, this process could determine that a reservation can be filled by a future reception, and that means the reserved product is available.

WM provides support for automatically converting between the units defined for the product. Thus a check for the availability of six bottles of soda could be filled by a single six-pack of soda.

Physical Inventory (Stock Take)

You use the inventory process when you count the physical stock. You use customizable business rules to determine which products should be included; when the results of the count are entered, the inventory is updated. (The stock balances are updated, the costing information is updated, and the General Ledger is notified of the financial status change.)

-Able/-Ing Processes

The following processes operate against product and warehouse and are intended to be combined by higher-level processes in order management, manufacturing, and so on. All of these follow the -Able/-Ing pattern (see Chapter 7) and are not complete: They are extended by each user. They are a part of the Warehouse Management CBP so that a warehouse application can work with all the extensions in a consolidated manner—for example, by doing picking for a shipment to a customer and picking to supply parts for the manufacturing line in a consolidated manner. Thus a single pick list for use in the warehouse can be generated even though items are being picked for two different reasons.

Reception

Reception, the process of receiving products, can be customized to be adapted to specific business and finance policies. For example, the physical properties of the warehouse locations can be used to determine the optimal location for stocking a product. The addition of products increases the inventory, and that in turn increases the assets of the warehouse, so the General Ledger is notified of the change.

Picking

The picking process is defined as picking products from stock (physically getting them from the warehouse). You can customize the picking process for specific business and finance policies. The picking process selection can include locations, lots, or serial numbers. Pick lists can be generated that include items to be picked for different reasons. When the actual amount picked is confirmed, inventory is adjusted (and that updates the General Ledger).

Planning and Replanning

The planning process is used to determine which warehouse will receive or supply products. The planning process can be customized to provide sophisticated processing. For example, the transport time (how long it takes a product to get from a warehouse to the delivery address) can be taken into account. WM allows transportation times to be established in a flexible and customizable manner. The address, transport zone, and manner of transport are used in what is provided by WM. This criterion is encapsulated in a key so that it can easily be extended to include whatever criteria your application uses when defining transport times.

Quality Control

The quality control process defines the basic process used to manage the inspection activity during reception—for example, inspecting every tenth item received to ensure that it adheres to some standard.

Shipping

The shipping process is used to handle shipping. You can define what must be shipped and what must be shipped together (shipping lists). The shipment process can be customized to your business practices.

Back Order

The back-order handling process is used to selectively incorporate back-ordering support within other processes, such as picking, by using customizable business rules.

The Order Management Core Business Process

Order Management (OM) core business process supports applications that handle order processing.

The Domain

Orders and the way they are handled take on many different forms. For example, in a retail store, the products being sold are picked up by the customer and brought to the cash register. In contrast, in a mail order industry, the products ordered by a customer are retrieved (picked) from the inventory by a picker and are packaged for shipment to the customer. You can see that depending on the business, its products, and its management policy, ordering and order handling can vary dramatically.

The next section focuses on a couple of these order types and the order processing they go through.

Sales Order

A sales order is used when a customer orders a product from you. For the example shown in Figure 10-14, the order processing consists of taking the order, determining how to fill the order (order analysis), retrieving the product from the warehouse to fill the order (picking), shipping it to the customer (shipping), and billing the customer (invoicing).

Figure 10-14. Sales Order Processing

When the customer calls, the information about the customer is taken or verified. This includes things such as the customer number and the billing and shipping addresses. Both addresses are needed because many businesses want the bill to go to an accounting office and the shipment to go to the warehouse. Then the information about this specific order is taken. First, the general information about the order, called the order header, is taken. An example is whether the order should be sent normally or expedited. Next, the specific products being ordered, called the order details (or order lines), are taken. For each product this information includes the quantity ordered, the price, and any discount.

Determining prices and discounts can be complex. It can take into account various factors, each one having a different (company-specific) level of importance. Factors for pricing include product cost, handling, storage, turnover, marketing, equipment, and so on. (Factors for discounts include customer ranking, inventory levels of specific products [high or low], stage of life of the products, turnover, popularity, out-of-season products, and so on.) This level of sophistication is required because prices and discounts directly affect the company's bottom line.

A credit check, using the customizable support in the CBO layer (see Chapter 7), can be done at this point to determine whether credit is to be extended to the customer. Depending on the business, a lack of available credit may not mean the end of the order because options exist such as changing the order into a cash on delivery (COD) order. Some companies also check to ensure that the customer order can be filled. This product availability check allows a business to work with the customer to determine whether the order should be changed (for example, using a substitute product), shipped in parts, or held until the complete order can be shipped.

After the order lines are complete, a determination of how to fill the order is made. This involves determining exactly what stock you are going to ship to the customer, such as which warehouse to ship from. This process is usually referred to as order analysis (or planning).

Then the items can be picked from the planned warehouse..A pick list that a person uses to go physically to the warehouse and get the needed product is generated.

Sometimes an entire order is picked; in other cases, the picking is split up among pickers assigned to particular parts of a warehouse. When an order is picked by multiple pickers, it is usually placed into a *staging area*, where, after the entire order is picked, it is packaged together and shipped. After the order is shipped, in this example, finance is notified, and an invoice is sent to the customer. Finance, such as an accounts receivable application written on the AR/AP CBP (discussed earlier), then ensures that the invoice is paid.

We have just described a perfect case in which everything goes right. Unfortunately, things can go wrong, and other actions may need to be taken.

For example, when the person physically goes to pick the product, there may not be enough to fill the picking request. In this case, you must either try to get the product from another warehouse or ship a partial order. If you ship a partial order, either the shorted items generate a back order, or the customer is notified that it is all that was available.

Figure 10-15 shows an example of a sales order. The customer orders 10 pencils and 42 robots. The customer's credit is good, and the products are available, so, as part of order analysis, it is determined where the product would be taken from. In this case, the pencils all come from one warehouse (A), and the robots come from two (B and C). When the products are picked, 5 of the robots are not available from warehouse C. The customer indicates, during order taking, that it wants 42 but that it will take whatever number is available, up to 42. So nothing will be done about the 5 that are not available (except that they aren't included in the customer's invoice). All the picked products are put into a staging area, where they are packaged and shipped. Then finance is notified,

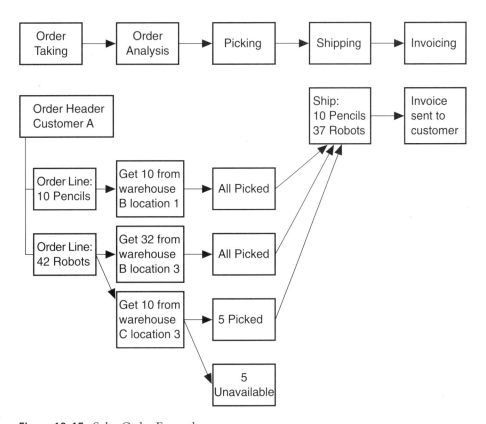

Figure 10-15. Sales Order Example

and an invoice is sent to the customer. If, on the other hand, the customer had requested a complete delivery, it could prevent the shipment of the order and result in a back-order or cause the order to be shipped with a substitute product (if one is defined and the customer allows it).

This example is only one of many ways a sales order can be processed. For example, the order may be invoiced at order time or at shipment time. Also, in some cases, steps are added or removed. If the sales order is recording a sale in a retail store, it deletes the steps of planning, picking, and shipping because the customer picks the item from the shelf, brings it to the cash register, where it is paid for (producing a sales receipt, which is a form of invoice), and then is taken by the customer.

A related Order Management process is the sales quote, which is used to quote a customer a price for an order. In many cases this quote is valid for a period of time and must be retained, or it may be sent to the customer to be available for discussion with the customer. Sales quotes can be thought of as sales orders that go through order taking and then are either deleted or suspended for some period of time.

Purchase Order

A purchase order is used when you want to order something from a supplier. As shown in Figure 10-16, typical order processing involves first determining which product you want to purchase, when you want to purchase it, and from whom you want to purchase it (supplier management). Next, the product is ordered from the selected supplier (creation), and then the product is received when it is shipped to you (receiving). You then perform some level of quality control to ensure that the product is acceptable (quality control). The product is then either placed in the warehouse, shipped to the group that ordered it, or put immediately in staging to fill a sales order.

Determining which purchase orders to create and when to create them (supplier management) can be complex. It can involve issues having to do with forecasting the future of the business as a whole as well as that of a particular product. Supplier management varies from business to business and can be proactive or reactive. In the *proactive* approach, purchase orders are driven by projections of future business. In the *reactive* approach, purchase orders originate in the need to replenish a depleted product.

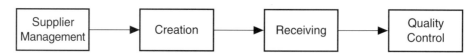

Figure 10-16. Purchase Order Processing

A purchase order requires information similar to that of a sales order. The order header contains information about the supplier, the billing address, and the shipping address. Each product has an order detail element that contains the quantity ordered, the price, and any discount. These details can be determined by negotiation, or they may be based on an established relationship with the supplier, such as a contract that stipulates that a certain product bought in certain volumes can be purchased at a certain price.

When the product is received, it goes to fill sales orders, to the warehouse, or to quality control; finance is notified so that it knows to pay the supplier's invoice. The management of quality control varies from business to business. Some businesses do not perform any quality control, whereas others put all products through quality control. Many businesses send new products or products from a new supplier to quality control for a period of time and then perform periodic spot checks.

The processing just described reflects an ideal case. In real life, the supplier may send a partial shipment and back-order the remainder of the order. Or it could send the wrong amount, or the shipment could be damaged. Also, quality control could determine that the product is unacceptable. Each business handles such situations in its own way.

Figure 10-17 shows an example of two purchase orders and their processing. The first step is forecasting, which determines that 300 phones and 50 fans will be needed next month to meet the expected demand. Looking at the suppliers and the agreements with them, we determine that the order should be split between supplier M and supplier T. A purchase order for 200 phones and 50 fans is sent to supplier M, and a purchase order for 100 phones is sent to supplier T. When the orders are received, we see that supplier M has completely filled the order. The phones are then sent to the warehouse. However, the fans are a new product for the company and are sent to quality control for inspection. Supplier T, on the other hand, has supplied only 50 phones. These phones are sent to the warehouse. The 50 that were not received were not back-ordered by the supplier because it has discontinued the product. So this information must go back to planning to determine whether we should create a purchase order to get the phones from another supplier.

There are a number of variations on a purchase order. One common variation is the addition of an approval step between the planning and creation phases. In some cases this step applies to all products ordered, and in other cases only to expensive items or capital purchases.

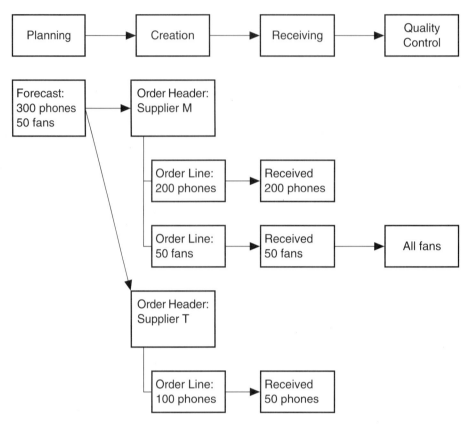

Figure 10-17. Purchase Order Example

Other Order Types

The sales order and purchase order are only two of the many possible order types, and the order processing described here is only one way an order can be processed. Order processing can even involve more than one type of order. For example, a *back-to-back* order is used for products that a company does not keep in its own warehouse but simply orders from a supplier. In this case, we take the order from our customer and issue a purchase order immediately to send the correct product and amount directly to the customer. Then we send an invoice. Two other common orders are sales credit orders and purchase credit orders. These order types are unique in that a sales credit order has many of the same characteristics as a purchase order. For example, the goods must be received into stock, and accounts payable entries must be created for the value of the goods.

The Core Business Process

The developers of SanFrancisco noticed that there were two aspects of order processing that were core to an order management application. The first was the underlying structure of the order, and the second was the processing of the order. Structurally, each order consists of an order header and order lines. As the order lines are processed, they can split into multiple pieces (picking parts of an order from two different warehouses), and each piece can also split into multiple pieces (some of the product is picked, and some is unavailable). This structure reoccurs as the order is being processed, creating a hierarchical structure. The SanFrancisco support for the structure is easily customized to support any order type and any order processing.

In addition to the core structure, the developers of SanFrancisco identified some of the core processes for typical orders. These processes, often built on top of the Warehouse Management CBP and Common Business Objects layer processes, can be used to build a particular order type. For example, an application might allow a supplier to be the replenishment source for a replenishment request in the warehouse, ultimately resulting in a purchase order or orders against that supplier.

Order Structure

The main business object provided by SanFrancisco is the *Order*. This object is used to capture the order header information. The order details are captured in two business objects: the OrderPriceDetail, which captures the product and price information, and the OrderRequestedDetail, which captures the quantity, delivery time, and delivery address information. This split allows product pricing and discounting to be calculated on the aggregate quantity of a product for a particular order because this quantity may affect both price and discount.

Figure 10-18 shows the structure of the sales order described earlier. The sales order's Order object is made up of two OrderPriceDetails (one for pencils and one for robots). Each OrderPriceDetail is made up of one or more OrderRequestDetails. In this example, all the pencils are being shipped to Newark, 30 of the robots are being shipped to St. Louis, and 12 robots are being shipped to Omaha.

This same structure can be used for a purchase order or any other type of order, and it is the core of all orders in SanFrancisco. What differentiates each order is its order type and the associated life cycle. This life cycle defines the allowed order processing and the business rules associated with that processing. For the sales order, this means that after the order is taken, it can be analyzed, picked, shipped, and invoiced. Figure 10-19 (which is a duplicate of Figure 10-14) shows the sales order life cycle.

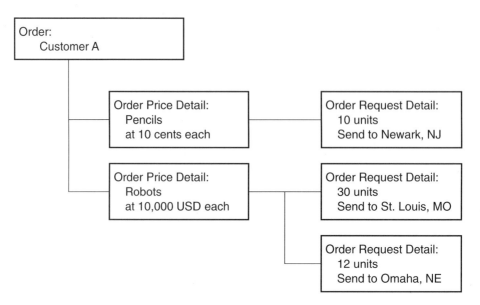

Figure 10-18. Order Example for a Sales Order

SanFrancisco supports this by using the LifeCycle generalized mechanism (see Chapter 7). The progression through the life cycle causes individual details to be created at each stage of the order processing. So for picking, Picking-Details are created; for shipping, ShippingDetails are created. Each of these details may be in a different part of the life cycle for the order. For example, suppose that only part of the product could be picked. One part can now be shipped, but the other part must be processed in another way, such as by being replanned. Rather than create one life cycle for the entire order—something that would be complex—SanFrancisco breaks the life cycle into the individual pieces, each with its own life cycle and the ability to interact with the other pieces. This is achieved by using the -Able/-Ing pattern (see Chapter 7).

Figure 10-19. Sales Order Processing Life Cycle

Order Product

OrderProduct is a business object used to provide an order-management-specific view of WM's product. OrderProduct adds three *views* of a product involved in order processing:

- Products that can only be purchased, such as office supplies
- Products that can only be sold, such as a product manufactured for sale
- Products that can be transferred internally from warehouse to warehouse

OrderProduct also makes it possible to restrict the use of a product (for example, for sales or purchase) to a limited set of units. For example, a business might purchase pallets of soda but sell soda only in cases. In this scenario, the business would set up a purchase order product to enable only the pallet unit of measure. Then the business would set up a sales order product for the same product to enable only the case unit of measure. The product itself would enable both units and define the conversion factor between them.

OrderProduct also supports replacement and substitute products. Replacement products are products that are automatically used in the place of the specified product (for example, special packaging during a promotion that gives the customer some additional amount of the product free of charge). *Substitute* products are products that can be offered as an alternative in case the requested product is not available. For example, if a customer asks for small bottles of aspirin, a larger-size bottle could be suggested as a substitute product if the small bottles are temporarily out of stock.

OM Business Processes

Following are the core business processes provided by OM. Many of these same processes are included in Warehouse Management, but WM focuses on the activities related to the warehouse and products, whereas OM focuses on the order- and order-detail-related aspects of these processes.

Prices and Discounts

The prices and discounts processes let you establish and maintain both inbound and outbound pricing information. OM pricing gives you the sophisticated capability of establishing both base prices and prices using limits. OM discounts give you the flexibility of establishing various types of discount structures for the various criteria, including discount limits. Both pricing and discounts are associated with business rules and business policies that designate the proper information to be used for the particular order situation. Both of them follow the Keyed Attribute Retrieval pattern (see Chapter 9) and can be customized to take into account criteria specific to your business.

Replenishment

Replenishment defines the replenishment resources for a product. OM defines external suppliers (via a purchase order) and internal warehouses. This process is used by Warehouse Management when doing replenishment.

-Able/-Ing Processes

The following processes operate against product and warehouse and can be combined to form the different order types. All of them follow the -Able/-Ing pattern (see Chapter 7) and are interchangeable in that they support being combined in any sequence for a particular order type. Many of them were introduced in the Warehouse Management core business process or Common Business Objects layer and are extended here to add the Order Management context.

Order Acknowledgment

Order acknowledgment supports notification of the customer as the order is processed.

Order Entry

Order entry supports the creation of the order (order header) and the related order detail information, including the policies and validation necessary to ensure the completeness, correctness, and integrity of the order and its content. This process can be completely customized for your particular order type. Order entry supports changing the order and order detail throughout its life cycle. This includes the creation of information, such as financial information, for use by other applications. It also lets you control when changes are prevented from occurring; for example, an order-requested detail cannot be changed after an order has been picked. Order entry supports the deletion of orders and all associated information according to the specifications established by the business. For example, you can customize at what point the order can no longer be deleted.

Planning and Replanning

Planning assigns the relation between an order detail and the warehouse it will be shipped to or delivered from. It also maintains reservations against (or future receptions for) the product directly related to the order detail. This functionality can be customized to your business needs. For example, you can customize the criteria used to select the warehouse so that it chooses the one closest to the customer location.

Picking

Picking associates the information about each stock pick with the order detail and maintains product reservations against the specific location, lot, or serial number used for the pick. These details are actually picked as part of the picking process in Warehouse Management.

Back-order Handling

Back-order handling provides tracking of the order detail that temporarily cannot be satisfied. How this is handled can be customized. For example, you can move the unhandled quantity back to plannable so that it can be planned against a different warehouse.

Supplementary Charges

Supplementary charges let you associate miscellaneous additional charges at any level of an order. These charges can be anything your application needs. For example, they can be used to record charges on an order that are not directly related to products, such as freight, special handling charges, invoicing fees, and so on.

Reception

Reception associates the information about each purchase order reception with the future receptions for the product and warehouse. This process is used as part of the Warehouse Management process.

Sales Order Invoicing

Sales order invoicing identifies the order line, or lines, that are to be invoiced and generates the inputs to the general invoice processing provided by the CBO layer (see Chapter 7). The financial status in the general ledger and AR/AP are also updated.

Quality Control

Quality control can be used to perform quality control when a particular order type is received.

Shipping

Shipping lets you mingle multiple order details into a single ship list. For example, you can combine all orders going to a certain location onto a pallet for transport by truck.

OM Order Types

The OM core business process provides seven order types. They can be either used as is, modified for your needs, or copied and used as a starting point for other order types.

- Full sales: standard sales order processing, including planning, picking, shipping, and invoicing.
- Full purchase: standard purchase order processing, including planning, receiving, and quality control.
- Direct sales: a sales order that progresses directly from order entry to invoicing.
- Credit sales: a sales order that is used to handle returned goods.
- Quotation: an order that represents a bid and can be converted to a standard order if the bid is accepted.
- Stock movement: the moving of goods from one internal warehouse to another.
- Direct back-to-back sales: a sales order that automatically causes a purchase order to be created. This order type specifies that the products are to be shipped from the supplier directly to the customer.

Summary

This chapter gives an overview of the domains supported by the core business processes and introduces the support provided by SanFrancisco for those domains. Chapter 11 explores the Warehouse management core business process further by looking at how it can be used to build an application.

11 Using the Core Business Processes

To better explain how to use the SanFrancisco core business processes, we now take a look at a sample application that uses them. Until now, we have been using the GPSE application (introduced in Chapter 5) as a sample. The GPSE application is built on the SanFrancisco Foundation and Common Business Objects layers and also uses SanFrancisco patterns. That may be a beneficial scenario for a solution developer using SanFrancisco when no appropriate core business process is available. However, the full power of SanFrancisco lies in being able to reuse the core business processes. The reuse is raised one level: from large-grained business objects and patterns to actual implemented business domain processing. This chapter focuses on the use of the core business processes in a sample application. Whereas previous sample application discussions included code samples, this discussion focuses on explaining the reuse of the SanFrancisco processes conceptually rather than getting into implementation examples. The actual implementation of reusing the core business processes is similar to the code examples in previous chapters; that is the beauty of the programming model and design patterns! Use of the Foundation and Common Business Objects layers is noted here to show how all layers of SanFrancisco are typically used in an application built on the Core Business Processes. This sample application uses the Warehouse Management core business process.

First we discuss an application case study, the business scenario in which the application will be used. In this scenario, a solution developer is providing a new physical inventory module, based on SanFrancisco, within their company's application portfolio. *Physical inventory* is the process of counting the quantities of inventory actually found in the warehouse. The primary function of physical inventory is to provide a mechanism for checking the accuracy of the system's inventory control measures by comparing system inventory balances with actual physical counts. The solution developer has two beta customers with differing physical inventory requirements. Here, we describe the exercise of mapping these application requirements to the SanFrancisco Warehouse Management core business process. During the development of the application, extensions are made to customize the existing SanFrancisco processes as well as to satisfy additional requirements not addressed by SanFrancisco. Some of these extensions are discussed to illustrate the various extension techniques that are available.

Application Case Study

Appliance Dealer Solution Source (ADSS) has been supplying scalable and flexible integrated software solutions to home appliance retailers for more than 10 years. By providing leading-edge solutions in a modular format, allowing its customers to migrate small pieces of their enterprise applications while maintaining integration with prior releases, ADSS has succeeded in building a significant customer base spanning four continents. ADSS has recently chosen IBM's SanFrancisco as part of its planned migration to an object-oriented, network-based architecture.

To begin this migration, ADSS solicited two customers from its current installed base to become beta sites for a new SanFrancisco-based Physical Inventory module.

Beta Customer 1: Home Entertainment Store

Home Entertainment Store (HES) is a family-owned chain of 15 retail appliance stores in a single major metropolitan market. HES prides itself on providing customers of its upscale line of appliances with reliable advice and a high degree of personal service. HES is ADSS's oldest and most loyal customer and has often served as a beta customer for new ADSS software modules. From ADSS's viewpoint, HES is an extremely valuable source for testing core functionality of new applications because of its small geographical scope and its focus on high-quality performance of basic business functions without much variation in response to new marketing fads.

Home Entertainment Store has one warehouse, which contains zones dedicated to receiving, storage, packing, and shipping.

Beta Customer 2: Big Electronics Superstore

Big Electronics Superstore (BES) is a strong international competitor in the consumer electronics and appliance markets, consistently ranking second or third in worldwide sales but well behind the industry leader. BES has been in existence for more than 12 years and has expanded to include more than 1,000 retail outlets worldwide, which are supplied from 20 warehouses in Europe, the Far East, Australia, and North America. Not all products carried by BES are stocked in every warehouse.

BES is also one of the most innovative chains of its type in developing alternative distribution channels for the products it carries. In addition to its own retail stores, the company has an agreement with the Court Shops (CS) department store chain in the United States to rent retail space within CS stores. The CS management wished to effectively outsource its declining-margin consumer electronics and appliances business in order to invest more money in upgrading its stores and improving the quality of its more-traditional product lines. As part of this outsourcing agreement, BES owns all CS inventory in the department stores.

Although these two major distribution channels are managed as separate profit centers, BES uses two strategies to minimize cross-competition. First, BES sells some slightly different models of selected high-price products (especially major appliances) through the department stores that it does not sell through its own outlets. The CS portion of BES's business has also chosen to cater to the convenience motive of most CS customers by bundling many other products into all-in-one packages. Following are examples of such bundles:

- Camcorder packages consisting of the camcorder, carrying bag, second battery, AC converter, tape, and tripod
- Computer packages, complete with processor, monitor, printer, speakers, and cables
- Home theater packages of several varieties, most of them including at least a surround-sound receiver, five acoustically matched speakers, 150 feet of speaker cable, and all connecting cables

The packages are boxed separately from the other CS (and BES, of course) products to conform to Court Shops' advertising campaign.

Application Requirements

As mentioned, ADSS has chosen to implement a Physical Inventory module as its beta SanFrancisco implementation. Following are the business activities that must be supported in the sample application:

- Set up and maintain business rules for taking inventory. An annual count of the entire inventory could be taken, but most businesses have instituted some form of cycle count in which items are counted at different intervals depending on their relative importance.
- Determine the stock to count based on the defined business rules.
- Perform the physical inventory count.
- Record the result of the count.
- Analyze the result of the count.
- Update the inventory figures with the final count.

Some additional requirements of the application are as follows:

- The sample application must take into account various *roles* in the counting process.
  - ◊ Counter: person doing the physical count of inventory.
  - ◊ Variance coordinators: people who are responsible for taking action when a difference (*variance*) has been detected between what was actually counted and what the system expected based on balances maintained.
  - ◊ Variance managers: people who are responsible for taking action on variances that a coordinator has *escalated* (sent up the chain of command). A large variance, for example, may be escalated for further investigation.
- When a count is recorded, if the expected quantity and the counted quantity are the same, the count is automatically accepted.
- When a difference is found between the expected quantity and the quantity counted, the following general rules should be used:
  - ◊ The counter should be prompted once to verify the count entered to allow for correction of typos and the like.
  - ◊ The count should be automatically accepted if the variance is less than a certain monetary amount (*variance threshold*) defined by the system.
  - ◊ Variances above the variance threshold must be moved to a list of variances to be acted on. The following actions can take place:
    - Request recount
    - Accept count
    - Optionally escalate the variance to get a manager's approval

Each beta customer also has specific requirements for carrying out physical inventory.

- Beta customer 1:
    - ◊ Counting cycle: Everything in the warehouse is counted at the end of a calendar quarter.
    - ◊ Multiple zones exist within the warehouse for receiving, storage, packing, and shipping.
    - ◊ Products are stored and tracked by locations within the warehouse. Each location has a location number.
    - ◊ Only items in storage are counted during physical inventory.
    - ◊ No products have lot numbers.
    - ◊ Some products have serial numbers.
- Beta customer 2:
    - ◊ Counting cycle: Products are classified, and the counting interval is based on a product's classification as follows:

Class	Interval
A	30 days
B	90 days
C	365 days

- Product characteristics that establish count cycles are not the same as those that determine physical stock location.
- Multiple zones exist within the warehouse for receiving, storage, packing, shipping, and quality control.
- Products are stored and tracked by location within the warehouse. Each location has a location number.
- Inventory includes products within product categories.
- Items in storage, receiving, and quality control are counted during physical inventory.
- Some products have lot numbers.
- Some products have serial numbers.
- Counting lists should consolidate items by warehouse and zone to support an efficient physical count.

Mapping to the SanFrancisco Core Business Processes

The SanFrancisco Application Development Roadmap is used as the development process for the application. The Roadmap defines a set of activities that should be performed during development. They are the typical activities in any development process: requirements gathering, analysis, design, implementation, and test. The most important advantage to following the Roadmap, however, is the *mapping stages* within the process. This step in the process ensures that you are fully utilizing the existing content of SanFrancisco wherever possible. See Chapter 5 for more information on the Roadmap.

The SanFrancisco Warehouse Management User Guide documents the core business process starting from a domain view and going through analysis and some design. In the sample application development, this documentation was used to determine that the Warehouse Management (WM) core business process covers physical inventory processing. The User Guide contains a process map that maps the logistics and distribution business domain to the WM processes. In WM, physical inventory is referred to as *Stock Take*. If we look at the main Stock Take process description in the documentation, it is as follows:

WM Stock Take

Domain background

Typical business counterparts

In SanFrancisco's Warehouse Management core business process, WM Stock Take covers the functionality provided for building the stock take features of an application. In the example logistics and distribution business domain, the stock take activities are located in stock take, *which is under* inventory control and acquisition.

Typical business usage

Stock take (or physical inventory) is the process of counting the quantities of specific inventory actually found in the warehouse. An annual count of the entire inventory could be taken, but most businesses have instituted some form of cycle count in which items are counted with different frequencies depending on their relative importance. The primary function of a stock take is to provide a mechanism for checking on the accuracy of the system's inventory control measures by comparing system inventory balances with actual physical counts.

Typical business process

The business rules that determine the schedule on which each inventory item is counted and the manner in which the count is conducted must be defined. At the start of a stock take the business rules identify the inventory items to count and set up details for a specific stock take process. The physical count is performed and the results are recorded. The results of the count are analyzed, especially as they compare to expected quantities based on stock transaction records. Discrepancies are resolved. The inventory records are updated, and any necessary stock or financial transactions are initiated.

Features of the SanFrancisco process

Description

The Stock Take process begins at the point where a set of products to be counted has been presented to the system along with business rules for conducting the count. The WM material provides support for taking over the physical inventory activities at that point by incorporating the information and business rules presented into stock take lists. These lists can be used to allocate, consolidate, and prioritize the items to be counted and can serve as the count tickets used on the warehouse floor.

The process as implemented in WM puts a flag and a lock on all inventories while they are part of a stock take. The flag prevents an item from appearing on more than one active stock take. The lock, which is set from the time the stock take is initiated until the final counts are accepted and entered into the system, prevents the items in the stock take from being used by other system stock movement processes such as picking or reception.

In the activities of confirming and committing the information entered onto the lists, the process provides support for recording the results of the count, for validating the results as entered, for updating inventories and stock transactions where necessary, and for initiating any financial transactions that result.

Stock transactions will be updated to record any inventory changes that are necessary and to record financial transactions.

Process analysis

1. *Establish physical inventory business rules (not part of WM).*
2. *Identify inventory to count for the particular stock take (not part of WM).*
3. *Set up details for a specific physical count.*
4. *Perform the count (not part of WM).*
5. *Record the result of the count.*
6. *Analyze the result of the count (not part of WM) and repeat from Step 4 (if necessary).*
7. *Update the inventory records and record the financial impact.*

This process description seemed like a good fit at requirements time. As the application was developed and the WM processes were researched in more detail, it was discovered that the WM processes provided good coverage for the application's stock take requirements. The Stock Take processes were used along with several other processes within Warehouse Management. Several extensions were also made to specialize the application and satisfy the business requirements. The three core concepts within Warehouse Management described in Chapter 10 were also used: product, warehouse, and inventory.

For illustration purposes, we focus on two extensions that were made to satisfy the application requirements. One involves customizing existing processes to accommodate the requirements; the other involves adding a new set of requirements to the existing business processing. A third extension is discussed briefly as an example usage of the List Generation pattern discussed in

Chapter 9. We also discuss the use of the common business objects and San-Francisco security to show how all aspects of SanFrancisco—the core business processes, the common business objects, and the Foundation layer—are typically incorporated into an application.

Application Use Case

To better explain the application that was developed, we now present an informal stock take use case. Here, a counter enters the amount of inventory counted. We also show the main dialog boxes the counter interacts with.

Actor: Counter

1. Counter is presented with the Logon dialog box (see Figure 11-1).

Figure 11-1. Logon Dialog Box

2. Counter enters user ID and password and selects OK.
   A. System verifies user is authorized to enter counts.

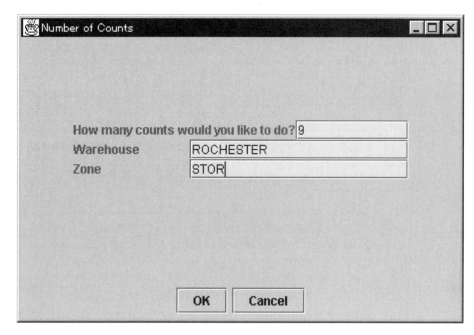

Figure 11-2. Number of Counts Dialog Box

3. Counter is presented with the Number of Counts dialog box and enters the number of counts he or she would like to do, enters the warehouse, optionally enters the zone (STOR indicates the storage zone in Figure 11-2), and selects OK. The number of counts entered is the number of inventory records the counter would like to verify by counting that physical inventory in the warehouse. The number may be based on how much time the counter has to do the counting assignment. For example, the counter may typically do 20 counts in one morning. The optional zone may be entered to limit the counter's work to one particular zone or area of the warehouse.

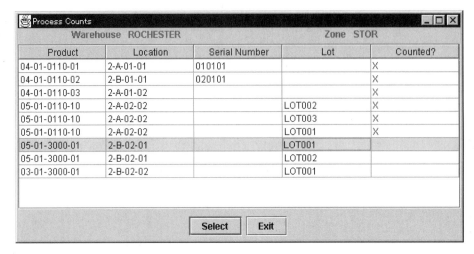

Figure 11-3. Process Counts Dialog Box

4. Counter is presented with the Process Counts dialog box (see Figure 11-3). Not more than the requested number of counts for the correct warehouse is included in the list displayed. (Note that in some applications this would be a count ticket that would be printed for use by the counter in the warehouse.) The counter processes each entry in the list.

   A. Counter selects a count that has not been recorded (as indicated in the "Counted" column) and select OK.

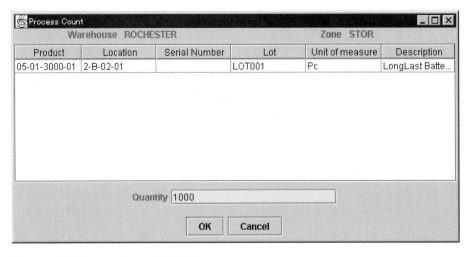

Figure 11-4. Process Count Dialog Box

B. Counter is presented with the Process Count dialog box displaying the product number, location, serial number if available, lot if available, unit of measure (Pc represents "piece" in Figure 11-4), and description. Counter enters the quantity counted and selects OK.

If the count entered matches the system's expected count, the system commits the count, the Process Count dialog box closes, and the Process Counts "Counted" column is updated.

If the count entered does not match the system's expected count, a message is displayed asking to verify the count. The counter can then reenter the quantity. If the count still does not match, the process Count dialog box closes and the Process Counts "Counted" column is updated. If the variance amount is above the variance threshold, the system adds this count to its list of variances.

5. When all entries are processed or the counter wishes to quit counting, the counter selects Exit.

Stock Take Structure

Now let's discuss the structures defined in WM that are used for physical inventory processing. A *stock take* in Warehouse Management refers to the master list of counts that must be done for the company. Beta customer 1 (HES), for example, counts all products once per calendar quarter. So at the end of a calendar quarter a stock take is created that contains all product inventory. A *stock take list* is the "counting assignment" for a person involved in physical inventory activities (a *counter*). So the master list of counts, the stock take, can be broken into several counting assignments, stock take lists, that are then processed by individuals doing the counting. Both the stock take and stock take list have details associated with them. A detail represents one count for a particular inventory. A stock take list detail knows which stock take details it is associated with. If we apply these terms to the beta customer 1 requirements, one stock take is created at the end of a calendar quarter based on all products. If 10 people are doing the physical inventory, 10 stock take lists are created. Figure 11-5 depicts the relationships.

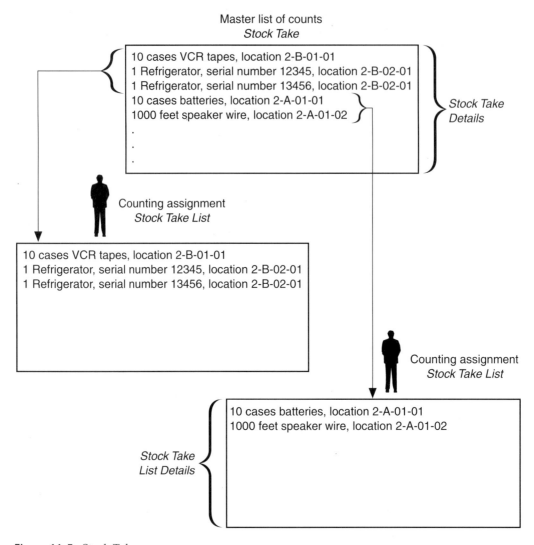

Figure 11-5. Stock Take

Stock Take Generation Extension

The *stock take generation* extension is an example of a way to customize the existing WM processes to accommodate application requirements.

Business Requirement

The requirements for the sample physical inventory application leading to this specific extension can be summarized as follows:

- HES must perform an inventory count on all products in storage in the warehouse at the end of a calendar quarter.

- BES, on the other hand, has a more sophisticated way of determining what must be counted. Products are classified in categories, and each product category has an associated counting frequency. Typically, expensive products must be counted more frequently than inexpensive products. There are three classes of products, and they are associated with a counting frequency of 30, 90, and 365 days. When a request for physical inventory is issued, the inventories that have not been verified within the counting frequency defined for the product must be included in the master list of counts (stock take). Items in storage, receiving, and quality control are counted during physical inventory.

Extension Description

The stock take generation implementation, which creates the master list of counts within the sample application, consists of several extensions made to existing processes to accommodate the application requirements. To satisfy the requirements, an existing policy was extended, two existing business object classes were extended, and a command was created.

SanFrancisco's Warehouse Management offers a way to create a stock take based on a collection of *stock take selections*. Stock take selections allow an application to specify which inventories must be selected for counting. A stock take selection contains the indication of a product, a warehouse, a stock type value, a unit of measure, and optionally of a serial number, a lot, and a stock location. SanFrancisco provides a mechanism to create the stock take via a *policy*, but there is no component that implements the creation of the collection of stock take selections needed by the policy to generate the stock take. Three WM scenarios were reused to satisfy the application requirements: Generate Stock Take, Create Stock Take Detail, and Create Stock Take Selection. The relationships between these scenarios is depicted in Figure 11-6.

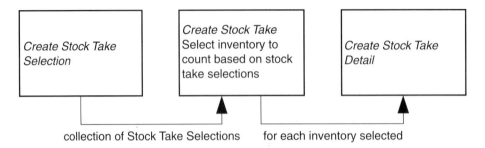

Figure 11-6. WM Scenarios

The default Generate Stock Take scenario is implemented as a policy. The business logic includes doing a scan of the inventories based on the content of each stock take selection. For example, if a stock take selection contains a reference to a certain product, unit of measure, warehouse, and stock type, all the inventories having these characteristics are selected for counting. Beta customer 2, however, has a requirement that the counting frequency for the product be taken into account when the stock take is generated. For example, for products with a classification of A, only those that have not been counted in the past 30 days should be selected for counting. Because of this requirement, the decision was made to extend the StockTakeSelection class to include date information (a new StockTakeSelectionDated class). For beta customer 1, the date can be set to null. The default Stock Take Details generation policy does not fit the application needs because it doesn't take into account any date information; therefore, a new, similar version of the policy is needed.

Because the application scenario required the reuse of multiple SanFrancisco scenarios, it was decided that the processing should be encapsulated in a *command* to increase the usability of the server-side processes. Figure 11-7 illustrates the StockTakeGenerateCmd class, which encapsulates the processing for creating a collection of StockTakeSelectionDateds and generating the Stock Take based on those selections.

StockTakeGenerateCmd

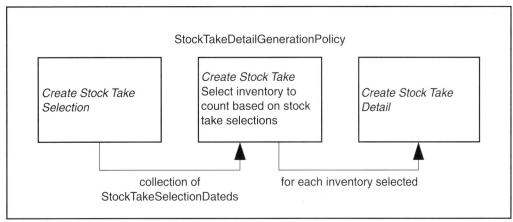

Figure 11-7. Stock Take Generation Extension

A second aspect of the requirements also calls for an extension, this one related to the counting frequency of a product based on its classification. The application requirements for company BES indicate that there is a need to classify products as A, B, or C and to assign a counting frequency, in number of days, to each classification. There is no direct match in the WM Product class that fits this requirement. WM does contain an ABCClassification class whose purpose is to let users subdivide their product portfolio into categories based on the product's popularity or value. All Products can contain an instance of ABCClassification. Because the counting frequency is related to this classification, ABCClassification was extended to include a counting frequency.

To summarize, to satisfy the Stock Take generation requirements within the sample application, the following extensions were implemented:

- The ABCClassification class was extended to include the counting frequency, in number of days, for a product classification.

- The StockTakeSelection class was extended to include date information to be used in selecting inventory to be included in a stock take.

- The StockTakeDetailGenerationPolicy was extended to take into account the date information in the StockTakeSelectionDated and the counting frequency assigned to products via their ABCClassification in selecting inventory to be included in a stock take.

- A command was created to encapsulate the processing for generating a stock take to simplify the client interface.

Variances and Recounts Extension

The variances and recounts extension is an example of adding a new set of requirements to the existing SanFrancisco processes.

Business Requirement

Variances and recounts encompass a large extension made to stock take for the sample application. At requirements time, the business rules determined for the application requirements consisted of the following:

- When a count is recorded, if the expected quantity and the counted quantity are the same, the count is automatically accepted.
- When a difference is found between the expected quantity and the quantity counted (referred to as a *variance*), the following general rules should be used:
    ◊ Counter should be prompted once to verify the count entered to allow for correction of typos, and so on.
    ◊ The count should be automatically accepted if the variance is less than a certain monetary amount (referred to as *variance threshold* and determined by the company).
    ◊ Variances greater than a certain monetary amount must be moved to a list of variances to be acted on. The following actions can take place:
        - Request a recount.
        - Accept the count.
        - Optionally escalate the variance to get a manager's approval.

Extension Description

Variances and recounts actually consist of several SanFrancisco extensions to implement a new set of requirements in the existing WM processes. To satisfy the requirements, two existing policies were extended, an existing controller was extended, an existing class was extended, two commands were created, and five business objects were created. Because this extension is quite large, we focus on a subset of the extension. We discuss it in two pieces to ease understanding.

- Update quantity in a count: This extension is an example of introducing a command to encapsulate two processes in WM that were logically one process in the sample application requirements. This extension also involves extending a WM policy to customize business processing.
- Variance lists, escalated variance lists, and recounts: This extension is an example of creating new business objects and extending the WM business processing to use them.

Update Quantity in a Count

An application scenario, to Update Quantity in a Count, was introduced during the requirements phase. The scenario was meant for recording the results of a count—that is, entering the counted quantity. During mapping, it appeared that this scenario mapped to an existing Warehouse Management scenario: Confirm Stock Take Detail. Because each stock take list detail is related to a stock take detail, it's the stock take detail that gets updated with the counted quantity. The stock take lists, the counting assignments, can be thought of as temporary. They can be deleted after a counter has completed the task. The stock takes can be thought of as the master physical inventory data. They can be retained for history. The WM Confirm Stock Take Detail scenario allows a counted quantity to be recorded for the count. A typical pattern within the San-Francisco processes is to break processing into a confirm step and a commit step. The confirm step typically involves updating business data, and the commit step finalizes the data and triggers any additional processing that should occur because of the updated data. There is a Commit Stock Take Detail scenario that occurs to commit the count or accept it and create any *stock transactions* that may occur because of a difference in the expected quantity and the confirmed quantity. A stock transaction causes a financial transaction to take place to record the unexpected increase or decrease in stock.

The application's Update Quantity in a Count scenario outlines its confirmation process as follows:

- If the counted quantity matches the expected quantity within a certain threshold (defined for the company), then the count is also accepted (committed).

- If the counted quantity is above the threshold, a *variance* is created in the *variance list*. When a variance is created, some history of the count is recorded.

The Confirm Stock Take Detail is implemented in WM as a policy. Because the application scenario varies from the WM scenario, it was thought that an extension would be implemented to specialize the confirmation policy with the application logic. But the application logic really breaks the confirm method contract by automatically doing a commit. In the sample application there was no requirement for the client logic to need to know about the confirm and commit semantics. The solution was to introduce a command for the client to use; the command encapsulated the confirm and commit processing in the Update Quantity scenario. The command scenario logic confirms the count, determines whether the confirm updated the count—meaning that the confirm was successful—and, if so, commits the count. The confirmation policy is still specialized to include creating a variance if necessary.

Figure 11-8 depicts the Update Quantity in a Count scenario extension.

CountQuantityUpdatedCmd

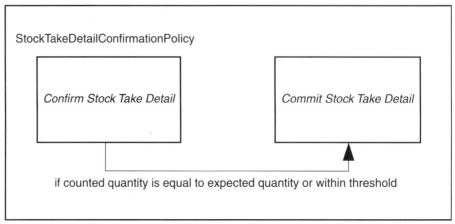

Figure 11-8. Update Quantity in a Count Extension

VarianceLists, EscalatedVarianceLists, Recounts

The sample application requirements documented a need to track counts as variances, escalated variances, or recounts. The requirements stated that when a counter entered a count, if the counted quantity was not equal to the expected quantity and it was greater than a certain monetary value, a variance was created. Variances can then be processed in three ways:

- The variance count can be accepted.
- The variance count can be escalated for further processing by a manager.
- A request for a recount can be made.

As discussed earlier, variances are created and put into a variance list in the Update Quantity in a Count scenario via the specialized StockTakeDetail-ConfirmationPolicy. To satisfy the preceding requirements, three application scenarios were introduced: Escalate Variance, Request Recount, and Accept a Count. Escalate Variance describes moving a variance from the variance list to an escalated variance list. Request Recount describes moving a variance from the variance list to the recount list. Variance lists, escalated variance lists, and recount lists, are maintained per warehouse. Because the existing WM Stock Take processes have no concept of variances and recounts, these scenarios involve adding new functionality. The processing for accepting a variance and escalated variance is contained in the Accept a Count scenario. The Accept a Count scenario mapped to an existing WM scenario, Commit Stock Take Detail.

A decision was made that variances and escalated variances would be specializations of StockTakeListDetail. This mapping was made because variances originated as part of processing a counting assignment, a StockTakeList. Recounts would be instances of StockTakeDetail. This mapping was made because recounts will later be processed to be included on another counting assignment similar to the master lists of counts, StockTakes.

Three new classes were introduced: VarianceList was added to hold variances, EscalatedVarianceList was added to hold escalated variances, and RecountList was added to hold recounts. During design, it was decided that the variance lists, escalated variance lists, and recount lists would all be owned by the StockTakeController. The reasoning was that StockTakes and Stock-TakeLists were already owned by the controller, and it would be convenient for the client if all stock-take-related lists were controlled by the same controller. It was also assumed that stock takes would not often be processed by several clients at the same time and so contention on the controller would not be a problem. This resulted in an extension to the StockTakeController. The logic in Escalate Variance was assigned to the controller as an escalateVariance() method. The logic in Request Recount was also assigned to the controller as an addRecount() method.

Figure 11-9 depicts this extension.

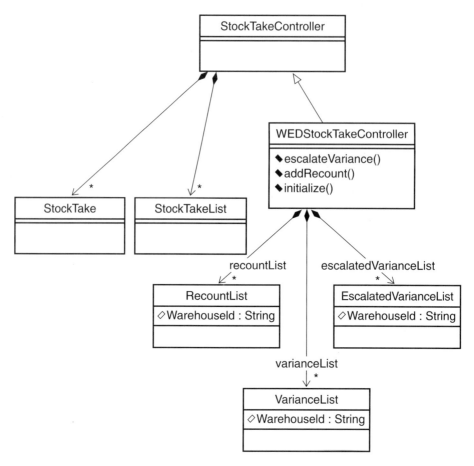

Figure 11-9. VarianceLists, EscalatedVarianceLists, Recounts Extension

This extension includes the implementation of four new Entity subclasses: VarianceList, EscalatedVarianceList, RecountList, and WEDStockTakeList-Detail. Although this sounds like a lot of work, these classes were completely generated by the SanFrancisco code generator.

Stock Take List Generation Extension

The stock take list generation extension is an example of using the List Generation pattern.

Business Requirement

Within the sample application requirements was the need to create a *counting assignment* that included counts from the *master list of counts* and also any *recounts* that were requested. There was also a requirement for beta customer 2 that counting lists should consolidate items by warehouse and zone to support an efficient physical count.

Extension Description

This requirement mapped to an existing WM scenario: Generate Stock Take Lists. This scenario is an example of the List Generation pattern discussed earlier (see Chapter 9 for more detail on this pattern). Generate Stock Take Lists takes as input a collection of stock take details. A Command, StockTakeList-GenerateCmd, was created to encapsulate the logic that goes through the master list of counts and recounts and invokes the stock take list generation. The input to the command is the warehouse, zone, and number of counts so that an appropriate list can be created. Figure 11-10 illustrates this extension.

StockTakeListGenerateCmd

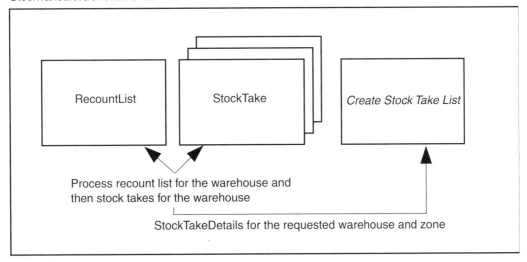

Figure 11-10. Stock Take List Generation Extension

Reuse of the Core Business Process

Although a few extensions were made to the stock take process supported in the Warehouse Management core business process, a vast portion of the application requirements were directly satisfied by the existing SanFrancisco functionality. This functionality includes all the product, warehouse, and inventory definitions that are supplied. Existing SanFrancisco processes provide all the logic for creating products and groups of products, defining whether a product is lot-controlled or serialized, defining which units of measure the product can be in (cases, boxes, pallets, and so on), creating warehouses and zones and locations within those warehouses, defining which products belong in which warehouses, receiving products into inventory, and so on. Also, the entire core stock take process was reused with the extensions described earlier.

Use of the Common Business Objects

The common business objects and SanFrancisco patterns are used extensively in the Warehouse Management core business process. These objects and mechanisms are also used frequently in application extensions and provide another level of reuse within the product.

Company

The Company hierarchy is used in the sample application. The Company common business object is used to represent an organization hierarchy. When the sample application is installed at the Home Entertainment Store, a Company object is created and used to represent information about the company. This object is also used as the owner for many of the controlled objects in the application, such as StockTakes, StockTakeLists, VarianceLists, RecountLists, and so on. The monetary amount used to determine whether a variance is created is also part of the Company. (See Chapter 6 for more information on the Company common business object.)

Initials

The Initials common business object supports the identification of certain roles of users of the system (see Chapter 7 for more information on the Initials common business object). When the application requirements were examined, it was determined that there were three roles for users within the application:

counter, variance coordinator, and variance manager. The individuals who take these roles were defined to be *system users*, an extension of Initials.

Initials should not be confused with the security services in SanFrancisco. Initials are used when a user of the system (Initial) must have certain abilities (*signatory ability*) to execute a process. The distinction made in the application was that the system user (Initial) function was used when a task required recording who carried out the task. For example, when a variance is created within the application, the person who did the count is recorded as part of the count history that is created. When a variance coordinator accepts a variance, that information may need to be recorded.

The use of Initials in the application involved creating a system user extension that contained the system user ID of the individual represented by the Initial. The user ID was then used as a *dictionary entry* within the Initials controller so that the correct Initials could be retrieved for the user of the application. Three *signatory ability groups* were defined as follows:

Ability	Signatory Ability Groups		
	Counter	Variance Coordinator	Variance Manager
Count	X	X	X
Process Variance		X	X
Manage Variance			X
WM_STOCK_TAKE_ COMMIT	X	X	X

These abilities were then verified when a count or variance was accepted, when a count was escalated, and when a recount was requested. Initials are also used within the WM Stock Take processes provided. To commit a count, for example, an Initials with the WHS_STOCK_TAKE_COMMIT signatory ability must be provided.

Policies

Policies are a type of SanFrancisco design pattern used extensively for extending the core business processes. Policies are a way to isolate business processing to allow it to be easily customized. Within the core business processes, much of the business logic that is a candidate for customization based on application requirements has been implemented as a policy. In the discussions of extensions implemented earlier, policies are used as an extension technique. See Chapter 7 for more information on policy patterns.

Controllers

A *controller* is also a type of design pattern supported in SanFrancisco. Controllers are objects used to track and manage primary business objects within a business domain. In the sample application, all the various lists of objects needed in the Stock Take process (StockTakes, StockTakeLists, VarianceLists, EscalatedVarianceLists, and RecountLists) are managed by the StockTakeController. This is a convenient way to organize object instances and associate them with the correct Company in the Company hierarchy. Controllers are also used to manage Initials and the SignatoryAbilities and SignatoryAbilityGroups that are used in the application. For more information on controllers, see Chapter 7.

Properties

Dynamic properties are another type of design pattern supported in SanFrancisco. Dynamic properties let you add attributes to an existing object instance at runtime. Properties are used extensively throughout the core business processes. Controllers, for example, are attached to Companies by property. Specific uses of properties in the sample application are the variance threshold and the stock take detail history. The variance threshold is a monetary amount that is used to determine whether a variance should be created when a count does not match the quantity expected. The variance threshold is defined as a property on the Company object and is created and attached to the Company when the application is installed. The StockTakeDetailHistory is an object that contains a set of count history details for each variance that is created for a particular count. The history detail includes information such as the counter's Initials and the counted quantity. The collection of count history details is attached to a StockTakeDetail (count) as a property when and if a variance is detected.

Use of Security

Secure tasks are used in the client user interface of the sample application. When the application is started, the user is presented with a logon screen. After the user has logged on, an initial menu is displayed; its menu items are enabled or disabled based on the access rights that have been created for that user. Figure 11-11 shows the main menu developed for the sample application with all menu items enabled.

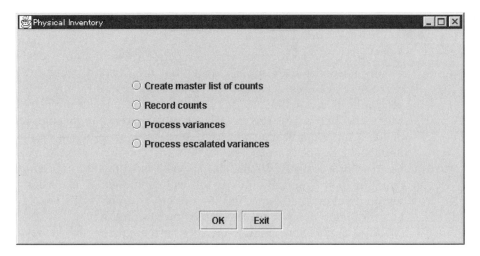

Figure 11-11. Main Menu

The beginSecureTask and endSecureTask APIs are used around each process. The following secure tasks are created when the application is installed:

- /whsed/RecordCounts
- /whsed/ProcessVariances
- /whsed/ManageVariances
- /whsed/MasterListGeneration

Part of the application administration includes the creation of user IDs and the configuration of access rights for each user of the system for the appropriate actions (secure tasks) and resources (Company within the Company hierarchy). Because the server-side processing also requires a system user (Initials extension) for each user of the system and because part of that system user is the user ID, a command to create the system user is provided. See Chapter 5 for more information on SanFrancisco security.

Summary

The core business processes in SanFrancisco provide a great deal of the processing needed for an application within the domain being addressed. The processes have been designed with a special attention to reusability. The sample application described in this chapter was built using the Warehouse Management core business process. The chapter presents application requirements of the sample application and discusses how some of the requirements are implemented. The sample demonstrates that the Warehouse Management core business process provides most of the core functionality needed to satisfy the requirements. Through the use of well-documented extension techniques within SanFrancisco—specifically, design patterns—satisfying the requirements did not involve a lot of complex programming.

Most applications built on the core business processes also take advantage of the common business objects, design patterns, and the Foundation layer to complete implementation. The sample application described in this chapter is an example of this complete use of what SanFrancisco has to offer.

Part V

The Client

Building and deploying an application involves technology and techniques that component developers seldom need to worry about. The reason for this disparity between component developers and application developers is that the two groups have substantially different requirements. Developers of the SanFrancisco application business components consider a component's versatility and extension characteristics and evaluate how it delivers the functionality required in a particular domain. By contrast, application developers consider technologies and solutions needed to deliver functionality to end users. To supply an end user application, the application developer must consider the most appropriate display technology, performance-enhancing techniques tuned for the deployment scenario, and many other characteristics that component providers aren't required to take into account.

Previous chapters have focused on the framework and methodology for customizing and extending the framework for use in applications. Part V is applicable to those people who are attempting to use SanFrancisco application business components in applications and subsequently to deploy those applications.

For the most part, building an application with SanFrancisco is an exercise in writing transactional Java applications. Chapter 12, Preparing to Build a Client Application, discusses a few technologies and scenarios that are unique to the SanFrancisco environment. If you have been following the examples in the source code and going further than what was described in the book text, you've probably seen some of this code. Items such as threading and transaction scope in user interfaces are addressed in Chapter 12.

Chapter 13 covers the SanFrancisco command object. (The command is also discussed briefly in Chapter 4.) Commands themselves become an integral part of populating data and enhancing performance in a final application. These uses go beyond the original intent of the Command class, which is to provide a way of building atomic business logic.

Chapter 14 discusses the topic of providing a user interface for your application. SanFrancisco provides its own flavor of user interface. Based on the Java Foundation Classes (JFC), the SanFrancisco User Interface framework creates a standard set of controls and techniques that are commonly used in creating an application that uses SanFrancisco application business components. (Of course, SanFrancisco does not prevent programmers from using user interface class libraries from other vendors.) This chapter presents a brief introduction to the SanFrancisco User Interface framework and explains how it fulfills its requirements. A sample application using a graphical user interface is also presented in the chapter, as are comparable techniques for building a user interface with the Java Foundation Classes. A short discussion on thin clients wraps up the chapter.

SanFrancisco covers the component territory very well with respect to the concept of an object-oriented class framework. This programming model does not correspond to Sun's JavaBean component model, which allows tool developers to construct robust development environments. The environments allow users to construct applications visually because the tool knows the contract and behavior that are expected of a component. Beyond visual construction, the JavaBeans contract offers a standard interface and behavior, which make components predictable and therefore easier for tools, and people, to work with. A set of JavaBeans that represents SanFrancisco application business components is shipped with the SanFrancisco product. Furthermore, a tool ships with the product that builds SanFrancisco JavaBeans (SFJB) from existing SanFrancisco classes. SanFrancisco JavaBeans are not trivial JavaBean widgets by any means. Chapter 15, SanFrancisco JavaBeans, discusses many of the interesting concepts introduced by SFJBs and walks through a sample that shows how to create and program with SFJBs.

Keep in mind that Chapters 14 and 15 discuss client technology that is in the process of creation at the time we are writing this book. It is nearly impossible to keep up with the pace of change in client display and application programming technologies. New technologies are discussed here when they are relevant, but they will likely be beta technologies at the time this book is published. We highly recommend looking at, and using, the newer technologies if they fit your needs. In the case of the SanFrancisco GUI framework, make sure you take time to understand IBM's commitment to supporting the two flavors of the framework that will be on the market simultaneously. The Web address for contacting IBM is included in the Preface to this book.

12

Preparing to Build a Client Application

It is rare that programmers will implement an entire program using a single-threaded model. More often than not, programmers will add a user interface to their client using classes shipped with Java (such as the Java Abstract Windowing Toolkit or the Java Foundation Classes), from the SanFrancisco User Interface framework, or potentially from some other user interface class library. No matter which user interface library is used, user interfaces are usually multi-threaded. Thread handling with the SanFrancisco framework can be tricky at first, but with a little guidance you can solve the issues early in development rather than later.

In addition to discussing the inherent multithreaded nature of user inter-faces, this chapter explains transaction boundaries and locking techniques. Because a transaction is a unit of work that commits or rolls back as a whole, it is crucial to plan what a transaction will encompass. In a sequential program, it is easy to determine the length and scope of a transaction. Unfortunately, when multiple windows and potential navigational paths are available for users, the resulting complexity can push transactional programming skills to the limit. For example, if two threads modify SanFrancisco objects independently of each other, do you want the entire application to run in a single trans-action, or should each thread manage its own transaction? Up-front knowledge of such transaction *boundaries* is also useful in maintenance tasks. If a single object maintenance window is presented to the user, should all changes in the maintenance window be kept within its own transaction? What happens if the maintenance window appears in the context of a larger collection management window? The answers to such questions are crucial if a client is using multiple frames to represent different objects, as you will see in future chapters.

This chapter provides a basic multithreaded sample program to address threading and transactional issues in SanFrancisco. The issues presented and solved here are used in subsequent chapters and have been used throughout the applications presented in the previous chapters.

An Overview of Multithreaded Applications

Most user interfaces have multiple threads of execution active, whether or not the threads are explicitly requested by a programmer. Specifically, a main thread often gets created at start-up time, and an event-handling thread becomes active when an interface is presented to the user. Typically, the event-handling thread takes over processing as user events occur, such as clicking a button or typing text into a text field. The result is that code in a typical program that presents a user interface is executed from two or more threads. Figure 12-1 shows the threads spanned by a normal user interface application.

In a *distributed processing* model, the creators of Foundation layer services must take into consideration that the process is actually a virtual process and lives across virtual machines or even across an entire network. The designers of the SanFrancisco Foundation layer had to take this distributed process into account. The process must be considered to be active across multiple Java virtual machines when you consider that objects actually live in a process that is separate from the process in which they are used. Consider the case of security. If the distributed process is considered one complete process, then security is validated across multiple Java virtual machines. On the other hand, if each Java

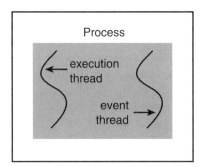

Figure 12-1. Single-process Application with User Interface

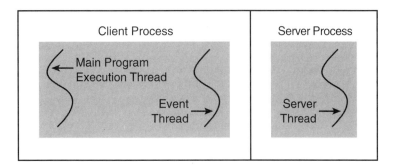

Figure 12-2. SanFrancisco Application with User Interface

virtual machine is allowed to be its own process, it becomes difficult to determine how to manage security given that a virtual machine may have stopped and restarted. Transaction management also becomes easier to build in a foundation that treats multiple virtual machines as a single distributed process. Some of the requirements in the Foundation layer for carrying information around with an application and between threads are reflected in how a developer programs an application.

Figure 12-2 more accurately shows what a process looks like in SanFrancisco. Portions of the distributed process exist on the client, and other portions of it exist in the server process. Allowing a distributed context to be passed around the network makes the multiple processes a conceptual whole. A *distributed process context* (DPC) is a shared workspace that is available from each of the separate process spaces.

This chapter forgoes discussion of specifics about user interfaces in favor of taking a more basic approach that illustrates thread handling in SanFrancisco. This approach eliminates the need to worry about the event thread but still allows you to see the basics of thread handling in SanFrancisco.

A Multithreaded Application without SanFrancisco Interaction

First, let's build a small multithreaded program that prints lines in an orderly fashion. The program is entirely Java based, with no SanFrancisco. Two threads are created; each thread has an opportunity to print the next occurrence of a string, and then control is ceded to the next thread in line. A primitive looping method is used to wait for control to return to the thread.

Producer.java

The Producer class sets up the mechanism that is used to wait for the opportunity to act on an object. The waiting is done through the static runner variable. A synchronized method to get and set the runner variable is used for access. When the runner is the same ID as a thread, it means that the thread can take off and work. The mechanism is primitive and CPU-intensive but simple and effective.

```java
public class Producer implements Runnable {
    private int id;
    private String prefix;
    private int nextId;
    private static int runner = -1;

    private Producer(){};

    public Producer (int id, String prefix, int nextId){
        this.id = id;
        this.prefix = prefix;
        this.nextId = nextId;
    }

    public void run() {
        for(char i='a' ; i < 'j' ; i++)
        {
            while(getRunner() != id);
            System.out.println(prefix + i);
            setRunner(nextId);
        }
    }

    public static synchronized int getRunner(){
        return runner;
    }

    public static synchronized void setRunner(int i){
        runner = i;
    }
}
```

ThreadManagement.java

The main() method in the ThreadManagement class creates two threads and then runs them. After the threads are started, the runner mechanism inside Producer takes over and the program takes turns executing within its run() method.

```
public class ThreadManagement {
  public static void main(String args[])
    {
     Thread t1 = new Thread(new Producer(0, args[0], 1));
     Thread t2 = new Thread(new Producer(1, args[1], 0));
     System.out.println("Starting...");
     t1.start();
     t2.start();
     Producer.setRunner(0);
  }
}
```

The program is instantiated with the command

```
java GPSE.ThreadManagement PROD1 PROD2
```

Following is the output:

```
Starting...
PROD1a
PROD2a
PROD1b
PROD2b
PROD1c
PROD2c
PROD1d
PROD2d
PROD1e
PROD2e
PROD1f
PROD2f
PROD1g
PROD2g
PROD1h
PROD2h
PROD1i
PROD2i
```

Note the strict alternating sequence that the runner mechanism forces on the program. The threads always switch when one line is printed. Keep in mind that there are really three threads that are involved in this program: the thread that the client starts in (otherwise known as the *main* thread) and the two threads that are spawned to create new ProductGroups.

Adding SanFrancisco Interaction to the Multithreaded Program—Almost

Now we can modify the preceding program to add SanFrancisco interactions to the executing threads. For the purpose of this example, the thread bounces back and forth, each thread getting a chance to create a new object. Three tasks must be completed to add the SanFrancisco interaction to the program:

- Add an initialization statement to the main thread.
- Add a transaction inside the run() method. The transaction begins and commits with each loop iteration.
- Add the object create within the transaction.

In addition to completing these tasks, this example differs in that the class names are slightly different. The name change allows the samples to be run without any changes.

SFProducer.java

Following is the new Producer class, now called SFProducer:

```
1   public class SFProducer implements Runnable {
2   private int id;
3   private String prefix;
4   private int nextId;
5   private static int runner = -1;

6   private SFProducer(){};

7   public SFProducer (int id, String prefix, int nextId){
8     this.id = id;
9     this.prefix = prefix;
10    this.nextId = nextId;
11  }

12  public void run() {
13    for(char i='a' ; i < 'j' ; i++)
14    {
15    while(getRunner() != id);
16      try {
17        // CREATE a ProductGroup object
18        Global.factory().begin();
19        Company c = CompanyContext.getEnterprise(
20          AccessMode.createNormal());
21        CompanyContext.setActiveCompany(c);
22        ProductGroupController pgc = (ProductGroupController)
```

```
              c.getDirectlyContainedPropertyBy("GPSE.ProductGroupController");
23            DescriptiveInformation description =
                DescriptiveInformationFactory.createDescriptiveInformation(
                AccessMode.createNormal(),
                Global.factory().getContainer("GPSE.ProductGroup"));
                description.addDefaultDescription("Created by Thread: "+id);
24            ProductGroup pg = null;
25            pg = ProductGroupFactory.createProductGroup(pgc,
                AccessMode.createNormal(),
                prefix + i,
                1,
                2,
                description);
26            Global.factory().commit();
27          } catch (SFException e) {
28            e.printStackTrace();
29          }
30          setRunner(nextId);
31        }
32    }

33    public static synchronized int getRunner(){
34      return runner;
35    }

36    public static synchronized void setRunner(int i){
37      runner = i;
38    }

39  }
```

The preceding code has the following characteristics:

- Line 18: Starts a transaction. Changes between this point and an associated commit or rollback point will occur as one logical unit.

- Line 19: Retrieves the Enterprise (the top-level company), which we know contains many of our dynamic properties. Typically, an object that doesn't have a natural owner is owned by a Company instance through dynamic properties.

- Line 21: Sets the Enterprise as the active Company instance. This isn't really necessary for this program, but framework components often use the current active company to store attributes or retrieve custom business logic. The active company is scoped to the entire distributed process.

- Line 22: Retrieves the ProductGroupController. This is an attribute that was added to the current active company, the Enterprise, via a dynamic property.

- Line 23: Creates a DescriptiveInformation instance for the new Product-Group object. A DescriptiveInformation object is a way to store descriptions for one or more locales.

- Line 25: Creates a new ProductGroup instance. The reference to the controller and the description are passed as parameters. The new Product-Group is automatically added to the controller because the new ProductGroup creation is tightly coupled.

- Line 26: Commits the entire transaction. With the commit, the new Product-Group, DescriptiveInformation, and the modified ProductGroupController (remember that a ProductGroup was automatically inserted into the controller at creation time) are saved to the underlying persistent store and are available for other applications to take advantage of.

- Line 27: Exceptions may occur, especially at commit time. Typically, this exception block would either roll back or mark the transaction as roll back only. For the sake of this example, a simpler approach is taken.

Note that the large code expansion occurs because we added SanFrancisco interaction and object creation rather than simply printing a line with concatenated data.

SFThreadManagement.java

The main class, now called SFThreadManagement, also has slight modifications to initialize SanFrancisco.

```
1  public class SFThreadManagement {
2    public static void main(String args[]){
3      try {
4        Global.initialize();
5        Thread t1 = new Thread(new SFProducer(0, args[0], 1));
6        Thread t2 = new Thread(new SFProducer(1, args[1], 0));
7        System.out.println("Starting...");
8        t1.start();
9        t2.start();
10       SFProducer.setRunner(0);
11     }
12     catch(SFException sfe){
13       sfe.printStackTrace();
14     }
15   }
16 }
```

Note the following about this code:

- Line 5: The Global.initialize() method initializes your application and any constructs that SanFrancisco needs for distributed processing. The try/catch block is added in lines 4, 12, 13, 14, and 15 because the initialization of SanFrancisco can throw exceptions.

WorkArea Exceptions

Running the program gives us our first reality check in thread management with processes that exist across a distributed process (the client and the server). An exception is thrown, indicating that the SanFrancisco WorkArea is not initialized.

```
Starting...

------>Beginning of exception trace(com.ibm.sf.gf.SmWorkAreaNotActiveException:
MSG_SM)
Transaction ID is  Unknown
[(1998.11.23 11:52:34:083) (9.5.168.21:1ed636:d44e1c6a2e:-7fd0)
(Thread[Thread-1,5,main]) (Client)]
com.ibm.sf.gf.SmWorkAreaNotActiveException: MSG_SM_230: The current thread should
be associated with a Work Area.
        at
com.ibm.sf.gf.SmDistributedProcessImpl.getDTC(SmDistributedProcessImpl.java:442)
        at com.ibm.sf.gf.BaseFactoryImpl.begin(BaseFactoryImpl.java:3232)
        at com.ibm.sf.samples.gpse.SFProducer.run(SFProducer.java:27)
        at java.lang.Thread.run(Thread.java:474)

------>End of exception trace(com.ibm.sf.gf.SmWorkAreaNotActiveException: MSG_SM)
```

SanFrancisco uses the concept of a distributed process (DP) to coordinate work that must be done across threads, virtual machines, and even networks. The distributed process serves to make separate virtual machines into one conceptual unit of processing. Information, such as a global thread identification, is shared by the distributed process via the distributed process context (DPC). Changes made to the context by one process are immediately available to other processes that share the distributed process.

In addition to the distributed process and its context, a *work area* exists that contains data used within a transaction as well as data that can be used outside a transaction. Data in the work area may contain the state of the current transaction, if one exists, and other details about the state of data that are needed to coordinate a unit of work. The work area is scoped to a single active thread. If two threads want to use the same work area, an object can be used to pass it between threads. The caveat is that the work area can be *active* in only one thread at a time. Furthermore, a single thread can have two work areas as long as it is active only in one at a time.

The model of distributed processes, contexts, and work areas is powerful. It is also one of the first complex concepts that a new SanFrancisco programmer encounters when assembling a user interface. We continue with this topic here, but many topics that require advanced programmer knowledge are handled in the SanFrancisco Programmer's Guide.

Handling the SanFrancisco Work Area and Finishing the Multithreaded Program

Now that we have described the process model and work areas, we can diagnose what went wrong with the sample. The distributed process, the context, and the main thread's work area are created with the Global.initialize() method in the first active thread. A work area can be active in only one thread at a time. Furthermore, we must actually access the work area from each thread to gain control of SanFrancisco from our active thread.

We can obtain the WorkArea, or Control, object by suspending a transaction. To do that, we call the suspend() method on the factory object that is being used by the process (accessed by the method on the Global singleton object factory()). To resume the transaction in another thread, or the current thread if a developer chooses, the resume() method is called. The resume() method is also accessed on the factory instance for the current application.

> **Note:** A singleton object instance refers to a single instance of a class that is always returned when a user attempts to create a new instance. Using this technique, only one instance of a class can exist in a virtual machine. The Global object instance is a singleton instance of the Global class.

After the Control class is obtained via the suspend() method, it can then be passed to any other thread that interacts with SanFrancisco. Here is the code to obtain the control information:

```
Control waControl = Global.factory().suspend();
```

Often, the communication mechanism between participating threads operates through static methods, through a singleton object, or possibly through a centralizing object that all threads have access to. This example uses the communication mechanism of static methods on the SFThreadManagement class. Threads can call the static methods to suspend and resume the transaction. Each time, they obtain control of the WorkArea by issuing the following method call:

```
Global.factory().resume(waControl);
```

There are two things to remember with this program sample. Because we are sharing only one work area across the whole process, only one thread can have access to the work area at a time. In our case, we've created a relatively safe mechanism for ensuring exclusive access. Second, our method of passing control around is inadequate for a user who is clicking around modal dialog boxes and window frames. This second point is addressed in the next section.

In the rewrite of the SFThreadManagement.java class, we add static methods as well as a static variable in which the Control object can be stored. In both the SFThreadManagement.java program and the SFProducer.java program, the appropriate suspend and resume methods are called in the SFThreadManagement class. Note that even though a single work area exists, many transactions are taking place over the course of a program. A work area, or Control object, can exist over the life of a process and beyond the bounds of a transaction. In fact, the Control object carries information with it about the status of the transaction itself.

In the SFThreadManagement class, we add the following static data and methods:

```
private static Control waControl = null;

public static void resumeWorkArea(){
    try {
        Global.factory().resume(waControl);
    }
    catch(Exception sfe){sfe.printStackTrace();}
}

public static void suspendWorkArea(){
    try {
        waControl = Global.factory().suspend();
    }
    catch(Exception sfe){sfe.printStackTrace();}
}
```

Next, within the body of the main() method in the class SFThreadManagement, after SanFrancisco is initialized, we call the suspend method to save the instance of the Control class for the first time:

```
t2.start();

// SAVE the main work area for access from other threads
suspendWorkArea();

SFProducer.setRunner(0);
```

In the SFProducer class, we add a method call to resume and obtain the work area. This code follows the code that obtains permission to create the new object. After the transaction commits but before we yield our right to be running, we suspend the work area. The following code must be added to SFProducer in the appropriate locations (we show only the lines before and after where the code is added):

```
while(getRunner() != id);
SFThreadManagement.resumeWorkArea();
try {
    // CREATE a ProductGroup object
    Global.factory().begin();

    // do good things

    Global.factory().commit();
    SFThreadManagement.suspendWorkArea();
} catch (SFException e) {
    e.printStackTrace();
}
```

The program works appropriately. Upon execution, 20 new ProductGroups are added to our ProductGroup controller. Typically, in the final calls to clean up an application—usually a WindowClosing event from the main frame—we call the SanFrancisco method:

```
Global.factory().uninitialize();
```

This call cleans up remaining threads and releases required objects to exit gracefully. Programmers often also call System.exit(0) to force program completion. In our case, we don't know which thread is the last thread to finish, so this call might have been dangerous.

A Simplified Mechanism for Handling the Work Area

As previously mentioned, the mechanism we have presented to move the work area from thread to thread is not robust in any sense of the word. The SanFrancisco User Interface framework introduces the Session class, which is meant to be a more robust mechanism for handling work areas and transactions. This class is not tied to the SanFrancisco User Interface framework in any way, but the user interface package was the most logical place to put it at the time the class was created.

The Session class adds several mechanisms beyond the SanFrancisco Foundation mechanisms.

- Methods for suspending and resuming WorkAreas
- Methods for handling transactions
- Reference counting for potential nesting conditions
- Event mechanisms to inform listeners of transaction and work area events

Note: A listener refers to an object that will receive notification when an event occurs in a system. Events are generated by an object, and any listeners that registered to receive the event notification will have an opportunity to process the event.

When you use the Session class, it is crucial that you use strict coding practices, mainly because of the reference counting that is built into the class. Reference counting accounts for nesting conditions that can occur when an object is brought up in the context of another accessed object. Nesting does not occur when an object is brought up on its own.

More documentation on the Session object is available in the SanFrancisco User Interface Programmer's Guide as well as in the JavaDoc for com.ibm.sf. gui.sfutil.session.Session. For the small threading example we've put together, we need to change only the static methods and data. Also, a call to resume-WorkArea must be added to the main thread of the program after SanFrancisco initialization takes place.

The static methods are modified as follows:

```
private static Session s = null;

public static void resumeWorkArea(){
    if(s == null)
        s = new Session();
    try {
        s.enterWorkArea();
    }
    catch(Exception sfe){sfe.printStackTrace();}
}

public static void suspendWorkArea(){
    try {
        s.exitWorkArea();
    }
    catch(Exception sfe){sfe.printStackTrace();}
}
```

Next, we add a call to the resumeWorkArea method right after the Global. initialize() method call in the main program. The program now works exactly as in the preceding section, and you'll add 20 more product groups to the product group repository.

Transaction Scope

Looking at the last two versions of the preceding program, you can note where transactions begin and commit. As the program is currently coded, each ProductGroup is created and committed in the same program segment. What would happen if the program encountered an exception halfway through creating our group of objects? In the program, as presented, half of the objects would exist, and the other half wouldn't exist.

To create a well-behaved system, you must understand window flow and know where client interaction takes place in a user interface. The visual flow of a user interface should be user-centric, but what occurs after a user completes interactions with a screen or series of screens must be respectful of the multiuser nature of SanFrancisco as a whole. Two areas are key to a well-behaved SanFrancisco client:

- Transaction scope: How long a client will keep a transaction open before committing changes to SanFrancisco

- Lock strategy: How long the client can wait before getting a pessimistic lock on an object, preventing others from accessing it

First, let's look at a couple of transaction scopes that can occur in an application. A *long* transaction scope starts a transaction at the first location where a user can change data in an object or at the first location where a user will want to access or start locking objects. The transaction ends when the user is finished with a sequence of changes. A *short* transaction scope focuses on committing changes as they occur, thereby keeping the system, as a whole, moving and also minimizing potential conflicts with other applications running on the San-Francisco network.

Remember, we are really not taking into account lock strategies at this point, only transaction strategies. Now consider the following scenario (also shown in Figure 12-3):

- A master window opens in a user interface. The window contains a list of available data (which users can change by editing the individual cells).

- More-specific data is obtained and changed in a secondary form-based window.

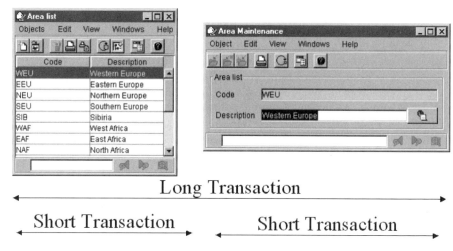

Figure 12-3. Transaction Scope with User Interface

Simply put, when does the transaction start, and when does it end? You can answer several questions to help with your decision, such as the following:

- Should a change in the second form be committed with changes in the table, or can the changes be committed separately?

- When should a change to an object instance be available to other users of the objects—immediately after each object is changed or after the user completes a series of object changes in nested windows?

With large, complex programs, many different strategies will be employed throughout the program as a whole. When you make the decisions about transaction length for the various flows through a program, you must also take into account screen reuse. For example, the frame that is opened from the table may also exist at another location in the application, but in the second location it may be the master of a transaction rather than being opened by a table that was in control of the application.

Often, programmers employ a singleton object that functions as a transaction entry point, much as was done in the earlier WorkArea examples. When a frame is opened, the frame asks the singleton to start a transaction. If multiple frames try to start a transaction, only one is started, but a reference count of the number of frames that are in the transaction is kept. When the final frame is closed, the transaction is committed. SanFrancisco contains the Session object, which can be used in the singleton object in this fashion.

What this approach does is to start to bridge short transaction scopes with long transaction scopes. This approach is useful if windows are not modal. Nonmodal dialog boxes often leave a user free to enter other portions of an application in ways that are not always expected by the programmer.

Looking back over the program presented earlier in the chapter, you could consider it as having a short transaction scope. Changes and objects created become immediately available because each create is bounded by a begin and commit of a transaction. You can change the behavior of the program by moving the separate begin and commit cycles out of the SFProducer run method and into the main program.

```
public static void main(String args[]){

    try {
        Global.initialize();

        resumeWorkArea();

        Global.factory().begin();

        Thread t1 = new Thread(new SFProducer(0, args[0], 1));
        Thread t2 = new Thread(new SFProducer(1, args[1], 0));
        System.out.println("Starting...");
        t1.start();
        t2.start();

        // SAVE the main work area for access from other threads
        suspendWorkArea();

        SFProducer.setRunner(0);
        t2.join();
        resumeWorkArea();
        Global.factory().commit();
        Global.uninitialize();
        System.exit(0);
    }
    catch(SFException sfe){
        sfe.printStackTrace();
    }
}
```

In addition to beginning and ending the transaction in the main thread, the second thread is joined so that the transaction does not commit until the second thread has completed processing. Also, note that the main thread must re-obtain the work area after the threads are completed. Passing the WorkArea around is a lot like a game of catch. After it has been passed off, you must behave like everyone else and wait for the opportunity to get the ball back.

Now the program has a single transaction. All objects created in the program become available only upon the final commit in the main thread. If an exception occurs in the program, the objects do not commit and therefore need not be cleaned up; they need only be re-created later.

Locking Strategies

Locking strategies are also crucial to a system and its behavior in the context of the larger SanFrancisco network. Consider an application that starts by displaying a table of all available ProductGroup objects in the current active company. When the table is displayed, should the application lock all the objects that are being displayed, or can an application risk having stale data displayed if another user has updated data?

You can develop locking strategies by answering certain questions that are similar to those asked about the transaction scope:

- How critical is it that data not be changed in the system while a user is looking at it?

- How long can an object be locked so that other users cannot alter the data? How long can it be locked to prevent reading of the data?

- Can an object be locked for an indefinite period if a user goes home for the evening, leaving a program window open?

- If an optimistic locking approach is used, how should the program behave if the optimistic lock fails?

Simple questions with honest answers often go far in helping you create both a lock strategy and a transaction scope strategy. Documentation, prototyping, and case studies of how your users will interact with the user interface go far in balancing network object contention with a fair response time and minimal lock and commit failures.

Summary

This chapter covers a lot of material that programmers should consider as they develop applications. The methods discussed here for passing work areas, scoping transactions, and locking objects are employed in the remaining chapters. There is no single way to complete these jobs, although the Session object supplied by the SanFrancisco User Interface framework attempts to simplify and provide additional mechanisms for complex clients.

Being aware that multiple threads are running within most user interfaces is crucial to the success of your client program. Further knowledge of the transaction boundaries that you wish to employ, the locking strategies, and the threads that are active in your application will prove extremely useful in employing various programming techniques.

13
Using Commands in an Application

As mentioned in Chapter 4, commands are SanFrancisco Dependent classes that bundle atomic units of business logic for execution. There are many places in applications where commands can be used to create logical units of work. System designers often locate commands and build them into an application's design models.

In reality, system designers usually find only those atomic processes and transactions that fit the implementation of the system and the requirements developed by the analysis team. So what is left for implementors beyond coding them? There are three primary areas in which system implementors may have a better view than the designers of possible uses of commands:

- System performance
- Graphical user interface (GUI) event processing
- System setup and initialization

As systems reach their first full prototypes or even as late as the first full system tests, characteristics of the system are discovered that may not have been predicted. For example, a full system test may reveal that population of a list box is particularly time-consuming. The implementors may find that a better way to populate the list box is to submit a command that retrieves only the required data from the server. If the command runs next to the location of the persistent data (near the database where the data is stored), less network traffic will result and client-side garbage collection will be minimized.

From the perspective of a user interface, imagine a button on the application that runs a large calculation or a complex business function. Typically, the interface waits for the event to be signaled by the button and then executes a method containing the business logic to be executed. If this logic is complex or computation-intensive or if it interacts with many business objects, it may be easier to encapsulate this logic in a command. You also gain better performance, as described earlier. In addition, the command can be class-replaced at runtime if the logic is changed.

Class replacement of commands can be especially useful when an application is installed at different customer sites. Processing implications for a calculation or user interface event may vary from one location to the next. Class replacement can be used to allow individual locations to modify a user interface event's result.

Commands are also useful for system setup and initialization, which can be wrapped in a command to create a logical unit of work. For example, the first time applications are installed, the site can set up all its financial calendars, periods, and business infrastructure, and then populate the business objects.

In this chapter we show a technique used with commands to set up and initialize a new installation of a SanFrancisco application. The commands populate the server data upon installation of the GPSE application (introduced in Chapter 5). Commands are used to logically separate the installation functions and improve the installation performance.

> **Note:** SanFrancisco Version 1 Release 4 introduces a Client Command framework that helps you realize the performance advantage of using commands throughout a client program. Object creation, deletion, and access are targeted in the first release of the framework. It is initially being released in beta form but should become stable in a follow-up fix release.
>
> The Client Command framework is not covered in this chapter, but if you understand the basic concepts of commands and some uses of them, you will be able to adapt your knowledge to the framework. The one additional technology it introduces is the ability to bundle parameters in a generic way; as a result, you are not required to create a command interface subclass, an implementation subclass, a factory, and method implementations. The command framework is generic in nature, and parameters are passed within generic transfer objects.
>
> Information about the Client Command framework is available in the SanFrancisco Programmer's Guide. The JavaDoc for the framework is also available in the full SanFrancisco Version 1 Release 4 CD. The package name for the commands is com.ibm.sf.client.cmd.

Performance Characteristics of Commands

The sample in this chapter is not geared toward the performance aspects of an application. As the sample is presented, keep in mind the logic that will be executed as the result of submitting the atomic unit of work, and think about where the execution of the command will take place.

You can create commands that execute at the location where an object exists. The commands use a SanFrancisco Handle as a target to access the object's location. After the target is set up at the location where the object exists, the access location of the objects manipulated with the command should be appropriate. Target objects can be accessed in two locations. Each has unique performance characteristics.

- HOME: The object and data reside on the server. A proxy object, created on the client, forwards requests for data from the client to the server and returns the appropriate data.

- LOCAL: The object is copied in its entirety to the client.

The first case, AccessMode HOME, is fast in the sense that you do not have to copy all the data to the client when you really want only a single field of data. Unfortunately, a proxy must be constructed, and there is always overhead for method calls because of the marshaling of data.

In the second case, AccessMode LOCAL, all the data is moved from the server to the client, creating considerable overhead. After the data is on the client, data access is very fast.

Now suppose that you must get the descriptions of 50 or 60 objects, or even 1000 objects. Both methods seem suboptimal when you consider the strain it put on the client's garbage collector in the long-running application.

Shipping the command to the best location for execution by using the Handle as the target makes the retrieval of the descriptions much less stressful on the application and the system as a whole. The client programmer sets the target of the command to be the server. Subsequently, all objects accessed by the commands should be accessed with the HOME access location. All code and data are executed in the same location, creating a much faster application.

With this setup, only a command object is created and executed at the client. The server is responsible for the object maintenance. No proxy objects have to be created, and that helps the garbage collector in the long run. Ideally, the application programmer also plans for reuse of the command. With object instance pooling, the garbage collector does not collect the command; instead, you keep it in a pool and reuse it every time you need a description of an object. You do not even need to call a factory to re-create the command.

Keep object location in mind when you read the remainder of the chapter and the example.

Setup and Initialization of an Application Using Commands

Setup and initialization of data are tasks that are well suited for SanFrancisco commands. Using setup and initialization commands, you can create units of work for the servers that set up the runtime infrastructure for your applications and then populate some initial data for the application to work on. The tasks for these commands are broken down as follows:

- Setup commands: Sample setup commands are supplied by SanFrancisco for all the common business objects and core business processes; you must set up any application requirements that are implemented as extensions. Controllers and default policies are examples of this type of infrastructure. Within the sample GPSE application, the Customer category setup command adds the CustomerController to the active company.

- Initialization commands: Initialization commands are not provided by SanFrancisco. This type of command is discussed here as an example of how to create the initial data necessary for an application. In some cases this data may already exist but not in a format that can be used by SanFrancisco. In that case, the data must be used to instantiate initial objects for use in the application. In the GPSE Customer example, the Initialization command is used to populate the customer base from data files.

A large portion of the code for commands is built by the SanFrancisco code generator. Each command implementation class has one method, the handleDo() method, that is responsible for the bulk of the work. This method cannot be generated completely because it contains the custom business logic. When going through this chapter, you may want to refer to the section "Creating a Command Subclass" in Chapter 5 to refresh your memory on the methods associated with a command.

Two commands are created in this chapter: one setup command and one initialization command. Splitting the two commands in this way serves to allow the structure of a company to vary independently of the data that is set up. For example, one company may set up its company hierarchy in a unique way but want the data to be initialized in the same way as that of other companies. This split of behavior and function is not required by the framework, but it is a technique you may find valuable, depending on your company's structure.

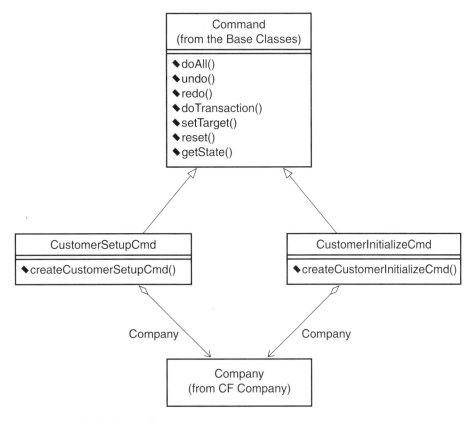

Figure 13-1. GPSE Setup Commands

Creating a Setup Command

The commands in this chapter use the Company for which the data is being created as its target. The setup command that populates the customers for our company extends the CommandImpl class. The code generator creates much of the code. Upon generation and some of our implementation, the setup command's outer scope in the implementation looks like this:

```
1   package GPSE;

2   import java.util.*;
3   import java.io.*;
4   import com.ibm.sf.gf.*;
5   import com.ibm.sf.cf.*;
```

```
6   public class CustomerSetupCmdImpl extends CommandImpl
       implements CustomerSetupCmd {
7      static final int versionNumber = GPSE.VersionNumber.CURRENT;
8      static final String realClassName = "GPSE.CustomerSetupCmdImpl";

9      // methods....

10     /**
11      * <P>not owned and mandatory attribute </P>
12      */
13     protected Handle ivTargetHdl; // for Company entity

14  }
```

Note the following about the preceding code:

- Line 6: Declares our setup command to extend directly from the CommandImpl class provided in the SanFrancisco framework. Like all classes that adhere to the SanFrancisco programming model, it implements a corresponding interface.
- Line 9: The methods are left for later in the chapter.
- Line 13: We will have an instance variable that stores the target object for the location where the command will run.

It is in the handleDo() method of a command that the action occurs. In the CustomerSetupCmdImpl, the method is responsible for attaching a Customer-Controller to the active company that is being used as the target of the command.

```
1   protected void handleDo() throws com.ibm.sf.gf.SFException {
2      try {
3         // retrieve the company from the target handle
4         Company company = (Company)(getObjectFromHandle(ivTargetHdl,
              AccessMode.createPlusWrite()));
5         //build a DescriptiveInformation object, which will be used to give
6         //  the object a locale-sensitive description
7         DescriptiveInformation di1 =
              DescriptiveInformationFactory.createDescriptiveInformation(
              AccessMode.createNormal(),
              Global.factory().getContainer("GPSE.CustomerControllerRoot"));
8         di1.addDefaultDescription("CustomerController");

9         // call the factory to create a controller instance
10        CustomerControllerRootFactory.createCustomerControllerRoot(
              company,
              AccessMode.createPlusWrite(),
              Global.factory().getContainer("GPSE.CustomerControllerRoot"),
              di1);
```

```
11   }  catch(SFException ex) {
12      try {
13        Global.factory().rollbackOnly();
14      } catch (SFException e2) { }
15   }
16 }
```

Note the following about the preceding code:

- Line 4: Assuming that the target of this command has already been set, this line retrieves the company for modification.
- Line 7: Constructs a DescriptiveInformation instance.
- Line 8: Adds a description to the DescriptiveInformation object.
- Line 10: Creates the customer controller. Note that the customer controller is created with the company as the first parameter. The controller will automatically be attached to the company. This is tightly coupled object creation.

Note that if any exceptions occur as the controller is being added to the company, the whole transaction gets marked as rollback only. This means that no changes that occur within this transaction will be saved. During setup and initialization, it is often easy to resubmit the entire string of commands after you correct the problem. The rollback-only mechanism can be a benefit in that you can abort all changes without leaving the network in a half-created state.

A DescriptiveInformation object is created for the controller. Descriptive-Information objects are a locale-sensitive way of creating object descriptions. When a user attempts to retrieve a description from a DescriptiveInformation object, the description matching the user's current locale is returned. If a description does not exist matching the current locale, the default description is returned. DescriptiveInformation instances are widely used in SanFrancisco business objects.

At the completion of the command, the CustomerController will be attached to the Company that was the target of the command.

Creating an Initialization Command

The CustomerInitializationCmd can now be created and executed using the same company as its target. In this sample, a single customer is created. The outer scope of the initialization command is as follows:

```
1    package GPSE;

2    import java.util.*;
3    import java.io.*;
4    import com.ibm.sf.gf.*;
5    import com.ibm.sf.cf.*;

6  public class CustomerInitializeCmdImpl extends CommandImpl
7    implements CustomerInitializeCmd {
8    static final int versionNumber = GPSE.VersionNumber.CURRENT;
9    static final String realClassName = "GPSE.CustomerInitializeCmdImpl";

10    // methods
11    /** <P>not owned and mandatory attribute </P>*/
12    protected Handle ivTargetHdl; // for Company entity

13  } // end of class CustomerInitializeCmdImpl
```

Note the similarities between this command and the preceding command.

As with the setup command, the complexity of this command is mostly in the handleDo() method. The company is, again, retrieved from the target handle that is stored in the command instance. From the company, two controllers are retrieved: the customer controller, which contains all our customers for this company, and the country controller, which contains a list of known countries for use in building the addresses of the customers.

After the controllers are retrieved, some initialization data is set up. Several addresses are built from the data, and all of them are used in the Customer object. After the addresses are built, the Customer object can be created from the CustomerFactory. The first parameter in the create method is the owning controller—in this case, the CustomerController we retrieved at the start of the method.

Next, some additional state is added to the created Customers for sample purposes, giving us a variety of customers with varying outstanding balances and credit lines.

```
1 protected void handleDo() throws com.ibm.sf.gf.SFException {
2    try {
3      // get the company from the target handle
4      Company company =
       (Company)getObjectFromHandle(
         ivTargetHdl,AccessMode.createNormal());

5      // retrieve the controllers from the company by property name
6      CustomerController owningController =
         (CustomerController)company.getDirectlyContainedPropertyBy(
           "GPSE.CustomerController");
```

```
7    CountryController countryController =
       (CountryController)company.getDirectlyContainedPropertyBy(
         "cf.CountryController");

8    // set up initial data for a customer
9    String name = "University of Wisconsin";
10   String creditLimit = "1500.00";
11   String outstandingBalance = "340.00";
12   String cAddressee = "Joe Football";
13   String cPhone = "368-245-9972";
14   String cFax = "368-245-9970";
15   String cEMail = "Joe Football @ UNet.com";
16   String bAddressee = "Billing Dept";
17   String bLine1 = "1439 Wheatland Boulevard";
18   String bCity = "LaCrosse";
19   String bState = "Wisconsin";
20   String bZip = "63019";
21   String bCountry = "US";
22   String bLocale = "en_US";
23   String sAddressee = "Athletic Dept";
24   String sLine1 = "1400 Sport Lane Bldg-D";
25   String sCity = "LaCrosse";
26   String sState = "Wisconsin";
27   String sZip = "63019";
28   String sCountry = "US";
29   String sLocale = "en_US";

30   // create the contact address
31   Address contact = AddressFactory.createAddress(
       AccessMode.createPlusWrite(),
       Global.factory().getContainer("cf.Address"),
       countryController.getCountryBy(bCountry),
       bLocale);

32   // set additional info in contact
33   contact.setAddressee(cAddressee);
34   contact.setPhoneNumber(cPhone);
35   contact.setFaxNumber(cFax);
36   contact.setEMailAddress(cEMail);

37   // create billing address
38   Address billing = AddressFactory.createAddress(
       AccessMode.createPlusWrite(),
       Global.factory().getContainer("cf.Address"),
       countryController.getCountryBy(bCountry),
       bLocale);
39   // set additional info in billing address
```

```
40    billing.setAddressee(bAddressee);
41    billing.addAddressLineBy(bLine1, "line1");
42    billing.setPostalCodeLocation(bCity);
43    billing.addAddressLineBy(bState, "state");
44    billing.setPostalCode(bZip);

45    // create shipping address
46    Address shipping = AddressFactory.createAddress(
        AccessMode.createPlusWrite(),
        Global.factory().getContainer("cf.Address"),
        countryController.getCountryBy(sCountry),
        sLocale);
47    // set additional info in shipping address
48    shipping.setAddressee(sAddressee);
49    shipping.addAddressLineBy(sLine1, "line1");
50    shipping.setPostalCodeLocation(sCity);
51    shipping.addAddressLineBy(sState, "state");
52    shipping.setPostalCode(sZip);

53    // now that relevant addresses are created, the
54    //   customer can be created
55    Customer customer = CustomerFactory.createCustomer(owningController,
        AccessMode.createNormal(),
        name,
        billing,
        contact,
        shipping);

56    // set additional customer information
57    CurrencyController currController = (CurrencyController)
        (company.getPropertyBy("cf.CurrencyController"));

58    DDecimal ob = DDecimalFactory.createDDecimal(outstandingBalance);
59    DCurrencyValue obCurrencyValue =
        DCurrencyValueFactory.createDCurrencyValue(
          currController.getBaseCurrency(), ob);
60    customer.setOutstandingBalance(obCurrencyValue);
61    DDecimal cl = DDecimalFactory.createDDecimal(creditLimit);
62    DCurrencyValue clCurrencyValue =
        DCurrencyValueFactory.createDCurrencyValue(
          currController.getBaseCurrency(), cl);
63    customer.setCreditLimit(clCurrencyValue);
64  } catch (SFException e) {
65      // Could not access necessary business object -- severe error
66      Global.factory().rollbackOnly();
67      throw e;
68  }
69  }
```

As with the setup command, the company is immediately retrieved from the target location that was stored in the command at creation time. Two controllers are retrieved in this command. The customer controller, created in the setup command, stores the customers that are created here. The country controller must exist prior to execution of this command. The country controller stores instances of Country classes, which are used throughout the framework.

- Line 4: Retrieves the company that was stored as a Handle in this instance at creation time.
- Lines 6 and 7: Retrieve the customer and country controllers, respectively, from the Company. They are dynamic properties.
- Lines 8–29: Set up data for an object. Typically, this data would be read from a file in the filesystem but were inserted here for simplicity and to increase the size of the book.
- Lines 31–52: Create a series of Address instances. Addresses are in the Common Business Objects layer.
- Line 55: Creates the Customer instance. Note that this is a tightly coupled creation. As a result, the new instance is automatically added to the customer controller at creation time.
- Lines 56–63: Set up additional data in this customer, relating to the balance owed and the credit limit. Note the distinction between the Currency and a DCurrencyValue. A Currency is a description of a currency, such as U.S. dollars. The various currencies that a location understands are maintained in the controller. In addition to the normal collection characteristics of a controller, the currency controller has a method to determine the base currency. The DCurrencyValue is a quantity of the currency of the base value. If a person interacts with this customer in the future and the currency types don't match, all the data and operations to take care of manipulating the data with its correct characteristics are maintained in the DCurrencyValue instance.

We now have atomic units of code that set up the structure of our data and initialize the data. These units of code can be run at customer sites after the application is installed. These setup and initialization commands are also likely to be used extensively during testing.

Running the Setup and Initialization Commands from an Application

After the commands are in place, a short program can be created to kick off the setup commands. The setup and initialization client presented here has the following flow:

- Initialize SanFrancisco and start a transaction.
- Retrieve the company that the customers are being set up for.
- Build the setup command.
- Start and wait for the return of the setup command.
- Build the initialization command.
- Start and wait for the return of the initialization command.
- Commit the transaction so that the data can be seen by other users and applications.
- Exit the program.

The following new class has a main() program to execute the command:

```
1    import com.ibm.sf.gf.*;
2    import com.ibm.sf.cf.*;
3    import GPSE.*;
4    import java.io.*;

5    public class GPSESetupAndInit {

6      public static void main(String args[]) {

7        // initialize SF
8        try {
9          Global.initialize();
10       } catch (SFException ex) {
11         System.out.println("GPSESetupAndInit: Error initializing SF: " + ex);
12         RuntimeException e = new RuntimeException(ex.getMessage());
13         throw e;
14       }

15       // initialize GPSE data
16       try {

17         // Begin the transaction
18         Global.factory().begin();
19         // get the Company
```

```
20          Company company = CompanyContext.getEnterprise();
21          CompanyContext.setActiveCompany(company);

22          // Customer
23          System.out.println("GPSESetupAndInit: Initializing Customer");
24          CustomerSetupCmd csc =
            CustomerSetupCmdFactory.createCustomerSetupCmd(
            company.getHandle());
25          csc.doAll();
26          CustomerInitializeCmd cic =
            CustomerInitializeCmdFactory.createCustomerInitializeCmd(
            company.getHandle());
27          cic.doAll();

28          // Commit the transaction
29          Global.factory().commit();

30       } catch (SFException e) {
31          try {
32            if (Global.factory().getTransactionStatus() !=
          Status.NO_TRANSACTION)
33          Global.factory().rollback();
34          } catch (SFException e2) {
35              System.out.println("GPSESetupAndInit::
            fatal error on rollback " + e2.getMessage());
36          }
37          System.exit(0);
38          }
39    }
40  }
```

There are a few lines in the preceding code that must be explicitly pointed out:

- Lines 24 and 26: Create the commands and the Handle of the target into the command. Using the Handle, the command executes at the location of the object. In this way, we minimize the overhead of creating proxy access and avoid putting a subsequent burden on the garbage collector on the client. If we use the lock mode of PESSIMISTIC with the location HOME, we set up an optimally performing command.

- Lines 25 and 27: Execute the commands. If the doAll() method is called, as it was earlier, the client program is in control of the transaction. If the command must be executed completely on its own, the client calls the doTransaction() method on the command. If the doTransaction() method were to be called in this case, the transaction started on line 19 would have to be committed before the doTransaction() method is called because SanFrancisco does not support nested transactions. Many other permutations for setting the active company can also be found in that case.

After execution of the main, Joe Football will be permitted to buy from our company. Both of the commands presented in this chapter use the Customer class and other existing SanFrancisco classes to get their tasks done. Commands can be used to speed setup and initialization and to execute tasks as one atomic action. Failure of one of the commands will force a rollback of all data that is set up.

Furthermore, sites where the application is deployed could replace the command with their own implementation via class replacement. No application code would have to be recompiled except the command that was being created.

Summary

Commands can play a crucial role in applications. They can improve performance in system bottlenecks, bundle large pieces of code into easier-to-manage work units (as is the case for the setup and initialization of data), and provide a more natural mechanism for bundling events that result from user interface interaction.

Discussion of the application characteristics of commands was deferred to the client portion of the book because the need for a command is often discovered only in the latter phases of development. Commands prove useful as user interfaces evolve and performance bottlenecks are found in an application.

SanFrancisco Release 1.4 will have new client-centric commands. This Client Command framework will center on the operations of client applications rather than the inner workings of the business framework.

14 The Presentation Layer

SanFrancisco provides a robust User Interface framework for use in building applications. Although SanFrancisco applications can be constructed with other user interface frameworks (such as the Java Foundation Classes (JFC) from Sun or the original Java Abstract Windowing Toolkit (AWT) classes), application developers will want to consider leveraging the capabilities in SanFrancisco. The most important reasons for using the SanFrancisco User Interface framework are as follows:

- The framework provides much infrastructure that is common to SanFrancisco applications.
- It gives your applications the consistent SanFrancisco look and feel described in the SanFrancisco User Interface Style Guide.
- You can use the built-in support for translatable text in the User Interface components.
- You can leverage components built with SanFrancisco patterns in mind.

Note: SanFrancisco Version 1 Release 4 includes a new version of the SanFrancisco User Interface framework based on JavaBeans and visual construction capabilities. The Version 1 Release 4 GUI framework (or *SanFrancisco GUI beans*, as they will likely be called) will probably ship as a beta and quickly evolve into a stable base.

This chapter deals with the "classic" SanFrancisco GUI framework, which will likely disappear in future releases of SanFrancisco. The Version 1 Release 4 GUI framework follows design principles similar to those of the current framework, so this chapter will remain relevant in the future. As you read this chapter, you will note the amount of code that must be handwritten to implement portions of this version of the GUI framework. Much of the need for this manual writing of code disappears with the Version 1 Release 4 GUI framework. It is based on the SanFrancisco beans, which are discussed in Chapter 15.

In addition to discussing the existing GUI framework, this chapter discusses the use of SanFrancisco with the Java Foundation Classes and the construction of applications with thin clients. So even though portions of this chapter will have to be rewritten, the design principles discussed here will not disappear. Rather, they will take on a slightly different form in the near future.

As you read about the SanFrancisco User Interface framework and the Java Foundation Classes, keep in mind that the code presented here is for an application and not an applet. Applet invocation of applications built with the SanFrancisco framework can require heavy bandwidth requirements because of the large installed base of SanFrancisco. Often, if an applet is going to be built, the clients must have the required SanFrancisco framework components on their systems.

The SanFrancisco User Interface Framework

The SanFrancisco User Interface framework goes beyond what most user interface class libraries provide in terms of interaction with business data models. A large portion of the implementation of complex applications is done within the framework implementation itself. Numerous items—such as default frames with a set of default menu actions, message bars, and automatic error dialog boxes—are already implemented when you start using the framework.

The motivation for including so much implementation out of the box is to provide a mechanism for rendering the same look and feel throughout suites of applications from different application providers. Furthermore, the framework helps guide the placement of transaction boundaries and common user interface interactions with business data.

In addition to providing default implementation of many common application processes, the framework enforces a strict programming model. All the various levels of viewable containers and widgets adhere to a strict model-view-controller (MVC) pattern. In many class libraries, adhering to the model-view-controller pattern is optional. In some cases the pattern must be built entirely from scratch. When you're dealing with transactional systems, the

MVC pattern is extremely valuable. The SanFrancisco User Interface framework enforces the pattern in all parts of the framework.

The Design

For many programmers using the SanFrancisco User Interface framework for the first time, the most important leap is the complete, and enforced, split of user interface function into distinct model, view, and controller pieces. A large percentage of this book is focused on the model portion of the triumvirate. The *model* represents business logic and the way data are acted on. The *view* is concerned with the presentation of screens and requests for data to and from a user. The *controller* moves information—whether in the form of actions on the user interface or data entry fields from the view into the model.

In multiuser systems, the controller takes on a larger role. It must place appropriate locks on objects and define transaction scopes for the various paths a user can take through the user interface. The SanFrancisco User Interface framework provides a series of overridable implementations and guiding concepts to drive large applications.

Again, the SanFrancisco User Interface framework is built as a true model-view-controller. If you've read the entire book, you've probably realized that the term *controller* is already widely used in the framework. As a result of the use of this term in the Common Business Objects layer, the term *maintainer* is used in the SanFrancisco User Interface framework. Using the term *maintainer*, the User Interface framework breaks down into the following high-level components:

- Model: The model is considered the data-centric portion of the framework. The model is represented by SanFrancisco business objects (or possibly objects or data models of another type) and their business logic. We will use the business objects that are described earlier without modification.

- View: The view is the graphical portion of the application. A view consists of the windows, frames, and forms that guide the application as well as the groups of widgets and controls that guide the user and represent the data in the model.

- Maintainer: The maintainer is responsible for the connection between the view and the model. Data is moved from the model to the controls in the view and vice versa. Considering that the business logic is complete and the view is often constructed visually, much of the work in building the final application is spent in the maintainer.

The trio of concepts is shown in Figure 14-1.

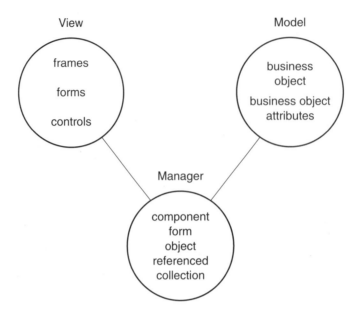

Figure 14-1. Model-View-Maintainer

This chapter spends time discussing a few of the mechanisms and conventions in the User Interface framework, but you should not expect to be an expert in the framework after reading this chapter. In addition to the JavaDoc information on the classes, which is available with SanFrancisco, there are three additional paths to learning more about the User Interface framework:

- SanFrancisco User Interface Programmer's Guide: This guide goes through all the mechanisms and concepts that you need to program with the SanFrancisco User Interface framework.

- SanFrancisco User Interface Style Guide: This guide goes through the style that was used to build the framework as well as the style that end user applications should adhere to. If the style guide is used, SanFrancisco applications from various vendors should end up with a common look and feel.

- SanFrancisco User Interface Framework Redbook. This is a step-by-step approach to building applications with the SanFrancisco User Interface framework.

- SanFrancisco samples: Most of the samples distributed with SanFrancisco use the user interface framework for interaction with the user. Several programming approaches are shown, and several of the samples are optimized for various kinds of access to the model.

Constructing a Client

The SanFrancisco User Interface framework should appear, at least visually, very similar to the Java Foundation Classes view components. The reason is that the components are subclasses and aggregations of JFC components, with added or slightly altered implementations. Having complete knowledge of JFC can be a boon in some cases, but in other cases it can be a hindrance. For example, if you leverage Java's Swing model support and have intimate knowledge of the widgets available, you will understand many of the details of the SanFrancisco subclasses. On the other hand, if you've become heavily dependent on some of the advanced event mechanisms used for communication in JFC, occasionally you will probably have to step back, take a deep breath, and remember that this is not pure JFC programming.

The view components can be split into three categories: nonvisual components, container components, and lightweight components.

Many SanFrancisco components go beyond the JFC implementations. A few forms are very common in SanFrancisco, such as displaying a collection in a table along with a more detailed object form. The framework often offers hybrid components to address specific SanFrancisco patterns of objects. The specific collection/object form control in the SanFrancisco User Interface framework is called the UITableForm.

Notice in Figure 14-2 that we are using five components: the UITableForm; a UITable that is constructed and contained in the UITableForm; a UIForm, also contained in the UITableForm; and a series of UILabels and UITextFields to build the view representation. Also notice the frame decorations surrounding the main contents: a toolbar, a menu bar, and a message bar. All these UI elements are implemented by the SanFrancisco User Interface framework with little or no extra code (depending on how you want the frame customized).

Two lines of code will set up and initialize the User Interface framework. Setup and initialization use the static methods on the UIInitializer class, which centralizes many of the default behaviors and implementations that are used by the user interface throughout an application. In this sample, two items are set up through the initializer:

- Factory: A default factory is used virtually any time the SanFrancisco User Interface framework is used with SanFrancisco business objects as the model. To use SanFrancisco with other objects as models, you replace the factory with one more appropriate to your scenario.

- Message dispatcher: The message dispatcher controls how the framework reacts if an unhandled exception occurs. With the default message handler supplied by SanFrancisco, an entry occurs in the message area, and a frame with a text field may appear.

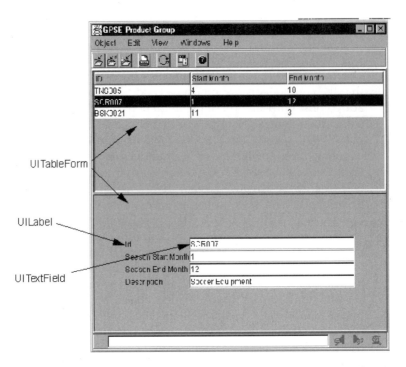

UITableForm

UILabel

UITextField

Figure 14-2. ProductGroup Maintenance with the SanFrancisco User Interface
Framework

After the framework is initialized, a series of parameters is set that determines
the look and feel of the frame to be shown. Parameters sent to the frame
include the desired toolbar, prebuilt menu bars, the viewable contents of the
frame, and various parameters that may affect the size and placement of the
frame. Note that the toolbar and menu bar are classes contained in the San-
Francisco User Interface framework. When items are selected from the toolbar,
predefined actions occur that are sent to the maintainers for the forms contained in the frame. Not only are default views given, but also communications
mechanisms defined that give consistent application behavior are.

- A UIFrame always contains a UIForm. Whereas the UIFrame is often
  used straight out of the framework, UIForms are usually subclasses of
  the class in the user interface framework. The UIForm subclass contains
  the widgets and visual elements to provide interaction with the user. The
  UIForm subclass is set into the frame through the open frame parameters.

- After the application's frame is configured, the frame is shown through
  the setVisible method.

```
1 public static void main(String[] args)
2 {
3    Session s = ApplicationContextBean.getDefaultSession();
4    try
5    {
6      Global.initialize();

7      // Initialize the SanFrancisco User Interface Framework
8      UIInitializer.instance().setFactoryClassName(
           "com.ibm.sf.gui.sfutil.UISFFactory");
9      UIInitializer.instance().setMessageDispatcherClassName(
           "com.ibm.sf.gui.sfutil.UISFMessageDispatcher");

10     // Create a SanFrancisco UI Fwk Frame
11     UIOpenFrameParameters ofp = new UIOpenFrameParameters();
12     ofp.setFormClassName(
           "com.ibm.sf.samples.gpse.GPSEProductGroupTableForm");
13     ofp.setFrameClassName("com.ibm.sf.gui.UIFrame");
14     ofp.setMenuBarClassName("com.ibm.sf.gui.UIObjectMenuBar");
15     ofp.setToolBarClassName("com.ibm.sf.gui.UIObjectToolBar");
16     ofp.setSize(500,500);

17     UIFrame frame = UIFactory.instance().createFrame(ofp, false);
18     frame.setTitle("GPSE Product Group");

19     // Suspend the threads access
20     s.exitWorkArea();

21     frame.setVisible(true);
22   }
23   catch(Exception e)
24   {
25     e.printStackTrace();
26   }
27}
```

There are a few interesting things about the preceding code:

- Line 3: We are using a singleton object that keeps a Session object for management of the thread and work area (as discussed in Chapter 12). This technique is discussed in Chapter 13. The singleton used here is provided in the SanFrancisco JavaBeans package.

- Lines 11–16: These lines customize the frame along with the decorations and default actions that it will contain.

As previously mentioned, the content of a UIFrame is a UIForm. A subclass of the UIForm is created that constructs the view, in this case the GPSEProduct-GroupTableForm. Within the UIForm subclass, a setupControls method contains initialization code for the view. Notice that a layout is set up for use, just as in JFC or AWT programming.

The UIForm subclass looks very much like any other JFC component. The widgets contained in the form are set up, a layout is set into the panel, and the objects are sized. Two additional things occur in the UIForm subclass:

- The maintainer class name is set into the UIForm via the setMaintainer-ClassName() method call.

- Each control, widget, or container gets an attached UIAttributeID.

The maintainer class name is set into the form via the method call:

```
setMaintainerClassName(
    "com.ibm.sf.samples.gpse.GPSEProductGroupCollectionMaintainer"
);
```

Whenever an event occurs in the view portion of the user interface, the event is passed to the maintainer. Unlike most class libraries, every SanFrancisco User Interface framework component can have a maintainer attached to it. In many cases, such as UIButtons, UITextFields, and others, a default maintainer is set by the User Interface framework. In general, the more-complex forms must have the maintainers written by hand.

In addition to the maintainer, UIAttributeIds must be attached to each of the components. UIAttributeIds are used as communication mechanisms between the view and the maintainer. An attribute is identified by both a string and an integer value. Typically, the integer value is a final static variable set up either in an interface or in the maintainer itself. Basically, any item that can contain a state that is managed by the maintainer will have an associated attribute ID.

```
UITable tblProductGroup = new UITable();
tblProductGroup.setAttributeId(
    new UIAttributeId("TBL_PRODUCTGROUP",
    GPSEProductGroupIds.TBL_PRODUCTGROUP)
);
```

In the preceding example, a UITable is created and a UIAttributeId is assigned to it. Now when the view must pass information about where an event occurred, the common language between the view and maintainer will be the attribute identifier.

For most components, that is the extent of the work to do in the view. In some complex components, especially the ones with collection interaction, additional maintainers must be set into them, or additional forms must be assigned. For example, the UITableForm interacts with collections of data as well as with single objects. For this reason, an object form (a subclass of UIForm) must be given to the UITableForm component.

The Maintainer

As explained in the preceding section, each viewable component has a maintainer attached to it. The maintainer is responsible for feeding data back to the view for presentation and is responsible for interacting with the actual data model. In general, each single object that has a view associated with it inherits from UIObjectMaintainer, which has a series of default implementations associated with it. A view control that has a collection of items represented has a maintainer that implements the UIContainerControl in addition to extending the UIObjectMaintainer.

Population and interaction with the UITable component occur, primarily, in the getElements() method that must be implemented in the maintainer. The method is responsible for retrieving the collection of items, in this case from the ProductGroupController, and moving it into a UICollection. This collection is returned to the caller of the getElements method; in this case, it is the SanFrancisco User Interface framework, which is busy coordinating view updates.

```
1  public UICollection getElements(UIAttributeId theId) {

2    UICollection uic = null;
3    QueryCollection resultCollection = null;

4    try {
5      startTransaction();
6      // retrieve the controller from the enterprise
7      Company c = CompanyContext.getEnterprise(AccessMode.createNormal());
8      ProductGroupController pgc =
         (ProductGroupController)c.getDirectlyContainedPropertyBy(
           "GPSE.ProductGroupController");
9      switch (theId.getValue()) {
10       case GPSEProductGroupIds.TBLF_PRODUCT_GROUP:
11         resultCollection = pgc.queryOwnedProductGroups(
             "select x from ProductGroups x;",
             "ProductGroups",
             null, //selectCompareObject
             null, //bind name for select compare
             null, //sort compareObject
             null, //bind name for sort compare
             false //accessResults
           );
12     }
```

```
13    uic = new UISFCollection(resultCollection);
14    stopTransaction(true);
15  }
16  catch(SFException sfe){
17    sfe.printStackTrace();
18  }
19  catch(Exception e){
20    e.printStackTrace();
21  }
22  return uic;
23}
```

Notice that the maintenance of the transaction is moved into a series of meth-ods on the maintainer (this is shown in lines 5 and 14). This is a common prac-tice in maintainer construction. Often, forms contain highly individualized transaction handling. In studying frame and form display within a particular application, you may notice that a form is sometimes displayed and is respon-sible for starting a new transaction. At another point in the application, the form may be instantiated and be inside another form's transaction. The result is some fairly complex transaction handling.

A UITable requires both a container maintainer and an object maintainer associated with it. The container maintainer is responsible for retrieving the collection as a whole and for passing it to the framework for processing. Indi-vidual attributes are requested for processing from the object maintainer. The order of processing for a UITable is as follows:

1. Request the collection from the UIContainerMaintainer associated with the UITable.

2. For each of the attributes set up as table columns, request the data from the UIObjectMaintainer associated with the table.

Whereas the getElements method is the worker in the UIContainerMaintainer, the getAttribute method is the worker in the UIObjectMaintainer. Again, a requested attribute is passed to the method. The method is responsible for determining and returning the data requested by the framework. In the case of the UITableForm, the UIObjectMaintainer can serve dual functions. The main-tainer can handle requests to fill column data from the UITable as well as han-dle data requests to populate the UIObjectMaintainer.

Just as methods exist to retrieve data in the maintainers, similar methods exist for manipulating individual attributes. They aren't covered here in depth, but they have a similar form.

As previously mentioned, one of the most difficult parts of building main-tainers involves transaction management and object locking. Even in our rela-tively lightweight example, transaction management is a large issue. Perhaps the most difficult problem for first-time SanFrancisco User Interface programmers is that the framework does much object manipulation in its own implementation.

Implementation and management of transaction handling inside maintainers are aided by several methods that maintainers can override. Preparation methods exist for various states into which the maintainer can be put. Specifically, three methods exist:

- prepareForOpen: Before the view is opened and data are requested, the prepareForOpen method is called. Often, a work area will be resumed here; a transaction may also be opened.
- prepareForWork: Many times the work area will be suspended here. The reason is that the next time the method is called, we could be inside an event handler thread.
- prepareForClose: Upon completion of view processing, the prepareForClose is called.

Using Java Foundation Classes in a SanFrancisco Application

As previously mentioned, user interfaces can be constructed with the Java Foundation Classes from Sun or from other user interface components that may be available. There are a few things that should be mentioned in the beginning:

- The components you choose to use with JFC can look and behave similarly to those in the SanFrancisco User Interface framework. This is because the objects in the SanFrancisco User Interface framework are, for the most part, subclasses of JFC Swing components.
- The model-view split in many of the JFC components allows you to separate the SanFrancisco interaction from your view construction, much as the SanFrancisco User Interface framework does.
- When model support does not exist for Swing components, it is often useful to build your own model support to isolate transaction and business object interactions from the view.

If you are not currently a JFC programmer, you probably won't become one now. On the other hand, this section is very light on user interface programming. The bulk of the chapter discusses centralization of SanFrancisco interaction in well-defined units. It is the units that are highlighted in the chapter.

Keeping these things in mind, let's jump right into component selection and view construction. No code is shown for the view itself, except for a short amount in the maintenance form where we must construct mechanisms for a model-view approach. After building the view, we add SanFrancisco interactions to our models and then present a brief comparison of JFC and the SanFrancisco User Interface framework.

Building the View

Most view components are built visually within one of the many integrated development environments (IDEs) available on the market. As a result, this chapter does not delve into the actual coding of the views. Rather, we discuss the components that are assembled to make up the view. Later in the chapter, code is written to make the views talk to SanFrancisco.

The view for the maintenance application (see Figure 14-3) comes in two parts, as with the comparable SanFrancisco User Interface Framework application:

- ProductGroupCollectionForm: The form is a subclass of com.sun.java. swing.JPanel. The JPanel contains a JTable (inside a scroll pane) that displays the list of items. ProductGroupTableModel, a subclass of Default-TableModel, serves as the link between SanFrancisco and the user interface.

- ProductGroupMaintenanceForm: A JPanel is again used as the basis for the form. The inside panel consists of a series of JTextFields and JLabels to represent the data.

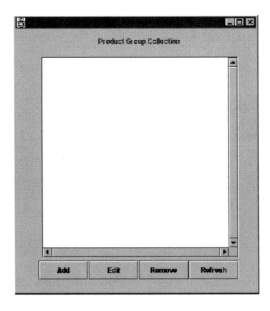

Figure 14-3. ProductGroup with JFC

Recall that the ProductGroup contains a DescriptiveInformation object. As with the UIForm built in Chapter 13, this object would be a great place for building a common form and reusing it. If a panel for DescriptiveInformation already exists, this would be a nice location to build a JTabbedPane. The first page of the tabbed pane could display the relevant ProductGroup details without the DescriptiveInformation. The second page of the tabbed pane could contain the DescriptiveInformation object and a series of fields and buttons that would allow separate manipulation of the DescriptiveInformation.

For the purpose of this example, the DescriptiveInformation is represented as a simple text field with some widgets to the actual data. To make the interface cleaner, we assume that we want to maintain only the current locale's description.

Building the Model

Construction of the user interface view is not very interesting. Various IDEs can be used to generate different types of code. The SanFrancisco interaction occurs in the table model for the JTable and not in the view. First, we build the subclass of the table model. The following methods should be overridden from the parent, DefaultTableModel:

- isCellEditable: For this collection form, none of the data is editable. In effect, the collection form is for browsing data only.

In addition to the overridden method, several new methods exist for taking action when one of the buttons is pressed on the panel:

- refresh: This method retrieves the data collection and refreshes the table.
- edit: This method presents the object form (in the next section) and allows the user to edit data in it.
- add: This is used to add a new ProductGroup to the collection.
- show: The object form is presented. No editing is allowed.

The refresh method is implemented in this section. The implementation is slightly less complex than the other methods because it deals only with the table and not with another frame and a different data representation. In addition to the refresh method itself, some additional class data is required for communication between the collection items and methods that act on a single item. Because the transaction scope is minimized to the course of single methods, we store the Handles of the ProductGroup items. An array works well to do this. During the refresh, the array is populated.

The following algorithm is used in the method:

- Populate the column data. This is a Swing mechanism. The column names are contained in a vector, which later is passed to the Default-TableModel for processing.

- Use the singleton object ApplicationContextBean to obtain a Session object. The Session class, discussed earlier, is basically used as a central location to deal with distributed thread management (otherwise known as WorkAreas) and transaction handling.

- Ask the Session object to start the work area for this thread. (Swing events are actually processed in a thread other than the main thread, so we must obtain the WorkArea for processing within the current thread.)

- Obtain the ProductGroupController from the Enterprise.

- Retrieve the ProductGroups contained in the controller.

- Iterate over the contained ProductGroups, saving the Handle for later use and populating the data vector with the required information for the table.

- Release the WorkArea back to any thread that may need it.

- Set the column and row data into the DefaultTableModel. This step fires an event to the view portion of the JTable telling it that the data are changed. The view retrieves the data and is updated.

The class will hold onto the handles of the Object instances represented in the table.

```
   private Vector productGroupHandles=null;
refresh
1 public void refresh() {
2    // Two vectors must be prepared for the labels and data
3    Vector rowData = new Vector();
4    Vector columnData = new Vector();

5    // set the column header data
6    columnData.addElement("Number");
7    columnData.addElement("Season Start");
8    columnData.addElement("Season End");

9    // use the beans session to simplify the work of transaction management
10   Session s = ApplicationContextBean.getDefaultSession();
11   try {
12     s.enterWorkArea();
13     Company c = CompanyContext.getEnterprise(AccessMode.createNoLock());
14     pgc =   (ProductGroupController)c.getDirectlyContainedPropertyBy(
          "GPSE.ProductGroupController");
```

```
15    QueryCollection pgs = pgc.getOwnedProductGroups();
16    Iterator pgIt = pgs.createIterator();
17    pgIt.setAccessMode(AccessMode.createNormal());
18    ProductGroup pg=null;
19    productGroupHandles = new Vector(10);
20    while (pgIt.more()) {
21      pg = (ProductGroup)pgs.getNextElement(pgIt);
22      Vector currVector = new Vector(3);
23      currVector.addElement(pg.getNumber());
24      currVector.addElement(new Integer(pg.getSeasonStartMonth()));
25      currVector.addElement(new Integer(pg.getSeasonEndMonth()));
26      productGroupHandles.addElement(pg.getHandle());
27      rowData.addElement(currVector);
28    }
29    s.exitWorkArea();
30  }
31  catch(SFException sfe){
32    s.exitWorkArea();
33    sfe.printStackTrace();
34  }
35  setDataVector(rowData,columnData);
36}
```

The code implemented in JFC should look very similar to that of the SanFrancisco User Interface framework. Much like the framework, JFC calls methods in the table model at certain points during the life cycle of the table. Other mechanisms, such as collection refreshing, saving, and exiting, must be created and hooked up through events.

You face a classic trade-off when choosing between the framework and JFC: How much of the implementation should be done without your knowledge? Looking at the difference between the refresh() method in the default table model that we implemented and the getElements() method presented in the SanFrancisco User Interface framework section, you can see that the trade-off appears to be about equal. Both techniques require about the same amount of code at this stage, and they appear to yield similar results.

Model, View, Controller

As controls and panels become more complex, glaring differences begin to appear between the JFC class library and the SanFrancisco User Interface framework. The SanFrancisco User Interface framework goes to great lengths to provide maintainers for every type of control and container. The Java Foundation Classes don't provide model support for everything.

As applications scale up to include multiple paths through the panel flow and, what's more, multiple ways to instantiate some views of data, the extensive maintainer support in the SanFrancisco User Interface framework becomes a strong ally.

If you choose to use JFC, the SanFrancisco User Interface framework is worth looking at, at least to understand how maintainers are used and where interaction with transactions occurs. For example, when an object form is opened in the SanFrancisco User Interface framework, the object form's maintainer methods are called. At this point, the application programmer has a chance to assume control of work areas, gather locks on objects, start transactions, or do anything else desired.

When you're using JFC, it is sometimes easy to forget that similar opportunities exist when using the JPanel. Many IDEs even make it easier to put interaction with business objects into the view rather than into separate maintainable units. This technique should be discouraged when developers are creating large applications. When you're considering scaling to a large, transactional-type application, take some time to learn the SanFrancisco User Interface framework. Even if you choose not to use it, you may see things that other class libraries have missed.

Thin Client Construction

SanFrancisco itself is very much a server-side technology. The SanFrancisco User Interface framework helps put an accessible user interface on top of the business components, but it is what could be considered a fat client model. A *fat* client model requires that the site where the application is installed have a large part of the framework installed on it. To perform the installation using an applet would be painful at best. Consider a minimum of approximately 40 MB of information being transferred into the local cache of the browser. From a client perspective, this scenario is unrealistic.

Using JFC, an application developer could trim the client substantially, but it is still difficult to get down to a true *thin* client model unless all, or most, of the SanFrancisco references are removed from the client application.

Before starting to build a fat client model, you should consider yet another construction model. One model that SanFrancisco framework customers are using more often is a servlet model (see Figure 14-4). The *servlet* isolates the SanFrancisco framework application code and interacts with a client via Web pages. With this model you can build a true thin client with little or no installation occurring from a Web browser.

This type of application tends to have very short transactions and very short, pessimistic locks. Usually, transaction and lock lengths last only long enough to interact with SanFrancisco and execute some business logic. A more

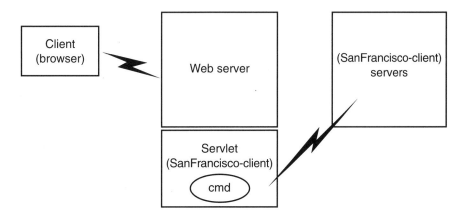

Figure 14-4. Servlet Model of Providing SanFrancisco Interaction

complex servlet would allow longer logical locks to be held also on object instances; this is somewhat like a reservation system. This type of construction is largely left to the servlet provider. Again, though, SanFrancisco Version 1 Release 4 provides a beta logical lock technology that may be helpful in this scenario. To read more about SanFrancisco logical locking techniques, refer to the SanFrancisco Version 1 Release 4 Programmer's Guide.

Thin client construction is centered in the servlet. The servlet will likely access the SanFrancisco framework services directly or via command classes. SanFrancisco framework command classes are a good fit for the thin client model. Furthermore, the SanFrancisco Version 1 Release 4 Client Command framework may be particularly well suited for this model for the following reasons:

- Commands for performance are best used in a short transaction with HOME access locations.
- You can offload work from the Web server to the SanFrancisco server processes by using command objects.
- Web requests can usually be turned into atomic actions, which fit the command model exactly.

In addition to the logical locking mechanisms and Client Command framework, SanFrancisco is also serving up a "Client Architecture" document. This document will endorse a servlet model for SanFrancisco framework interaction. It is clear that thin client models provide many characteristics to end user applications that are necessary for some clients:

- Minimal installation time
- Small client footprint
- SanFrancisco framework interaction on centralized, high-powered computers

The net message, no pun intended, about thin clients is that they play a crucial role in many application environments. The SanFrancisco framework documentation, samples, and client support are embracing this strategy more with each release. You should consider it as an application deployment model for your own application.

Summary

The SanFrancisco User Interface framework is extremely useful for large-scale applications. The complexity level of the framework is high at first, but in a typical large application the amount of reuse can be high. Numerous components exist, all of them derived from the JFC viewable components. Additional components exist that are tailored to the SanFrancisco Programming Model.

The framework enforces a strict model-view-controller split (the controller is renamed the *maintainer* to avoid overloading the term *controller*). The view can be set up with traditional mechanisms, such as a layout and the typical container/contained relationships available in other user interface libraries. The maintainers communicate with the view through the use of attributes associated with the view components. You implement a maintainer by overriding a set of methods according to the functionality required by the application. One of the most difficult tasks of the user interface programmer is to determine the transaction scopes and locking strategies. This job can be greatly eased if the paths and plans for user interaction are laid out up front.

The SanFrancisco User Interface framework is not the only way to build graphical applications using the classes built in previous chapters. The Java Foundation Classes can be used, as can a thin client approach built from a Web client and servlets. The important thing is to determine the best approach for your development needs.

It should be noted that the SanFrancisco GUI framework is evolving very quickly. Many of its shortcomings are being addressed rapidly. This chapter only scratches the surface of writing a user interface and final client application. In no way is this treatment meant to minimize the effort of putting together user interfaces. A complex user interface in a transactional system is a beast—difficult to plan for and fully understand. Make sure that your project team has ample time to carefully plan the screen flow, transaction scoping mechanisms, threading capabilities, and lock characteristics for the final applications.

In addition to the work going on to make the SanFrancisco User Interface easier to use, a substantial amount of work is being done to make SanFrancisco JavaBeans more useful for certain types of applications. SanFrancisco Java-Beans consist of visual representation in the form of a collection form, an object form, and a nonvisual JavaBean. The trio of JavaBeans also has simplified wiring mechanisms to create certain types of applications. More information on this topic is presented in Chapter 15.

15 SanFrancisco JavaBeans

There is a fundamental difference between the target audience of the SanFrancisco application business components and that of parts built with adherence to the JavaBeans specification. The SanFrancisco component framework classes are designed with object-oriented extension capabilities in mind and are built for ease of use for potentially complex business domains and built in a way that hides the persistence, distribution, and foundation capabilities. JavaBeans, in contrast, create a common interface and patterns that ease integration with integrated development environments (IDEs) and often provide techniques for assembling applications visually. SanFrancisco component framework classes do not adhere to Sun's JavaBean specification, but the SanFrancisco JavaBeans do.

A substantial amount of work is being done in SanFrancisco product development to find the critical balance between providing SanFrancisco framework components that are fully functional, robust, and flexible and providing JavaBeans components that are quick to learn, simple to use, and suitable for visual construction. SanFrancisco offers to users what is best termed SanFrancisco JavaBeans. SanFrancisco JavaBeans are bigger and more complex than the average JavaBean, but in many ways they are "friendlier" than the SanFrancisco application business components for beginners.

SanFrancisco JavaBeans target a particular type of application for rapid application development. Most installed applications require *maintenance applications,* smaller applications that must be built to support data entry and maintenance. Maintenance applications typically function against one or more business objects with a very rigid screen flow and technique. Maintenance applications tend not to be performance-sensitive, and they look very much alike. Because general rules exist to build such applications, they are a natural target for rapid application development.

You should, by now, have at least a passing understanding of the concepts that make up the SanFrancisco Programming Model as well as the patterns and classes that are in the Common Business Objects layer. The SanFrancisco Java-Beans that are currently packaged with SanFrancisco represent many of the SanFrancisco classes that are often used for building maintenance applications. Classes such as Address, Company, BusinessPartner, Currency, Country, and many others come with prebuilt JavaBean components that you can start using right off the shelf.

SanFrancisco is constantly expanding its catalog of SanFrancisco Java-Beans. In addition, a SanFrancisco JavaBean wizard allows a developer to take on the role of a JavaBean creator, building new SanFrancisco JavaBeans or rearchitecting existing SanFrancisco JavaBeans. The potential complexity of a bean is extremely high. As the complexity of the interface to a SanFrancisco JavaBean increases, a richer set of functionality will be available from it. On the other hand, a SanFrancisco JavaBean can be built with a tight role focus, at the expense of versatility.

How SanFrancisco JavaBeans Work

A SanFrancisco JavaBean has the potential to expose as many as five different *modes*. Each mode represents one or more different SanFrancisco concepts. The component creator has the responsibility of deciding which modes he or she will expose and, consequently, the complexity that the application assembler will be forced to endure.

Following are the modes that a SanFrancisco JavaBean can expose:

- Controller mode: This mode retrieves data from a controller. The controller is either attached to the currently active company or set as a property on the JavaBean.

- Owned collection mode: The application assembler will wire the collection owner to this bean unless the owned collection is saved by user alias; in the latter case, the user will type in the alias. Methods that manipulate the collection will call back to the collection owner.

- Collection mode: In this mode, no callbacks occur to the owner of the collection after the collection property is set. The behavior as a whole is very similar to that of the owned collection mode.

- Owned business object mode: As with the owned collection mode, the bean will call back to the wired owner of the business object for method calls. In effect, this object will be committed and retrieved based on the owner of the object.

- Business object mode: The business object mode acts independently after the connection is wired. It will be committed and manipulated independently of the object that gave the bean the reference.

All modes expose an interface that contains the properties of the SanFrancisco application business component that the JavaBean represents. If the mode selected is a controlled or collected mode, the data in each property will be the currently selected item. You select an item in a controller or collection by using the iteration interface or by setting keys on the JavaBean. If the JavaBean is in one of the single business object modes, the values of the property represent the business object that is active in the JavaBean.

When a component creator chooses one mode for the bean to exist in, pre-configures most of the details, and strips the properties that allow the bean to be attached and set into other modes, a *simple* SanFrancisco JavaBean is created. If a component creator exposes the properties that allow the SanFrancisco JavaBean to be hooked up in different contexts, the SanFrancisco Java-Bean is considered a *complex* SanFrancisco JavaBean. The simple bean offers minimal flexibility and maximum ease of use, whereas the complex bean gives the maximum flexibility and the least usability. As SanFrancisco JavaBeans are required to take on more-complex tasks, usually a complex bean is required.

We've discussed the modes that a SanFrancisco JavaBean can fulfill, but combining the functions of many SanFrancisco objects into a single location is not the only function SanFrancisco JavaBeans undertake. They also attempt to simplify the task of programming with SanFrancisco. Let's look at a simple example: transaction management.

Normally, SanFrancisco programmers must take care in managing their transaction boundaries. This is not the case with SanFrancisco JavaBeans, which have a default locking and transaction management scheme. An example of how this works can be shown with a method that changes a property of the object. When a set method is called on a SanFrancisco JavaBean that will change one of the underlying business objects (whether it is a collection or a business object), the SanFrancisco JavaBean starts a transaction, makes the change to the business object, and commits the transaction. Of course, having such fine-grained transactions increases the overhead of an application and also decreases the ability of a programmer to control the level of what defines an atomic set of changes that will occur to one or more business objects.

For a beginner, not having control over the granularity of transactions is not a problem. Eventually, a SanFrancisco JavaBean user will want two business objects to be changed at the same time or to fail in their change together.

Programmers can take advantage of Session objects provided by SanFrancisco JavaBeans. The Session object organizes transaction start and commit points. The object has methods and properties that give programmers access to transaction methods and to details about how exceptions and debug information flow. It also fires events to notify listeners when transaction boundaries are being hit by one of the components that is using a particular Session.

SanFrancisco JavaBean Tools

SanFrancisco comes with a set of base classes for SanFrancisco JavaBeans to inherit from, a set of starter beans that you can start using off the shelf, and the SanFrancisco JavaBean wizard, a tool for building SanFrancisco JavaBeans from existing SanFrancisco classes. The wizard can also be used to modify existing SanFrancisco JavaBeans. Although it is conceivable that a component creator could hand-program a SanFrancisco JavaBean, using the SanFrancisco JavaBean wizard will greatly simplify the task.

The SanFrancisco JavaBean wizard guides the component creator in one of two modes: simple or advanced. In simple mode, the wizard attempts to observe the environment and determine the modes that a SanFrancisco Java-Bean is intended for. For example, if a user chooses to build a SanFrancisco JavaBean for the interface GPSE.Product, the wizard will observe the Product class.

- A class called GPSE.ProductController exists. This indicates that the Product will likely be used in controlled mode.
- A set of properties that follows the SanFrancisco Programming Model is offered on the Product. The properties will be offered to the user as pure JavaBean properties with property change events attached to them.

In simple wizard mode, the component creator will now be required to add more information about the SanFrancisco JavaBean—items such as the properties that should be exposed, the icons associated with the bean, and a definition of which properties must be used to create a new instance of the wrapped business object. The last item is the most difficult to get correct, and JavaDoc or the interface for the class's factory should be kept handy.

In advanced wizard mode, the decisions made by the wizard are exposed to the user, who can alter those decisions. Things that can be changed by the advanced user include the following:

- The component creator can change modes in which the bean can be used. For example, suppose that a component creator knows that one of his or her objects owns a single instance of an area. The component creator would then choose to allow the new bean to be an owned business object. The creator can choose to maintain the bean as a simple SanFrancisco Java-Bean by removing the ability to be in controlled mode, or the component creator can choose to expose both modes, thus making it a complex San-Francisco JavaBean.

- A component creator can add properties that are not a part of the San-Francisco class that is being turned into a bean. As a result, a new property is added to the SanFrancisco JavaBean along with an appropriate get/set interface. The underlying class interface is not changed. Instead, the data is attached to an instance through the use of property containment. As a result, only objects that implement the PropertyContainer interface in SanFrancisco can have properties added to them by the SanFrancisco JavaBean wizard.

- The component creator can choose which methods are visible to the user. Methods are typically added for collection manipulation, creation, saving of new instances, and so on. If some of these methods are unnecessary in a particular JavaBean, they can be reused, thus making the job of the component assembler a little less confusing.

A document on the SanFrancisco Evaluation CD discusses SanFrancisco Java-Beans in detail. Look for the SanFrancisco JavaBean Handbook from the documentation entry page.

Using the SanFrancisco JavaBeans with the Sample Application

In this example of a maintenance application, the SanFrancisco JavaBean wizard creates a default user interface for the Product class. The Product is used to show some of the advanced capabilities of SanFrancisco JavaBeans.

Instead of constructing an all new interface for the object, we build the JavaBean with the SanFrancisco JavaBean wizard. We then wire an application together inside VisualAge for Java Enterprise Edition.

Building a New SanFrancisco JavaBean for Product

Classes to be used in the SanFrancisco JavaBean wizard must be in the classpath. The wizard is available inside the JavaBeans folder of the SanFrancisco installation. After it is started, the wizard gathers necessary information such as which interface the JavaBean will represent and whether you are modifying an existing bean or creating a new bean.

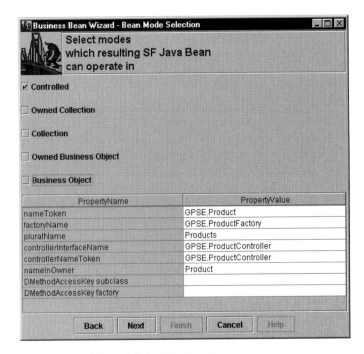

Figure 15-1. SFJB Wizard, Bean Mode Selection Screen

Following the class selection screen, a screen appears that shows the specific modes that the SanFrancisco JavaBean will support (see Figure 15-1). The modes represent all the different contexts into which the JavaBean can be assembled. If you did not use typical patterns for dynamic property key names, you should alter any incorrect guesses made by the wizard.

For the Product, preconfiguring the JavaBean to be in controller mode—and not making visible the capability to switch to other modes—is sufficient and perhaps optimal. It may be optimal if Products are used only in relationship to their controller. If this is the case, the bean creator can reduce the complexity of the bean that the application assembler will be using.

Look at the other properties that can be set on the bean. The data for the controller key can be compared to previous samples, but you should notice that the wizard made its guesses accurately. On later screens, various properties that were discovered through reflection are offered to the wizard user. For this sample, we omit the discount selection policy from the JavaBean. To do this, the wizard offers tables that contain checkboxes where you can add and remove properties as you judge necessary for the consumer of the JavaBean.

Much data in source code does not get put into class files. Data such as parameter names and context information are not available. As a result, it is always useful to have JavaDoc nearby to help you understand class factory

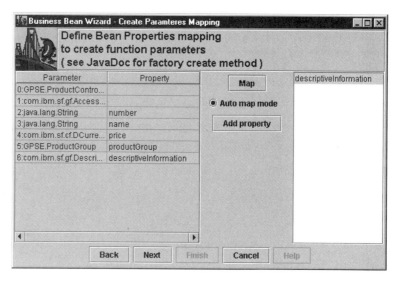

Figure 15-2. SFJB Wizard, Create Parameters Mapping Screen

methods. As you can see in Figure 15-2, some of the screens are fairly complex and require knowledge that should be available in the JavaDoc for a given class and factory. From the factory documentation for Product, note that the createProduct method takes the following parameters:

- String number
- String name
- DCurrencyValue price
- ProductGroup productGroup
- DescriptiveInformation description

These parameters match our properties very well. The wizard allows you to map the parameters to their correct properties from the bean. Leave the first two values in the mapping blank; the JavaBean wizard takes care of these. They are left in the screen to create parallelism with the actual factory methods.

> **Note:** The wizard, which is profiled here, was available in SanFrancisco Version 1 Release 3, the beta version of the wizard. Many modifications and usability changes were put into the Version 1 Release 4 wizard, and more are scheduled for later versions of the wizard.

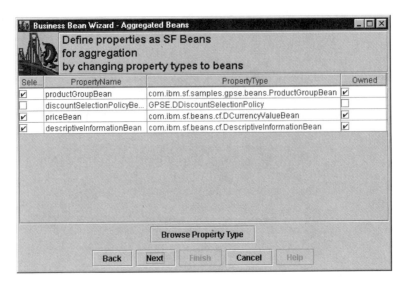

Figure 15-3. SFJB Aggregation

The aggregation screen is another interesting place where knowledge of the actual class design can be useful (see Figure 15-3). Aggregation of properties allows a single SanFrancisco JavaBean to function and display interfaces for multiple complex types. A Product contains several primitive types that are supported by default, as well as several more-complex types. The three that we will aggregate are as follows:

- productGroup: Supplied with the example in this book, the class name is GPSE.ProductGroupBean. The Product does not own the ProductGroup.

- price: The price is a DCurrencyValue, which is supplied by SanFrancisco as a prebuilt bean. Place the bean class in the correct field.

- descriptiveInformation: The DescriptiveInformation SanFrancisco Java-Bean is again supplied by SanFrancisco. Enter the class name in the property field.

If one of the fields is set incorrectly, it is likely that the Next button will not be enabled. Accept the defaults in the rest of the screens until you get to the final page, where you locate your beans. Other screens that you can fill out include the following:

- Visual Beans: This page determines the appearance of the default forms for the Product. Notice that the aggregated beans have default form names entered here. They will be presented as tabs on the final Product maintenance form. If the class for the form is incorrect, the field is editable so that changes can be made.

- Bean Icons: Select any custom icons that you would want displayed in an IDE here.

- Bean Metadata: Add any contextual information here. This information is used to create a special documentation format called BeanDoc. BeanDoc is not discussed in detail here.

Finally, the Beans Location Definition screen appears; here you enter packaging information for the JavaBean. Then the resulting jar file can be distributed to SanFrancisco application assemblers, assuming that they have SanFrancisco and the supporting framework installed on their system.

Building an Application

The creation of the SanFrancisco JavaBean requires knowledge of how the Product class was built. Much of this knowledge is no longer necessary when the application is assembled. SanFrancisco JavaBeans attempts to minimize the knowledge application assemblers must have of how SanFrancisco classes are used and how classes are built.

As you assemble the application, notice the following:

- No explicit information is seen in the application relating to locking or transactions.

- No factories, interfaces, or SanFrancisco-specific information is in the application.

- The user interface is a combination of the SanFrancisco UI framework (with the default form built by the SFJB wizard) and Swing components.

JavaBean environments differ substantially; some of them allow completely visual programming, and others require that you fall into actual programming. The goal of SanFrancisco JavaBeans is to make coding obsolete for simple business applications. Thus VisualAge for Java is a good choice of IDE.

To assemble an application, you first need the ProductBean from the ProductBean.jar file created in the preceding section. The ProductBean is nonvisual in nature and is not contained in a user interface. Some IDEs do not work as well as others with nonvisual beans. In VisualAge for Java, the nonvisual bean is presented with its icon.

The visual form for our application contains the following:

- JButton (or similar widget): Label should read "Reset."
- JButton: Label should read "Next."
- ProductBeanObjectForm: Available from the ProductBean.jar file created earlier.

Note the mixing of Java Foundation Classes with classes built using the San-Francisco User Interface framework. Because both types of classes are Java-Beans, they function well together within the same visual form.

In a visual environment (shown in Figure 15-4), *wires* are created that connect events and properties between JavaBeans in the application. Some Java-Bean development environments allow coding techniques only for connecting JavaBeans. If you are working in one of those environments, the wire consists of some combination of event listeners and method calls.

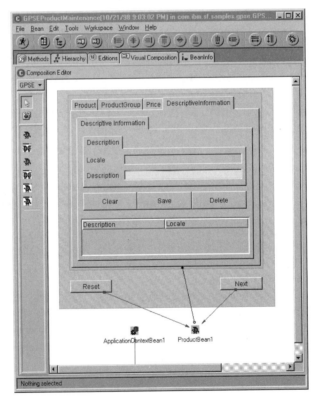

Figure 15-4. Application Assembly in VisualAge for Java

For example, to create an event-to-method connection, build an event listener that contains a method call to the target method that occurs when the correct event is fired from the source component. To build a *bound* property in code, attach to the source component an event listener that waits for a propertyChange event. When the event is received, retrieve from the source object the property that is bound and set it into the target object.

This application wires together the button events and methods on the nonvisual JavaBean.

- Connect the Reset button's actionPerformed event to the ProductBean's doReset method.

- Connect the Next button's actionPerformed event to the ProductBean's doNext method.

- Connect the ProductObjectForm's businessObjectBean property to the ProductBean's this property.

Those are all the connections that are required for a basic product-browsing application. It is evident that the last connection has some interesting things going on behind the scenes. The forms that are generated by the SanFrancisco JavaBean wizard have special connection properties that allow the form to be attached to the nonvisual JavaBean with only a single wire. In typical complex user interface forms, a series of wires must be connected from the source components to the individual graphical representations of the data.

Summary

SanFrancisco JavaBeans simplify the SanFrancisco programming environment. They are especially useful with maintenance applications.

SanFrancisco JavaBeans simplify SanFrancisco by hiding parts of the full SanFrancisco programming model that are not part of traditional JavaBean development. And because SanFrancisco JavaBeans are large-grained and expose various modes to component assemblers, component creators use a wizard to create them and to manage their complexity.

After you have created specific SanFrancisco JavaBeans, you can wire simple applications together visually in almost any IDE. More-complex applications can be a combination of wiring and programming. Application creators can wrest expanded functionality from the SanFrancisco JavaBeans to tailor an application's performance and behavior. As application assemblers gain more knowledge about SanFrancisco, they can take greater control of the environment. Eventually, the desired capabilities may exceed the capabilities of the

SanFrancisco JavaBeans model. At this point, the developer can transition into more traditional SanFrancisco programming while keeping the SanFrancisco JavaBean for some tasks. The SanFrancisco product comes with increasing numbers of JavaBeans that are available for use off the shelf.

A

Tools

There are many tools that can be applied to day-to-day SanFrancisco administration and development. In general, such tools fall into two categories: tools that aid in development of SanFrancisco classes and applications, and tools that help manage a SanFrancisco installation (see Figure A-1). Earlier chapters cover several of the tools provided by SanFrancisco: the Configuration tool, the Schema Mapper tool, the User (or Access Rights) Administration tool, and the SanFrancisco JavaBean wizard.

The Configuration tool makes classes available to your SanFrancisco Logical Network. The Schema Mapper tool allows you to create custom mappings of classes to persistent storage. The User Administration tool helps you to define security in your SanFrancisco Logical Network. These tools are discussed in more detail in Chapter 5. In addition to the tools presented in the Foundation layer, the SanFrancisco JavaBean wizard is discussed in Chapter 15. The SanFrancisco JavaBean wizard helps you build JavaBeans that access San-Francisco application business components.

If you are looking for tools to use with SanFrancisco, a good place to start is the SanFrancisco Tools Catalog. This document is available from the SanFrancisco Web site and should also be included in SanFrancisco Release 1.4 and beyond.

The SanFrancisco Tools Catalog attempts to document the wide variety of tools that are known to work with SanFrancisco. It is by no means comprehensive because the Java tools market is moving much too quickly. Nor does it

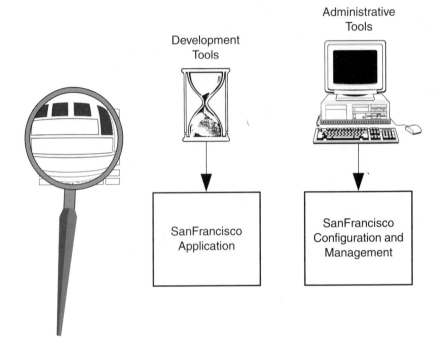

Figure A-1. SanFrancisco Tools

make recommendations about tools. With that said, the catalog is a good place to start looking for information about supported tools. It contains a short description of the tools that are known to work with SanFrancisco as well as information about how to contact vendors.

Note that many of the tools are not formally tested by IBM. Thus IBM does not support many of the tools in the catalog directly.

Development Tools

Chapter 15 discusses the SanFrancisco JavaBean wizard, which is designed for use on existing classes that adhere to the SanFrancisco Programming Model. As you may have noticed by this point, creating a SanFrancisco class requires a substantial amount of code, several support classes, and rigid adherence to the programming model.

Programming by hand is tedious on the best of days. This Appendix discusses tools that substantially cut down class creation time and class maintenance.

Modeling Tools

Most modeling tools are supported by the SanFrancisco environment. To use a modeling tool, you should be aware that the component models shipped with SanFrancisco are in Rational Rose format. If you intend to use these models, ensure that the modeler you choose can import Rose models.

To use the SanFrancisco code generator, ensure that the modeler also can export into Rational Rose formatted files and can import the correct format.

Always check with IBM to determine whether the modeler you are using is directly supported. The SanFrancisco Tools Catalog lists tools and utilities that SanFrancisco works with.

The SanFrancisco Code Generator

Although we've alluded to it, a full treatment of one of the most important tools has not yet been given. The SanFrancisco code generator produces Java code based on the SanFrancisco Programming Model. Each release of SanFrancisco provides an updated generator that adheres to any new or changed rules for SanFrancisco code.

The SanFrancisco code generator acts on UML models produced by Rational Rose. In fact, the code generator is a wizard built by Rational, and it must be instantiated and installed separately from SanFrancisco. Although Rational Rose models are the most common input to the code generator, in theory the SanFrancisco code generator will work on any model that adheres to the Rational Rose format.

The SanFrancisco code generator is used throughout the SanFrancisco development process by the domain developers at IBM. It goes through a rigorous workout before each release, generating thousands of lines of Java code that must adhere to the programming model.

To use the code generator, you must have an ODBC datasource available to the tool. This datasource is used to create a database based on the Rose model, which it reads in upon request. When the database is ready, you choose one or more of the classes in the Rose model from the list boxes. The tool generates the Java code necessary to implement the selected classes. Typically, the classes fan out into many more classes. For example, choosing the ProductGroup class to generate (based on the UML model in Figure A-2) would generate the following classes:

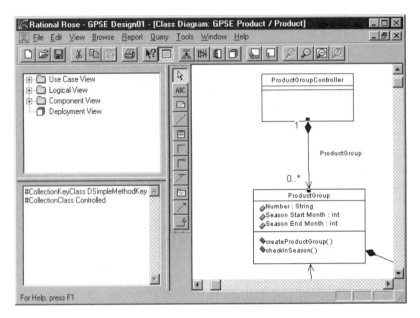

Figure A-2. Rational Rose Wizards with ProductGroup

- ProductGroup.java: The interface for the ProductGroup class.
- ProductGroupImpl.java: A concrete implementation of ProductGroup with as much implementation filled in as possible (such as initialization methods, serialization methods, copy and destroy methods, and so on).
- ProductGroupFactory.java: The complete factory for creating new Product-Groups. This file is usually 100% complete from the code generator, although occasionally some editing is needed.

Typically, there are a few lines of code that are left to be changed for which information is not available in the Rational Rose model. A sample of the generated code can be seen in the dialog box.

After the class is generated, developers must also put the customized business logic into the implementation files. Developers often use their favorite IDE, or even a customizable editor, at this stage. It's not unheard of to see a developer using Windows Notepad to implement a class quickly.

A drawback of the IBM SanFrancisco code generator is the lack of round-trip code generation. Furthermore, IBM's code generator does not support regenerating code from the existing Rational Rose model into existing files. Although IBM and several third-party tools providers are working to implement this kind of support, it is best to keep your development environment in mind when using the code generator. Always ensure that you have two locations for code: one for generated code, and a second one for code you have implemented. Watch the tools catalog for the release of a code generator that supports round-trip code generation and/or code merging.

Meanwhile, if class designers decide to alter a Rational Rose diagram, they must generate new class implementations. Any customized code from the last iteration the programmers were working on must be merged into the new files.

Rational Rose Directive Assistant

SanFrancisco designers often need to supply information to the Rose model that will help the code generator make correct decisions. For example, the ProductGroupController class has a containment relationship to one or more ProductGroups. There are many ways that SanFrancisco code could reflect this containment relationship: lists, sets, maps, and, in this case, controllers. The name of a controller need not contain the string "Controller." To help the code generator understand the type of a controller and how to collect the Product-Groups, #directives are used in the Rose model.

A #directive is basically a text string that contains information that goes into a class or relationship's documentation section. The SanFrancisco Directive wizard works inside Rational Rose to help place directives on classes. The wizard is instantiated, based on a selected class, from the Tools menu. Selecting whether the directive should go on the class, attribute, relationship, or method follows instantiation. Finally, based on the selection, the user can choose the needed directive.

The ProductGroupController has the #ControllerType directive placed on it. This directive has an associated value that tells the code generator which type of controller to generate: simple, aggregating, or hiding. The relationship between the ProductGroupController and the ProductGroup class itself also has two associated directives. The first directive, #CollectionKeyClass, tells how collected items will be retrieved from the collection, in this case by a derivative of the DSimpleMethodKey class. The second directive, #CollectionClass, tells the code generator which type of collection will be used, in this case a controller (the ProductGroupController).

As previously mentioned, the Rose model does not have a one-to-one correspondence with Java files that are generated according to the SanFrancisco Programming Model. Based on the classes and directives, the single Product-GroupController class in the Rose model produces the following Java classes:

- ProductGroupController.java
- ProductGroupControllerImpl.java
- ProductGroupControllerRoot.java
- ProductGroupControllerRootImpl.java
- ProductGroupControllerRootFactory.java

The SanFrancisco code generator, when used correctly and in conjunction with the Rational Rose Directive wizard, can be one of the best productivity aids for creating SanFrancisco framework code. Users do not have to worry about many of the SanFrancisco programming model rules and requirements because they are automatically adhered to when the code is generated. Much of the burden of the details of the programming model disappears. Although the code generator does not eliminate the need for programmers to put a Rose design into use, their job is reduced to creating custom business logic rather than sweating the details of SanFrancisco.

Integrated Development Environments

Integrated development environments (IDEs) are made by many companies. IBM does not test the various IDEs directly, but if an IDE supports 100% Java development, it should be usable by SanFrancisco. There are several things to look out for as you set up your development environment.

Java Development Kit (JDK)

- Does your IDE support the level and Swing user interface level used by the current SanFrancisco version?

- Does the IDE use its own Java version, particularly the String class available in the JDK?

- How does the IDE make use of classes in the development environment?

- RMI stub and skeleton generators shipped with IDEs are not sufficient for the SanFrancisco environment.

Although these topics seem trivial, it is crucial that you be aware of them. The JDK that is used by SanFrancisco undergoes rigorous testing at IBM. The currently supported JDK and user interface library are shipped on the SanFrancisco CD. This version of the JDK should be installed in the environment whenever possible and used as the basis for development.

IBM VisualAge for Java

The IBM VisualAge for Java is mentioned in a previous chapter. Thankfully, because this IDE is an IBM product, it receives some special treatment.

IBM VisualAge for Java is not a file-based IDE. This means that the IDE maintains its own version of the SanFrancisco code in its own repository (which could also be loosely called a database). Java class files, or source files, must be imported into the environment through a special import step. After that, classes are developed in a fashion similar to that of other IDEs.

It takes a little while to get used to the IBM VisualAge environment, but after you do, you learn that it has a powerful debug environment, a very nice customizable workspace environment, an easy-to-use development paradigm, and so on. After classes are imported into the VisualAge repository and placed on the workspace, class developers go about building their SanFrancisco applications.

IBM VisualAge for Java Enterprise Edition has team management capabilities that help large groups of developers to work on the same project. After source code is developed and tested with the IBM VisualAge for Java environment, the application and code must be exported from the environment into a more portable format, such as class files or jar files.

The SanFrancisco CD comes with two items that make the environment easy to use:

- IBM VisualAge SanFrancisco features
- IBM VisualAge SanFrancisco wizards

The feature package allows a VisualAge user to access SanFrancisco in the native VisualAge format. It is a prepackaged VisualAge repository file. This feature is very useful because it reduces the import time of SanFrancisco from approximately 8–10 hours to about 40 minutes on a good-sized machine. This alone is a significant improvement in productivity.

The wizard package adds SanFrancisco-specific tools to the IBM VisualAge menus. The tools do daily jobs such as starting the SanFrancisco servers within VisualAge, starting a code generator that is built into VisualAge, and running the SanFrancisco samples within the VisualAge environment.

IBM VisualAge for Java SanFrancisco Code Wizard

The IBM VisualAge for Java SanFrancisco Code wizard is a useful way to build quick classes that you may have missed in your Rational Rose model. Also, many SanFrancisco evaluators do not yet have a fully licensed copy of Rational Rose and the full set of development tools installed. For these people, the wizard is a nice way to get their feet wet.

The wizard focuses on constructing classes based on the Foundation layer of SanFrancisco. A user of the wizard can choose the option of building subclasses, Entities, Dependents, commands, and other low-level classes. The user is then guided through the process of adding primitives to the class and adjusting the interface.

Completed code is generated into the VisualAge project that the user selected in the wizard. The code generator builds code that adheres to the SanFrancisco Programming Model, but it should be noted that the code generator is different from the code generator discussed earlier in this Appendix.

Server Management

Icons exist on the server machines to start and stop servers. Finer-grained control of the servers is possible with the server management tools. The various servers that are required in a network can be configured and maintained from the Server Management Configuration Console. The console is one of the base utilities available in the SanFrancisco Base Utilities folder. After the console is started, a list of all available servers, their status, and customizable settings is displayed. By selecting one of the active, or inactive, servers or services, the console user can change settings in the server and perform other valuable operations on the process itself.

If the console user has selected one of the factory processes available on a server, the user can adjust the heap size available to the server or select one of many different configurable parameters. In the event that IBM service needs to take traces within your network, IBM will ask you to alter the trace settings. Notice that on several processes, the classpath can also be altered.

This book does not purport to give a full lesson in how to administer server environments for SanFrancisco. Administration and configuration receive detailed treatment in the SanFrancisco on-line documentation. The Administration and Configuration Guide discusses the parameters that you can use to set up a server and server network.

Problem Manager

The Problem Manager exists to record unexpected problems that can occur in a SanFrancisco network or in the code for a SanFrancisco framework component or application. The Problem Manager runs in a separate server process that is started automatically if a problem occurs that is tracked by the Problem Manager. Often, data recorded in the Problem Manager should be sent to IBM for service and additional help with debugging.

Other times, enough information is contained in the Problem Manager to identify and resolve a problem that exists in your own server setup or configuration. If a problem is identified as an internal error that IBM should be notified about, you will use the information presented in the Problem Manager window to start your discussions with IBM service.

The Problem Manager can be started from the Base Utilities folder in SanFrancisco. Figure A-3 shows how you want the Problem Manager to appear: no problem recorded.

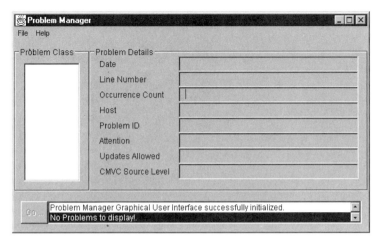

Figure A-3. SanFrancisco Problem Manager

HTML Documentation Print Tool

SanFrancisco documentation is presented almost entirely on-line in the form of thousands of pages of HTML documentation. The HTML Print tool attempts to generate books based on the table of contents files. Basically, a user can select sections to be printed.

The HTML Print tool can be started from an applet version in the header of each of the printable documents, or a subset of the documents can be printed from an application version of the print tool available in the main SanFrancisco folder.

If you choose to use the applet version of the HTML Print tool, you should be hooked up to the Internet during the first attempt. The JavaScript that invokes the print tool retrieves the Java plug-in, which is available from Sun. The plug-in gives a single JVM implementation, rather than the various browsers, and gives a single security mechanism to be used for the HTML Print tool. You can also retrieve the plug-in directly from Sun and install it before or after the first attempted plug-in load. After the plug-in is loaded, the print tool is accessible from Microsoft or Netscape browsers.

When the applet is invoked on a manual, a screen similar to the one in Figure A-4 is displayed. Choose the sections, or all sections, that you want printed. The print tool outputs a single HTML file that contains all the Web pages in the sections you have chosen. The resulting HTML document can be imported into a word processor for additional formatting or can be printed from a Web browser as a single document.

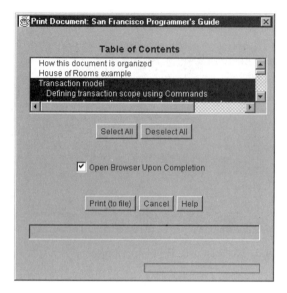

Figure A-4. HTML Documentation Print Tool

Summary

There are more tools available for use with SanFrancisco than can be presented here. Tools distributed with SanFrancisco are documented in the SanFrancisco product. For more information, look at the on-line documentation—specifically, the Administration and Configuration Guide—as well as the other on-line manuals.

Third-party tools can often be found in the Tools Catalog provided by San-Francisco. Although this is not a comprehensive list of tools that can be used with SanFrancisco, it gives you an idea of the type of tools SanFrancisco works well with.

B

The CD-ROM

Installing the Software That Accompanies the Book

Contained on the back cover of this book is a copy of the SanFrancisco Release 1 Version 3 Evaluation Edition CD. This evaluation edition is not the currently released edition of SanFrancisco, but it is the final version of the Evaluation Edition. Later SanFrancisco business component framework releases add more function and have substantial performance improvements.

The CD contains a substantial amount of documentation on the SanFrancisco business component framework as well as running samples and source code for many of the samples.

Before installing the software, read the following documents (available on the CD):

1. The SanFrancisco Evaluation Kit (V1R3): Getting Started redbook. The redbook is from IBM and guides you from the installation of the CD all the way through using several samples. It is available in the directory \SF_Redbook\sg24-5182-01. The file name is sg245182.pdf. You will need an Acrobat Reader to read the PDF file. You can download Acrobat Reader at http://www.adobe.com/. Ensure that you have at least the 3.01 version of Acrobat Reader.

2. Read the installation instructions available in the root directory of the CD. The file name is Install.htm. Load the file into a Web browser for reading.

If you are ready to install the software, keep in mind that when running San-Francisco, you are running a complete server-side framework. You must adhere to the minimum requirements for installation:

- Processor Speed: Pentium 200 MHz
- Main Memory: 128 MB RAM
- Available Disk Space: 100 MB (substantially more if you choose to install all of the documentation, and even more if you install the documentation in multiple languages)
- Display Resolution: 1024x768, 256 colors

Finally, each version of SanFrancisco is tested with specific versions of the Java Development Kit (JDK). The JDK that was tested with this version of SanFrancisco is JDK 1.1.6. This JDK and the accompanying JIT compiler are also available on the CD. We strongly recommend that you install the Java version that is available on the CD.

For more information on future evaluation editions or for additional documentation on SanFrancisco, see the IBM SanFrancisco Web site: http://www.software.ibm.com/ad/sanfrancisco

CD-ROM Warranty

Addison Wesley Longman, Inc. warrants the enclosed disc to be free of defects in materials and faulty workmanship under normal use for a period of ninety days after purchase. If a defect is discovered in the disc during this warranty period, a replacement disc can be obtained at no charge by sending the defective disc, postage prepaid, with proof of purchase to:

Editorial Department
Computer and Engineering Publishing Group
Addison-Wesley
One Jacob Way
Reading, Massachusetts 01867-3999

After the ninety-day period, a replacement disc will be sent upon receipt of the defective disc and a check or money order for $10.00, payable to Addison Wesley Longman, Inc.

Addison Wesley Longman, Inc. makes no warranty or representation, either expressed or implied, with respect to this software, its quality, performance, merchantability, or fitness for a particular purpose. In no event will Addison Wesley Longman, Inc., its distributors, or dealers be liable for direct, indirect, special, incidental, or consequential damages arising out of the use or inability to use the software. The exclusion of implied warranties is not permitted in some states. Therefore, the above exclusion may not apply to you. This warranty provides you with specific legal rights. There may be other rights that you may have that vary from state to state. The contents of this CD-ROM are intended for personal use only.

More information and updates are available at: http://www.awl.com/cseng/titles/0-201-61587-8

Index

Numbers followed by the letter *f* indicate figures.

Addison-Wesley Computer and Engineering Publishing Group

How to Interact with Us

1. Visit our Web site

http://www.awl.com/cseng

When you think you've read enough, there's always more content for you at Addison-Wesley's web site. Our web site contains a directory of complete product information including:

- Chapters
- Exclusive author interviews
- Links to authors' pages
- Tables of contents
- Source code

You can also discover what tradeshows and conferences Addison-Wesley will be attending, read what others are saying about our titles, and find out where and when you can meet our authors and have them sign your book.

2. Subscribe to Our Email Mailing Lists

Subscribe to our electronic mailing lists and be the first to know when new books are publishing. Here's how it works: Sign up for our electronic mailing at http://www.awl.com/cseng/mailinglists.html. Just select the subject areas that interest you and you will receive notification via email when we publish a book in that area.

We encourage you to patronize the many fine retailers who stock Addison-Wesley titles. Visit our online directory to find stores near you or visit our online store: http://store.awl.com/ or call 800-824-7799.

3. Contact Us via Email

cepubprof@awl.com

Ask general questions about our books.
Sign up for our electronic mailing lists.
Submit corrections for our web site.

bexpress@awl.com

Request an Addison-Wesley catalog.
Get answers to questions regarding
your order or our products.

innovations@awl.com

Request a current Innovations Newsletter.

webmaster@awl.com

Send comments about our web site.

mikeh@awl.com

Submit a book proposal.
Send errata for an Addison-Wesley book.

cepubpublicity@awl.com

Request a review copy for a member of the media
interested in reviewing new Addison-Wesley titles.

Addison Wesley Longman
Computer and Engineering Publishing Group
One Jacob Way, Reading, Massachusetts 01867 USA
TEL 781-944-3700 • FAX 781-942-3076